'A Very Private Diary'

A Nurse in Wartime

MARY MORRIS

Edited by Carol Acton

W&N

WEIDENFELD & NICOLSON

A W&N PAPERBACK

First published in Great Britain in 2014
by Weidenfeld & Nicolson
This paperback edition published in 2015
by Weidenfeld & Nicolson,
an imprint of Orion Books Ltd,
Orion House, 5 Upper St Martin's Lane,
London WC2H 9EA

An Hachette UK company

1 3 5 7 9 10 8 6 4 2

Diaries © The Mary Ellen Morris Trust 2014
Introduction and editing © Carol Acton 2014
Photographs © The Mary Ellen Morris Trust

The right of Mary Morris to be identified as the author
of this work has been asserted by her in accordance with
the Copyright, Designs and Patents Act 1988.

The editor and publisher are grateful to the Trustees of the Imperial
War Museum for allowing access to the original diary transcript and
photographs from their archives.

A CIP catalogue record for this book
is available from the British Library.

ISBN 978-1-7802-2738-2

Printed and bound in by CPI Group (UK), Croydon, CRO 4YY

The Orion Publishing Group's policy is to use papers that
are natural, renewable and recyclable products and made
from wood grown in sustainable forests. The logging and
manufacturing processes are expected to conform to the
environmental regulations of the country of origin.

vwww.orionbooks.co.uk

CONTENTS

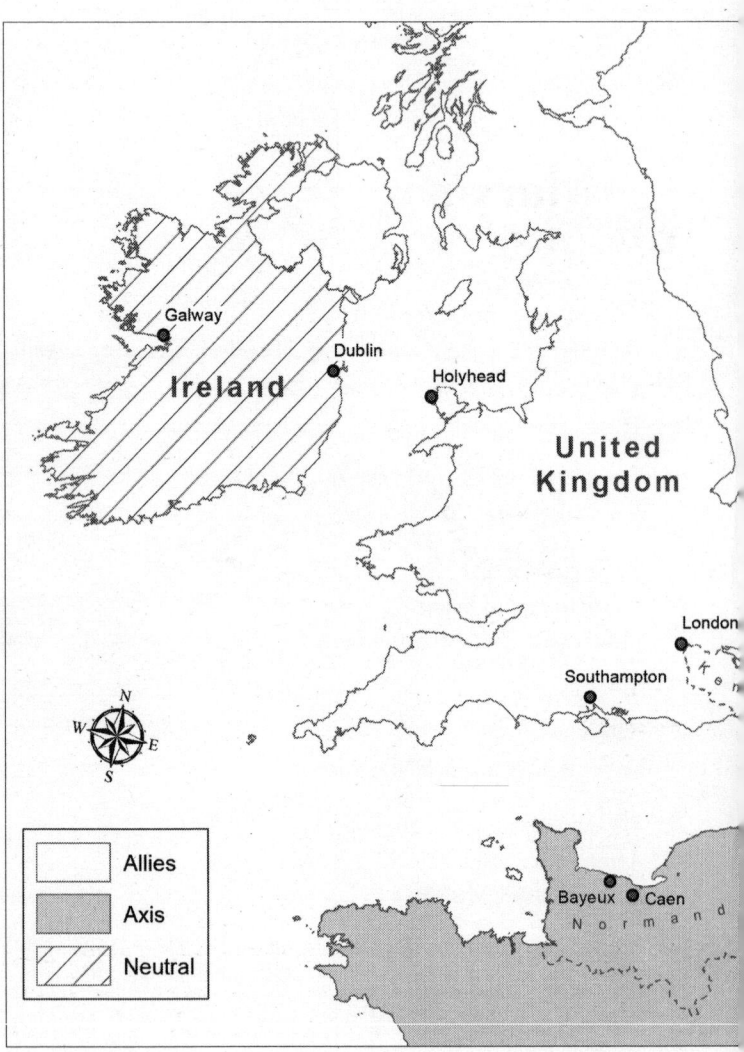

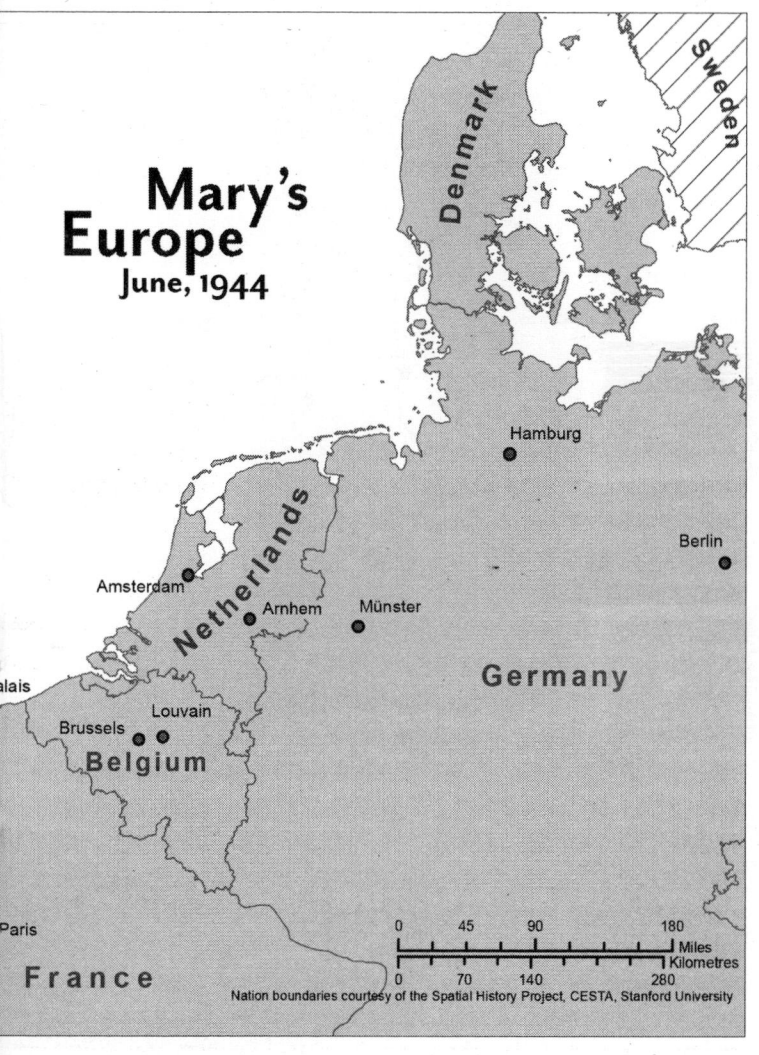

Mary's
Europe
June, 1944

Sweden

Denmark

Hamburg

Berlin

Amsterdam

Netherlands

Arnhem   Münster

Germany

alais

Louvain

Brussels

Belgium

Paris

France

0	45	90	180

Miles
Kilometres

0	70	140	280

Nation boundaries courtesy of the Spatial History Project, CESTA, Stanford University

Lt Mary Mulry displaying her 'two pips'

INTRODUCTION

We tend to remember the Second World War in dramatic images: the frantic evacuation of Dunkirk; Spitfires fighting Messerschmitts and leaving trails of vapour against the Kent sky in the Battle of Britain; fires raging in ruined buildings in the Blitz; troops wading ashore in the D-Day invasion. Yet we rarely glimpse the private thoughts and feelings of the individuals caught up in these dramas. This is the world we enter in the secret wartime diary of Mary Mulry (later Morris).

As an eighteen-year-old trainee nurse going on duty at the Kent and Sussex Hospital in June 1940, Mary would be 'faint with hunger' by lunch time, and get told off for going out to dinner with an attractive, recently discharged Dunkirk survivor by the terrifying Matron – with 'starched cap with frilly edges and a large bow tied under a medley of chins, all of them voicing disapproval'. But her duties also meant unquestioning dedication, self-sacrifice and compassion. 'Private Mullins is one of the most severely burned,' she writes of her first war-injured patient. 'He is about eighteen years old – my age. His . . . arms are propped up in front of him on a pillow, the fingers extended like claws and his naked body hangs loosely on straps . . . we give him morphia every three hours.'

The pages of this extraordinary diary bring together Mary's private thoughts with eyewitness accounts of some of the most public events of the twentieth century. With the exception of occasional gaps, which occur when she was working hard, ill or had let her entries drop for a time as diary writers so often do, we share her joy, fear, sorrow and anger, her romances, losses and friendships. We also see a young woman coming of age, from the breathless enthusiasm of her early entries, when 'Staff Nurse Jones reduced me to tears twice before the 9 a.m. break', to the understated courage and confidence of the nurse who devised her own protocols in her tent ward in Normandy.

Mary's entries can be humorous, sharp, thoughtful and sometimes subversive. Once on active service keeping a diary was forbidden, but Mary always delighted in challenging the rules – especially when they seemed to stand in the way of the humanity of nursing or her own common sense. 'Should have headed this "Somewhere in Southern England"', she writes on 15 June 1944, on her way to Normandy, 'but this *is* a very private diary.'

The glamour of dances, parties and constant male attention never seems to be far away for Mary, but we also feel her accumulated sense of loss at romances that were continually cut short: 'I always seem to be saying good-bye to men whom I might have loved had there been enough time.' Yet, as we shall see, love did not elude her, even if it did bring with it the extremes of exultation and heartache that mark a relationship forged through brief meetings and frequent separations.

We are often reminded of the threats to her own life too, when she narrowly escaped death in the bombing of the Alexandra Hotel in London, when her sister hospital ship was blown up as they waited to disembark at Normandy, or when her hospital near Bayeux came under German bombardment. Although Mary does not have time to reflect on these events for long, they surely contribute to her growing maturity, and were a world away from anything her childhood in rural County Galway could have prepared her for.

Mary Mulry, like many young Irish women, came to train as a nurse in England in 1939, since there were few opportunities for young women in an economically depressed Ireland. Mary had seen her older brother Michael (whom she meets later in the war) emigrate to America like many local young men; her cousin Delia marry for lack of other options; and the grinding poverty and poor health endured by women through

An Irish childhood: a young Mary with her father and brothers Patrick (*front right*) and Michael (*back right*)

constant childbearing. Mary had been brought up by her aunt after her mother's death from puerperal fever when Mary was only three weeks old. Well educated, but with few prospects for work at home, and encouraged by her cousin Julia, who was married and living near London, Mary applied for a position as a nursing probationer at the most prestigious nursing school in Britain, Guy's Hospital, London. She passed their entry examination and began training there in August 1939 in spite of her family's concerns about the prospect of war.

Nursing training began with probationers placed on the wards, tasked with the menial duties of bedpan washing and locker scrubbing while they learned hospital routine and discipline as well as medical care. There were medical lectures and study in addition to long hours on the wards. When, in September, sections of Guy's Hospital were evacuated out of London, Mary found herself continuing her probation at the Kent and Sussex Hospital in Tunbridge Wells. It is here that her diary begins.

War first came to her in the survivors of the evacuation of Dunkirk in late May 1940, when the British Expeditionary Force had been pushed back to the coast by the German army and forced to evacuate. Later that year she watched 'dogfights' overhead and socialised with pilots stationed nearby at Biggin Hill. Mary found escape in visits to London where, in spite of air raids, she was determined to enjoy dinners out and the theatre. In May 1941 she was caught in the worst recorded night of the Blitz, narrowly escaping with her life when her hotel was hit and split in half. Yet, as a young probationary nurse, Mary often seemed more daunted by her Matron than by the London bombs. Her long shifts and studies for her exams were punctuated by occasional holidays in Ireland where she could delight in meals unmarred by rationing: seemingly unlimited butter, eggs, bacon and rich fruit cakes were a short-lived delight before the inevitable sea-sickness of the ferry back to Holyhead.

In 1943, after passing her State Registered Nurse (SRN)

examinations, Mary moved to the Brook Hospital, Woolwich, London, to specialise in fever nursing. Although the most severe Blitz had ended in 1941, there were still intermittent air raids, and this period brought Mary closer to the realities of war on a daily basis. Her diary also shows how necessary this now more-or-less forgotten area of fever nursing was in the days before antibiotics, when children routinely suffered severe complications from diseases such as measles. With the constant threat of bombing raids, Mary often faced the impossible choice between moving critically ill patients from their beds and oxygen tents to the security of the shelter in the hospital basement, or of exposing them to possible death or injury by bombs. When Mary herself contracts diphtheria we realise the risks that medical personnel constantly took as they cared for the sick in a time before antibiotics and generalised immunisation.

At the end of her training in spring 1944, Mary joined the Queen Alexandra's Imperial Military Nursing Service Reserves (QAs). The QAs had been founded in 1902 to establish and maintain a workforce of trained nurses available to serve in military hospitals at home and abroad. QA nurses (Sisters) served in the First World War, but in 1939 there were only 640 members. By the end of the war this had risen to 12,000 (including the reserve). The army was actively encouraging the recruitment of nurses as preparations to invade Europe mounted, and Mary was determined to join up, in spite of the opposition of her Matron who, like many administrators of civilian hospitals, was concerned about the increasing shortage of medical personnel on the Home Front.

In joining a branch of the British Army Mary also faced opposition from her family back home. Her father, an idealistic republican, had fought the British during the Easter Rising in 1916 and in the War of Independence. She could have returned to Ireland to avoid being eligible for call-up or have stayed in England as a civilian nurse, but Mary was proud of her role defined by her QA uniform, particularly when she was saluted smartly by male soldiers in response to her officer's 'pips'. She could now also claim membership of the 'Irish Volunteers', the Irish citizens who joined the British forces, whom she would constantly meet during her time in Europe. Although what was then the Irish Free State, or Eire, was neutral, thousands of Irish men and women elected to join the British forces to fight in the war or to participate in war work on the Home Front. In addition to those working in factories or nursing on the Home Front, approximately 165,000 Irish were in the British Services in 1944.

Although most of Britain knew something momentous was about to happen, plans for the D-Day invasion of 6 June 1944 remained secret, even in military circles. When, after a brief period of army training at Hatfield House in Hertfordshire, Mary and her fellow QA nurses were sent to the south coast of England to await embarkation for Europe, they were stepping into the unknown. Following the male-only medical teams who landed with the troops on D-Day, five General Hospitals, including female nurses, landed in Normandy on 16 and 17 June. Mary's unit, 101 British General Hospital, was prevented from leaving because of bad weather, but sailed with a calm sea from Southampton at 11.30 p.m. on 18 June. By the time they arrived on the coast of Normandy 'the seas were mountainous', and, as Mary vividly evokes it, disembarking onto a landing craft was an act of faith as well as gymnastics.

In Normandy Mary quickly learned to cope with minimal hospital equipment and embraced the most basic of living conditions. Her matter-of-fact tone and dogged courage make it easy to forget the danger that even those officially behind the lines faced. Although she describes the grotesque details of the battle-scarred landscape in Normandy, the necessity of wearing tin hats and being strafed by German planes, she does not mention – and may not have been aware of – the precarious situation she was entering.

Whether in the tented hospital close to the front lines, or

later at a makeshift hospital in a convent in Louvain, Belgium, Mary records not only her story but those of the patients she nursed – both Allies and enemies – and of the other nurses and orderlies. Throughout the diary we witness the savagery of the war, but also what she calls 'the lovely spirit of warm friendliness which exists between all of us', and then her sadness at its loss when her hospital is moved and she is forced, once again, to try to build a new life. This was the world of young men and women at war, where close relationships that offered support in the harsh and dangerous conditions could be severed abruptly.

At the end of the war Mary remained in Brussels before being posted to Hamburg. Her diary from this period reminds us that the war did not end the moment the fighting stopped. Her own joy at being in love and then pregnant with her first child was set against constant reminders of the devastation of a war that reached far beyond wounded bodies and shattered cities. We see the guilt she feels at the starving German civilians and the state of the German prisoners emerging from prisoner-of-war camps, in contrast to the lavish entertainment at Allied parties. We glimpse the early Nuremberg trials, the controversy surrounding the creation of a Jewish homeland, and the horrific accounts emerging from concentration camps such as Bergen-Belsen. Yet the diary ends with her looking forward into the future with the birth of her son, delivered, with a storybook sense of completion, by a friend and doctor from her days in Normandy.

A typescript of this diary is housed in the Imperial War Museum. Very few nurses' diaries survived the Second World War, and this one is unusually complete and sustained. As Mary narrates this long war and its aftermath we are fortunate that, in defying regulations and writing for herself, Mary was also inadvertently recording for future generations. At one point she is frustrated by her seeming inability to articulate her thoughts: 'I do not seem to be at all creative. Have tried to write but the ideas in my head will not convey themselves to my pen.'

But her creativity *was* in that very pen. Reading the diary from a distance of seventy years it is easy to forget that each date she records at the top of her day's entry is the most recent date in history. Diaries take us into the experience of life as it is lived from day to day precisely because, unlike memoirs, the events and feelings recorded are immediate; they have not been revisited and rewritten through the lens of hindsight, nor can time blur their intensity. The vivid and candid entries of this young woman, who combined the practical with the adventurous, the vivacious with the thoughtful and empathetic, are a lasting testimony of what it meant to be a nurse and a young woman caught up in those long years of war.

Carol Acton,
December 2013

EDITOR'S NOTE

My first encounter with Mary Morris's diary was in the Reading Room of the Imperial War Museum, London, where the original typescript is housed (Department of Documents 80/38/1). I hope that readers will share the excitement I felt when I first read Mary's diary and the life of a young woman came into being under each succeeding date. Although it has been necessary to reduce the length, I have retained as much as possible of the original. Cutting has been limited to inconsequential events or repetitions. I have separated the diary into parts and added occasional notes to give context or historical background. I have also included notes to clarify the meaning of a term or to provide a specific context for a diary entry. While these have necessarily been brief, the Further Reading section provides more information on specific subjects.

One

'The real war started for me today'

Training at the Kent and Sussex Hospital, Tunbridge Wells

Eighteen-year-old Mary Mulry from Co. Galway, Ireland, had begun her nursing training at Guy's Hospital, London, in August 1939. In September, in preparation for war, sections of Guy's had moved out of London, and Mary continued her probation at the Kent and Sussex Hospital, near Tunbridge Wells, Kent. In May 1940 she confronted the war for the first time.

31 May 1940, Kent and Sussex Hospital

The real war started for me today. It was routine early morning on Men's Surgical – the usual old men with supra-pubic cystostomy, urine draining into Winchester bottles on the floor by their beds. Staff Nurse Jones reduced me to tears twice before the 9 a.m. break. I try not to let her see me cry.

Matron and Mr Horden and one of the Consultant Physicians were talking in Sister's office as I reported back on duty at 9.30 a.m. After they had gone, Sister called us all into the office to say that our ward was to be evacuated at once. No questions were to be asked. She would order ambulances and make the arrangements. We were to get on with packing the patients' personal effects and change the dressings if that was necessary.

There were disgruntled mutterings from most of the men, but within a short time relatives appeared on the ward and helped us to get them ready to depart. Staff Nurse had a good time bossing everybody about. Eventually the ward was empty, clean and beds made up. We were ready, but for what?

It was about 2 p.m. that the ambulances started to arrive. I was ordered to report to Casualty Sister, a being who terrifies me. She looks so efficient and rustles with starch when she dashes about.

As I entered the Casualty department, I was astounded to see so many wet, dirty and injured people there. Some were soldiers (I guessed they must be Dunkirk survivors), the others were civilians. They were all laid out on stretchers on the floor, and most of our surgeons and physicians were there, assisted by several senior Sisters and Staff Nurses. I was given the job of removing dirty, wet clothing. Several of the men had their skin flayed by oil burns, a very painful condition, others were injured by bomb splinters, and some were injured by machine-gun fire from the air as they came across the Channel. There is one badly shocked middle-aged man, a Captain Hermes, a Belgian boat owner. They were all very tired, cold, wet and hungry. All the surgical cases are now on my ward.*

1 June

There is a completely different atmosphere on the ward now – more cheerful. Staff Nurse chats to the BEF [British Expeditionary Force] soldiers and has less time for making my life a misery. Capt. Hermes is still exhausted and shocked and is under sedation.

The small ward is now occupied by the burns cases. Private Brian Mullins is one of the most severely burned. He is about eighteen years old – my age. His face and hands have been sprayed with tannic acid, which has set into a hard black cement. His arms are propped up in front of him on a pillow, the fingers extended like claws and his naked body hangs loosely on straps just clear of the bed. His eyelids are coated with a thick layer of gentian violet and we give him morphia every three hours. He was involved in an explosion on his way back from Dunkirk.

John Evans, the captain of the old *Brighton Belle*, got off

* In May 1940 Anglo-French forces were unable to mobilise a counter-attack against the German invasion of the Netherlands and Belgium and were forced to retreat to the coast, primarily Dunkirk. The evacuation of a total of 338,226 British and French forces was assisted by myriads of privately owned vessels. However, 11,000 British soldiers were killed, 1,400 wounded and 41,000 deemed missing or taken prisoner.

lightly with a fractured tibia and fibula. His leg is in a plaster and he talked to me as I helped him to have a blanket bath. He sadly misses his ship. She was certainly versatile. John told me that she used to carry holiday crowds across the Channel before the Boer War, swept mines in the Great War, and swept mines again last winter. This great old ship went over to Dunkirk to collect the soldiers, deposited one load safely on the Kent coast and went back for the second. It was on the return journey, with four hundred exhausted soldiers aboard, that she struck the wreck of a ship and slowly sank. John managed to transfer the soldiers to another boat and also rescued his dog Jock before the old *Belle* disappeared from view.

The story of the Dunkirk rescue operation is an extraordinary one. John told me how he and his crew met up with French and Belgian fishing boats lying off Ramsgate – boats from Caen, Le Havre and Antwerp. They had all helped before at Calais and Boulogne in the preceding days at Dunkirk, but when they heard the new orders they set out again. The fishing boats were the leaders of the procession, for they were slow and with them went some Dutch 'scouts', stumpy little coastal vessels, commandeered at the collapse of Holland. Each little boat was flying the white ensign of the Royal Navy, and fitted with *one* Lewis gun. Next went coasters, paddle steamers and tugs. There was a car ferry and lots of yachts, large and small. There were sloops, trawlers and, rolling and pitching in a cloud of spray, open speedboats, wholly unsuited to the Channel chop.

John told me as I washed his good foot that there was never such a fleet that went to war before. Some were tatty with old car tyres for fenders, others were bright with new paint and chromium. It was apparently the queerest and most nondescript flotilla that ever was, and manned by all kinds of people, English, Belgian, French. There were bankers and dentists, taxi drivers, yachtsmen and fishermen, even dockers, engineers and civil servants.

4 June

Private Mullins is to be transferred to Mr McIndoe's skin-grafting unit at East Grinstead as soon as he is well enough to be moved. He is still in a great deal of pain and there is a great deal to be done before grafting.[*]

Some of our Dunkirk evacuees are feeling better, and talking much more. They were extremely tired, and have slept for nearly two days and two nights.

There are several French soldiers here, but most of them are very quiet. They are, I think, still stunned by the collapse of their country.

Our own soldiers are far more bitter. They are angry because they feel let down by the RAF. Most of them allege that they did not see any of ours over there. They had spent days on the road and the beaches of Dunkirk. They have nothing but praise for the Royal Navy destroyers and the small ships that pulled them out of Dunkirk, but they will never forgive the Air Force. The newspaper headlines read 'Unceasing vigil of the RAF in France'.

12 June

Went on duty at 7 a.m. The ward was much quieter than usual, none of the loud cheery greetings which I usually received. Pierre was sitting on his bed crying, the tears rolling down his cheeks. I was appalled. Pierre is slim and dark, with beautiful brown eyes and masses of Gallic charm. I checked that Staff Nurse was not around, pulled the curtains round his bed and asked what was wrong. He took my hand and said in French, 'The honour of my country is at stake. Paris has fallen to the

[*] At the burns unit at East Grinstead Hospital, later the Royal Victoria Hospital, Archibald McIndoe pioneered burns treatment and reconstructive surgery for wartime burn victims, especially RAF aircrew. His RAF patients famously became 'The Guinea Pig Club'.

Boche."* He told me that he would remain in England and become a member of the Free French Army. He is being discharged from hospital tomorrow and invited me to have dinner with him tomorrow evening. We are not allowed to go out with patients, or even speak to them on matters other than their treatment. Pierre is charming. I shall go out with him. No one need know about it.

14 June

Went out to dinner with Pierre last night. His fractured English is delightful. We went to a restaurant near the Pantiles. Tunbridge Wells never ceases to astonish me. It seems to be populated by retired colonels and their ladies, who have spent most of their lives in the Indian sub-continent and other far-flung parts of the Empire. Their snippets of overheard conversation are liberally sprinkled with words like the Punjab, Sahib and Raj. They walk tall and straight, and tend to speak with loud, straight, self-confident voices with a strong undercurrent of authority. They seem to be a little ill at ease as they mix with the remnants of our brave BEF men in the shops or pubs. The class-consciousness in this country is still very new to me. It appears to be a matter of accent rather than social position. Have discovered that the type of colonel's lady who looks down her nose at my soft Irish brogue will be charm itself if I teasingly adopt an Oxford drawl.

Pierre poured out his heart to me about all the sorrows of his beloved La Belle France as he held my hand in the candlelight, and added that I must be partly French as I am so 'sympathique'. It was at this moment that I saw Staff Nurse and one of the seniors sitting at a table in the corner glaring at me. Pierre said, 'There are too many people here', and we went out into the warm June evening.

* The collapse (or capitulation) of France to the Germans resulted in occupation by German troops in the north and west zones, with the French Vichy (collaborative) government controlling the central and southern zones.

It was still quite early (I had to be in my room by 10 p.m.).
We held hands as we skipped along the road leading to Happy
Valley.* We lay on the grass, laughed and listened to the song
of the birds. Pierre goes away tomorrow. I may never see him
again. He too comes from a Roman Catholic background and
was brought up on a farm in Normandy. Soon it was nearly
dark and almost 10 p.m. We ran all the way back to the K.
and S., and crawled round the grounds in the hope of finding
an open window in the Nurses' Home. We found one eventually and in fear and trembling I said 'Au Revoir' to Pierre as
he helped to push me through. It was a real cloak-and-dagger
effort to get to my room without being spotted by the eagle-
eyed Home Sister.

15 June

Staff Nurse and her awful friend had a malignantly triumphant
look about them at breakfast this morning. I was soon to discover what they had been up to! Sister called me into her office
in the middle of bottle round. She looked very severe and said
that I was to remove my elbow frills and put on my starched
cuffs and wait outside Matron's office until I was called. She
then added, 'Finish the bottle round first'. I tore round as fast
as I could, my heart beating with fear and anxiety. What had I
done wrong? I had two more years of training to do. It would
be awful to be sent home in disgrace. I tried to tidy my hair
underneath the starched cap, but it is long and thick and keeps
escaping.

I waited in the queue outside Matron's office. Joyce Bale came
out in tears. What hope could there be for me, when Joyce is
always impeccably tidy and came top in the Prelim exams? The
next girl to go in was Audrey, clutching a broken thermometer
and a 2/- piece. She looks fed up too. It is hard enough on our

* Happy Valley is an especially scenic area of Rusthall Common (near Tunbridge
Wells), known for its caves and ancient steps.

tiny salary to have to pay for all accidental breakages – but in addition to that Matron seems to enjoy humiliating us. We are entirely at her mercy – examination results and references are essential in this job.

Matron was sitting behind her large desk as I entered and she left me standing there for nearly fifteen minutes while she carried on writing. She looked as if she was going to don the black cap at any moment, and said that a responsible senior nurse was 'horrified' at seeing me dining in a public restaurant with a male patient. It was useless for me to protest that he was in fact an ex-patient, discharged two days ago. I knew that I had already been tried and must now await judgement. Matron is to ask the Ward Sister for a full report on my work and behaviour on duty.

17 June

Slept very little last night. Am worried about my annual leave which is due on the 20th. Will I be sacked and sent home in disgrace? Will they understand in Ireland?

When Sister came on duty she told me that I must report to Matron's office at 9 a.m. I tore round madly to get the work done, dashed over to the Nurses' Home to find a clean, starched apron and cuffs, and then ran back to wait outside in the queue. It was a hot, sunny day, but I shivered with fear and anxiety as I waited to be admitted to the <u>presence</u>. She is such a terrifying figure as she sits behind her large desk in full regalia – severe navy dress with stiff starched collar, starched cap with frilly edges and a large bow tied under the medley of chins, all of them voicing disapproval. She said, 'Nurse, you are to go on holiday on the 20th as arranged and when you return we shall review the situation'. She added, 'Your work report states that you spend too much time talking to the patients. We do not allow such behaviour in this hospital. You are here to work and train. You are far too flighty.'

I returned to the ward feeling that I had least received a temporary reprieve.

Joyce Bale invited the girls in our set to her room this evening after duty for a midnight feast. She had received a food parcel from a relative in America. It was bliss to see a rich fruit cake and a whole packet of butter. Our ration is so minute I use up my ration in one meal and then go without for the rest of the week.* I've had to give up sugar completely – as it never reaches the lower echelons of our long dining-room table. This long table plays a large part in our lives. It is symbolical of the hallowed procedures and jealously guarded seniority of our profession. We are always hungry and I find that serving the patients' dinner is personal torture. We have breakfast at 6.30 a.m. and more often than not the juniors have to go to the second sitting for lunch at 1.30 p.m. I am usually faint with hunger by then.

Our party was great fun, and we were giggling away at 10 p.m. when we heard the bossy footsteps of Night Sister coming along the corridor calling, 'Lights off, nurse'. We put the light out and lay on the floor, terrified that she would enter and book us all for being out of bounds after hours. We had great difficulty in controlling Maggie Lee, who was choking on her biscuits with laughter.

In June 1940, Mary returned home to Ireland for the first time since arriving in London for her training the previous August.

20 June, Holyhead

Travelled up to London this morning, the beginning of my annual holiday. The train was full of soldiers and airmen, sitting

---

* Food rationing had been introduced in January 1940. The butter allowance was four ounces per person per week, and sugar twelve ounces per week.

on their kit bags in the corridor, whistling and chatting me up as I struggled to find a seat.

Met Pierre in the West End. We had luncheon in Lyons Corner House in the Strand. He seems happier now that he is a part of the Free French Army. Was amazed at the number of noisy Australian soldiers in the West End. They are our allies, over here to train I suppose, but I dislike their uncouth manners and atrocious voices.

My train left Euston for Holyhead at 11 p.m. and Pierre suggested that we book seats for a show in the evening. The only available tickets were for a new show at the Aldwych called *Women and Angels*. One can't be too fussy in wartime but I did not enjoy it, and was definitely put off by the loud guffaws of the Aussie diggers.

Pierre was quiet and said that he would miss me as we wended our way by taxi to Euston. He waved good-bye to me from the platform until his figure was a small lonely dot in the distance.

The Irish Mail to Holyhead is almost a part of the Emerald Isle, familiar Irish voices, the happy laughter of people going home to their families, glad to get away from the black-out of London, and looking forward to the bright lights of Dublin. We trundled northwards across a blacked-out Britain.

21 June, Galway

Arrived in Holyhead at around 3 a.m. feeling tired and stiff. There were large numbers of Red Caps [Military Police] on the quay – looking for deserters I suppose.

The smell of the boat to Ireland always excites me. It is taking me home. There was very little scrutiny of my papers, considering that we are travelling to a neutral country. I wonder how many spies find this an easy outlet for information to be passed on to the Germans.

There is quite a chop on the Irish Sea as usual. I've never

known it calm. Wish I could avoid being sea-sick. It was dark on deck, the boat chugging along without lights. How are we to avoid collision? We stopped twice on the way over. It may have been a floating mine. We were not told. I went below to lie down and felt very frustrated to see such a quantity of food – no rationing here and I was feeling sea-sick!

The atmosphere became more noisy and relaxed as we left wartime England behind and I went back up on deck again. I could pick out the lights of Dublin and Kingstown in the distance. These lights, such an irritation to the Royal Navy, are to me a part of the warmth and gaiety of Dublin.

We pulled alongside the quay of Kingstown or Dunleary as it is now called.[*] I stood on deck and scanned the faces of the waiting crowd. There was no familiar face there. It was a moment of bitter disappointment, until I saw my cousin Tom push his way through the crowds and wave to me. Dear Tommy, he is always there when I need him, his dear face puckered with lines of humour and sadness. He is such a lovely vulnerable human being.

It was a bright beautiful morning, with clouds thundering across the sky, and drops of rain falling through the sunshine, so we decided not to take the train but walk in to Dublin. Tom gave my bags to the train driver whom he knows. Everybody seems to know everybody else over here.

We talked and laughed and talked again all the way to O'Connell Street. There is always time in Dublin to talk, recite poetry or sing. The people we met wanted to know how England was coping with the war and were not at all convinced that they could manage it without the Irish.

We reached the S Hotel in time for breakfast. This is a lovely homely place, the staff never change. The waitress Kitty is a friend of ours and within minutes we were sitting at a round

---

[*] Dun Laoghaire (anglicisation: Dunleary) had been named Kingstown in honour of the visit of George IV in 1821. In 1921, after the Irish War of Independence, it was renamed Dun Laoghaire, but many people still referred to it as Kingstown.

table with a snowy white cloth, tucking in to the type of breakfast which I would dream about at the Kent and Sussex – lovely rashers of Irish bacon, two eggs, sausages, mushrooms and tomatoes, delicious home-made wheat bread and lashings of butter artistically sculpted into twirls and butterfly shapes, and all accompanied by hot strong tea. It was bliss. I was home.

I put my feet up in Kitty's room while Tom fetched my bags and put them on the Galway train. The driver will keep an eye on them.

Left Dublin waving good-bye to Tom about 10.30 a.m. The atmosphere here is very relaxed, never any rush. Time is totally irrelevant – only people matter. The driver knows everybody all along the line, and stops the train if he sees someone, to enquire about their health, or that of their family, or to pick up a few squawking chickens to take to a friend. You can go off for a picnic in a field at any small station, knowing that Pat won't move without you. My poor dear native land is far too easy-going ever to become a force to be reckoned with.

We trundled along through the middle of Ireland to Athlone. It is the least interesting part of my homeland, although they are inordinately proud of their Shannon Scheme – which brings very cheap electricity to most of Connaught. We eventually reached the open field and one station house that is Woodlawn. As we neared the station I noticed our ass John leaning over the gate. He had one ear cocked as usual and looked ready for a mad gallop. Auntie was there too looking apprehensive. I had a sudden pang as I realised how old she looked. Age in a loved one seems to show up after a period of separation. She had to be comforted by the Stationmaster and his wife, because she cried so much with joy at the sight of me.

We packed my bags into the ass's trap and set off for Caltra. Auntie is now blissfully happy and so am I. The roads are empty, except for the occasional farmer bringing home a load of turf with his horse and cart. John too is happy and the clop of his newly shod hooves on the road is music to my ears.

The countryside is flat but not uninteresting. The open fields and boglands are restful and peaceful, with a strange poignant loneliness that is intensified by the cry of the corncrake and the curlew and the musical swish of wild geese and ducks in flight. There are hares and rabbits playing in the fields, and happy-looking cows – just chewing the cud – in all, nature minding its own business. This is another world from the one that Pierre was talking about only yesterday in London – the horror and suffering of war and the defeat and surrender of France.

John is a very strong-minded animal and despite our efforts to reach home as soon as possible, he was determined to visit old friends. We dropped in on people for a cup of tea, because our ass refused to move on until we did. Anyway it is considered unfriendly in Ireland to pass the door without visiting. We received a Céad Míle Fáilte everywhere we went. They are always happy to substitute work for talk. Talking is a national disease and it is pleasantly infectious.

On reaching home we found that some relatives and friends had put on a spread for me, again lots of lovely good food and a warm welcome. Now it was my turn to cry. These were the friends of my childhood. We talked and talked until I literally fell asleep on the settle bed in the kitchen.

24 June

I seem to have been just eating and sleeping in this comforting cocoon of home for days. I do exactly as I like, come and go when I wish, no fixed meal times. We eat when we are hungry. Auntie is so hospitable, the kettle is always on the hob and the turf fire burns so brightly. All the cooking is done on this fire – a bad summer for the turf is a disaster.

The house is untidy as always, chickens and young turkeys come in and are shut out by the half-door. I can remember when that half-door looked like Everest, the whole world was beyond it. There is a sack of turf in the corner, a whole side of bacon hanging in the hob, and a picture of the Sacred Heart with a small shelf and a little red lamp lighted below it on the wall. The Shannon Scheme has not reached us yet so we make do with paraffin lamps. The kitchen is the focal point for family living, and when the sun goes down, friends and neighbours come to visit. There is laughter and music, the tin whistle and the fiddle, and the old story-telling folk songs are sung over and over again. There is an atmosphere of sadness and humour, and a strange mixture of Gaelic and colourful English.

Tonight my father was talking about Northern Ireland. He fought alongside Michael Collins and Sean McKeon in the 'Troubles' and to this day feels betrayed by the people who signed the treaty with England. He feels that the British Government will live to regret this alliance. I pointed out that HM Government have enough to worry about at present.

My father is something of a radical, a man of peace but strongly motivated by injustice, whether by the British or his own Catholic Church.

He once openly denounced our parish priest, Father Donnelly, for taking food from the mouths of children, because of the priest's demand from the pulpit at Mass for money for foreign Missions. My father pointed out that charity begins at home and 'what good were the missionaries doing in Africa anyway' and sure 'weren't the Africans being killed by pneumonia through being forced to wear clothes'. I'm sure that must be logical, because my father is a sensible man, but these sentiments made him very unpopular with the clergy. The local shopkeeper who was well in with the priest would not give him credit to buy seed after that. He was abused and vilified by all the holy toadies.

My father is constantly quoting the poetry of W. B. Yeats and Rudyard Kipling. Can't imagine how a man who loves the one can love the other! He is a man of ideas, never a man of action, and the broken-down appearance of the farm proves my point. He needs a great cause, and a small farm in a remote part of the west of Ireland is not his true habitat.

28 June

Enjoyed walking around the fields today, renewing my friendship with our dog Sammy Laddy. Auntie tells me that when I left home last year to go to England, he sat waiting for me at the gate for nearly a week. Sammy and I have been friends since I was a small girl. We ran round the fields as we used to do, and re-discovered all our favourite places, flushed out rabbits, picked wild strawberries, chatted to the hens and ducks, dug up new potatoes for lunch and had a lovely time.

We had cally for lunch, new potatoes straight from the earth thrown into a pot of boiling salt water, chopped spring onions also freshly picked and the lot pounded together until light and fluffy. The aroma is wonderful – and oh the delight of making a well in the centre and filling it with a small mountain of golden freshly churned butter. We drank buttermilk with this delicious meal.

Mick McLoughlin dropped in for a chat this evening, bringing a huge salmon as a present. 'Caught it only an hour since,' he said with a twinkle in his eye. We are all too polite to ask where he had caught it. There is so much good living here where food is concerned and so little money. The small farmer receives very little for his labour. The traditional customs of salutation are still preserved here. It is nice to hear the Gaelic 'God save all here' when people come to the door and the 'May God and Mary go with you' when a guest departs.

Went to visit [cousin] Delia in Cloonfaries today. It was a lovely bicycle ride, along the old deserted bog road. The road was very bumpy and I was glad to reach the tiny remote village. There are only three houses occupied there now. The others are deserted, the young have emigrated to America and the old people are dead. There is nothing so sad as an empty derelict house that was once a happy home bursting with the laughter of children.

Delia's two boys led me to the squat thatched cottage with the traditional half-door to keep out the hens. I had brought presents for the boys, and Betsy their pet lamb (now a fully grown sheep) was determined not to be left out of the festivities. She joined us as we had tea in the kitchen, her bright little eyes looking adorably at the boys as they fed her with pieces of cake. Betsy's mother rejected her after her birth and she was reared on diluted cow's milk fed to her by the boys when she was tiny. Delia said that she is a very nosy sheep and would have carried on grazing in the field had she not seen me arrive.

As I cycled home in the twilight that evening, I mused on the fact that the war has had no perceptible impact on my native patch of Ireland.

1 July

Went to Mass in Caltra this morning. The Catholic Church is a very dominating force here and always has been. Father Donnelly is a great Gaelic revivalist. He sent me to spend a week in Kilkieran, a Gaeltacht district in Connemara, to improve the use of my native tongue, when I was twelve years old. That was great fun, but I have never forgiven him for making me stand up at a Feis and recite twenty-four verses in Gaelic of a dreary depressing tale relating to the sad demise of the people who drowned at Annaghdown.[*]

It will soon be time for me to leave this haven of peace and return to my duties at the K. and S. Have refused to read the papers so do not know what is going on there.

On her return to the Kent and Sussex, Mary was still waiting in trepidation to hear what Matron might have to say about her transgression.

---

[*] A lament called 'Eanach Dhuin', written in memory of twenty people who drowned on Lough Corrib travelling between Annaghdown and Galway.

28 July, Kent and Sussex Hospital

Left home this morning. It was a great sadness for me to wave good-bye to Auntie and John as the train puffed out of Wood-lawn Station. It took me a long time to persuade my relatives and friends that I was not returning to a hornets' nest of evil, danger and Godlessness. They brought me small presents last night and were sad to see me go – but this is a country that has become accustomed to losing its young people. There is no money on the land, and to the youth the streets of Boston and London are paved with gold. I have not found much gold in England. The pay is 30/- per month, long hard hours of work, and lectures and study on one's days off. I love the work and caring for the patients is the best part.* The food is insufficient and on my day off I go hungry as I can't afford to go out for a meal.

Tom met me in Dublin and accompanied me out to Kings-town. It was almost dark as I went aboard and I felt a sense of trepidation as I waved good-bye to my cousin. What am I returning to at the Kent and Sussex – a disapproving Matron, an uncertain future and a war? I am leaving behind the family I love and they fear for my safety.

I watched the bright lights of Dublin until the last glimmer had disappeared, and then turned my face to the blacked-out shores of England and settled down to sleep. It was a calm night and the crossing to Holyhead was uneventful. There were many delays on the train journey down to London and Euston was in darkness as the Irish Mail pulled in to the station.

Telephoned Pierre after breakfast. He was delighted to see me, rather gratifying, and we mingled with the multi-national crowd in the West End for a couple of hours. There are many Polish and Czech soldiers here at present, and the raucous voices of the Aussies are still recognisable.

* Relative income value translates Mary's salary of 30 shillings into approximately £250 a month, based on the value of the pound sterling in 2011.

Was exhausted by the time Pierre put me on to the train for Tunbridge Wells. It was nearly 11 p.m. by the time I reached K and S. I had written to Matron in advance for permission to come in late.

2 August

It is hard to get back to the old routine after my lovely home leave. I invited some of the girls, including Maggie Lee and Joyce Bale, round to my room for a beano last night. I had brought back a rich Irish whiskey fruit-cake, and 1/2lb butter each for our set, also fresh eggs. They were delighted, sang 'You Are My Sunshine' at the top of their voices, and brought me up to date with the news. Matron had been a B as usual and I have been allocated to Women's Medical Ward. We are all, excepting Bale, down for night duty in three weeks.

Was sad to leave my Dunkirk heroes on Men's Surgical, but many are fit for discharge now; some have already returned to their units. I was not sad to see the back of <u>that</u> Staff Nurse and her <u>responsible</u> friend who reported my goings-on to Matron.

7 August

Have been working on Women's Medical now for a few days and like it very much. Sister Wolfe is in charge of the ward and is about twenty-eight years old. She and her scientist father left Germany in 1930 and they are both naturalised Britons. Gerta Wolfe is tiny, dark, intelligent and fair-minded. She takes her teaching role in the ward seriously, and I find these medical case histories fascinating. I can now relate the medical diseases in my text books to the real-life women on my ward. This creates a double interest – the women themselves, their personalities, home background and attitudes, and the illness that is confining them to bed.

Mrs Joan Kelly is in the first bed inside the ward door. She is in her early thirties, and an unwilling Catholic, married to an Irish labourer. She has six children, one for every year of their marriage. The Kelly children are well known in Casualty. They are constantly coming in with runny ears and chesty coughs. They are plainly under-nourished and in need of shoes and clothing. Joan is a good mother and loves her children dearly, but they are too much for her to cope with. She is in here suffering with acute anaemia, and she is pathetically grateful for the treatment we give her and the rather inadequate food that is provided.

We are giving her iron and liver injections but soon we shall send her home to have another baby and to start the whole cycle of family deprivation all over again. Women should not be forced to have babies unless they are strong enough to bear them and rear them successfully.

The women on the ward are lovely. Most of them are tolerant, easy-going Mum types, so self-sacrificing and always considerate to us nurses. Why are women so self-abnegatory and so grateful for everything we do for them?

Sister Wolfe has helped to improve my self-confidence. She assumes that I am capable of passing a Ryles tube into a stomach or taking a blood sample for the laboratory and because of this I find I can do these things.

There was a great deal of air traffic last night. They sounded like heavy bombers.

9 August

The weather is lovely, bright and sunny. Took my text book and notes out to Happy Valley yesterday and sat in the sunshine writing up medical lectures.

The air-raid warning sounded as I walked back to the hospital, and a Local Defence Force man approached and told me to get under cover. There was a sound of bomber planes again. They must have been German for the ack-ack mobile anti-aircraft guns were soon in the street and it became very noisy.

The All Clear sounded in a little while and I made my way back to the Nurses' Home. The phoney war seems to be coming to an end.* Hope it does not become too active over Kent.

12 August

Off duty 2 to 5 p.m. and decided to walk out to Happy Valley again. It is one of my favourite places. It was a very warm afternoon, and as I gazed up at the clear blue sky, I noticed the vapour trails wending their way across. It was then that I recognised the Spitfires – there were about a dozen up there and their agility in the sky was staggering. They were manoeuvring in and out creating more and more complicated vapour trails spinning and diving. I watched in amazement and then I heard the bombers – they must be German. I suddenly realised that the Spitfires were trying to buzz off the Messerschmitts, which were accompanying the bombers. I could not see the bombers – they must have been high – but suddenly there was a blur of twisting machines sparkling in the brilliant sunshine, and then a plane came spinning down in a sheet of flame. Was rooted to the ground in horror and then I saw a parachute open. Hope it was not one of ours.†

Met a small group of Local Defence Volunteers on the way back. They were accompanied by the Fire Brigade and ARP [Air Raid Precaution] men obviously on their way to the burning plane, and also to arrest or rescue the parachutist.

Reported for duty at 5 p.m. and Sister Wolfe said that Matron wished to see me. This was unusual and I hoped that it

* Officially, the Phoney War refers to the period between September 1939 and April 1940 when anticipated attacks on Britain did not occur and there was little sense of the immediate effect of the war on the civilian population.

† German attempts to disable British air power in preparation for an invasion resulted in the Battle of Britain, with dogfights between British and German fighter planes in the skies over Mary's hospital.

did not have any connection with the dinner with Pierre episode. I was terrified as usual but she merely said 'Will you go to bed at once, nurse, and report for night duty on Men's Surgical at 9 p.m.?' I whispered 'Thank you Matron' and went to my room.

It was a beautiful evening and I could not possibly sleep so decided to write some letters on the balcony. There is a fabulous view from there, right across the rich rolling weald of Kent, beautiful Cobbett country. Have enjoyed reading his Essays since I came here. *

It is twilight and beautiful now, remarkably peaceful – the birds are twittering happily but I sense a feeling of apprehension, maybe a fear of the unknown.

14 August

The Dunkirk men have gone home now or back to their units. In addition to the usual civilian surgical cases, we have several young RAF officers, most of them with burns. They are Spitfire and Hurricane pilots. They usually remain with us for a few weeks' treatment prior to being transferred to Mr McIndoe's unit at East Grinstead Hospital. Have heard a great deal about his incredible prowess in rebuilding faces for these young men who are so disfigured.

Dick was admitted to our ward at 1 a.m. today – a twenty-one-year-old Spitfire pilot. He had been picked up in the Channel having baled out after a dogfight with some Messerschmitts. He is in a very bad way, blind with a fractured jaw and severe burns of the face and head. He was taken to theatre on admission and bits of bone and loose teeth were removed from the remains of his face and a stitch put through his tongue so that it could be tied to a button on his pyjama jacket – otherwise he would have choked to death.

---

* In the early nineteenth century William Cobbett rode the English countryside and published essays on the value of farming. These 'Essays' may refer to his collection *Rural Rides* (1830).

I sat beside his bed all through the dark hours of the night. The pain and thirst were unquenchable – his mouth too burnt for even a sip of water, and the intravenous drip was too slow to replace the lost fluid. I gave him morphia every three hours. In the early hours his parents came to visit him and before their arrival I placed a gauze mask over the remains of his poor face.

15 August

The early mornings here are beautiful. I went out on to the balcony at dawn just before waking the patients. The beauty was indescribable – blue skies, the happy activity of birds, the peace and the poignant sadness which is an integral part of nature's beauty in wartime.

There is little time for philosophising these days and very little opportunity for sleep. The air-raid warning usually goes off after our meal at 9.30 a.m. and soon afterwards we hear the planes and the ack-ack guns.

Today I have been unable to sleep at all. It is so noisy. Will we win this battle in the skies? People are becoming rather depressed. The papers say 'we are unprepared'. Will there be an invasion? We feel particularly vulnerable here in Kent.

This is another beautiful day – a day for happiness and gaiety. I watched another dogfight this afternoon, the plane bursting into flame up there in the blue sky and the white parachute opening up like a flower and then dropping gracefully on to a field. Sometimes the parachute becomes entangled in a tree or even a church tower. All this has become a commonplace everyday event now. We switch on the wireless to listen to the BBC nine o'clock news and wait avidly to hear about the day's score. Are we killing more of theirs? Who is winning?

Felt extremely tired as I came on duty tonight. The horror of having to face a hard twelve-hour stint of duty without sleep. It is impossible to describe how I long for sleep.

We had four German POW patients admitted today. Three

were Messerschmitt pilots, the fourth a crew member of a Dornier, a 'flying pencil' bomber. All four young men had made parachute escapes from their aircraft. Helmut is a typical blond Aryan German youth. His parachute landed on top of a church steeple, and there he sat refusing to come down despite the help of ladders provided by the Fire Brigade. Our LDF [Local Defence Force] and ARP [Air Raid Precaution] boys then decided to ignore him and got out their flasks of tea and sandwiches. He came down eventually when he was hungry, and is now in a side ward here under the guard of a nervous young LDF man. He was busy reading his safe conduct leaflet when I went in to see him. These booklets, in German and English, are handed out to all German prisoners as soon as they arrive on our shores.

We had a monthly orange tonight. It seems almost too valuable to eat. It is so difficult to avoid gaining weight these days as the food is so stodgy. Am due for some nights off soon and hope to go up to London to see Pierre.

Told off by George, the Air Raid Warden, last night, for showing a chink of light in the sluice. He made me feel like a fifth columnist. There is talk of a German invasion, possibly along the coast between Folkestone and Bognor.

17 August

Maggie Lee invited me to her home in Tonbridge for lunch. She managed to get some petrol for her Baby Austin and we set off about 10 a.m. A beautiful day – very few people on the road. The air-raid siren sounded almost at once. We heard the usual banshee howlings in the distance, first the 'whee' rising to an hysterical shriek and the 'oo-oo-oo' sinking to a low-pitched gurgle – then sirens nearer at hand took up the lugubrious sound. Eventually the local sirens burst forth and the air was filled with sounds of souls in torment. It was almost more than nerves could stand after a hard night's work on duty.

We heard the sound of planes and the sirens were still wailing when anti-aircraft guns joined the unholy symphony.

We stopped by the roadside, and looking up saw thin vapour trails of German planes. We saw them clearly, about twenty in arrow formation, looking like silver fish in the bright sunlight. There was a rattle of gunfire and we saw two Spitfires attacking a straggling Heinkel. The latter swayed dangerously and then to our horror burst into flames and plummeted straight down on to a clump of trees . . . We drove to lunch.

Maggie's father is a butcher and we had a super meal of traditional roast beef and Yorkshire pudding, followed by apple pie and custard – a meal to be remembered.

The All Clear sounded soon after lunch and we returned in the afternoon to go to sleep in preparation for duty tonight.

We were stopped by Red Caps before entering the hospital and had to show our identity cards, then we saw it: Casualty and Out-Patients had a direct hit – it was a terrific shock. We were ushered across to the Nurses' Home, so we do not know if there were any people killed or injured.

18 August

There was a great hubbub of chatter in the dining room this evening. No dead or injured in the Out-Patient fracas. It was quite miraculous as that is the only afternoon and the only time of the week without a clinic session. There were a few patients and staff in Casualty and they too escaped injury. I must watch my black-out instructions tonight. Heard on the wireless that in the event of invasion all the church bells would ring up and down the country. There has been a great deal of bombing today in East London and the Channel Ports.

The ward is very busy at present and we still have our German POWs.

George the ARP warden woke up most of my patients when he came round to check on the black-out. He is clumsy and heavy footed, and clatters around wearing his steel helmet, and carrying his gas-mask, torch and haversack.

20 August

Listened to the Prime Minister's talk on the wireless. He said in referring to the RAF, 'Never in the history of human conflict, has so much been owed by so many to so few'. I remembered Paddy Finucane,* Dick Hilliard and some of the other pilots from Biggin Hill† whom I know. They are a special kind of people, outwardly talking in clichés and using their own 'in' language. They are a law unto themselves, top tunic button undone, droopy moustaches. I had dinner with Paddy at the Fantail Restaurant in Farnborough some weeks ago – and afterwards went on to his local pub in Biggin Hill. Paddy played the game of nonchalance as usual, as he drank beer from his own special pot. The pilots have their mugs hanging above the bar, and if somebody fails to return from a mission, the mug remains there, but his name is never mentioned, not even by his closest friends. They are a strangely superstitious bunch of boys, many just down from Oxford. The 'few' are now becoming fewer so we must hope that Jerry eases up for a while. They are all so brave and so desperately tired.

Seen by the surgeon today. I have an abscess on the coccyx and am to be admitted to Women's Surgical tomorrow for treatment.

* Brendan 'Paddy' Finucane was an RAF flying ace, nicknamed Paddy because of his Irish background. Whether or not he and Mary knew it when they met, both their fathers had fought against the British with Eamon de Valera at Boland's Mill during the 1916 Easter Rising in Dublin.

† Biggin Hill was the nearby RAF base that played a major role in the Battle of Britain.

21 August

The abscess was lanced in theatre this morning and I am back on the ward lying on my stomach. Matron came to visit me this afternoon and was quite pleasant and kind after telling me I must lie in this position for three weeks. It is very difficult to write or read, but at least I have headphones for the wireless.

The ward is crowded as usual. I am in the bed just inside the door, and there is a very sick girl about my age in the next bed. Her name is Julie and she looks rather pretty and fragile. She is on intravenous saline and is vomiting persistently. Connie Beale told me that she came in as an acute appendicitis yesterday. They took her down to theatre, removed her appendix (although it looked OK) and returned her to the ward on a drip. She was seen by the Consultant Physician this morning and is now diagnosed as acute salpingitis.[*] It is suspected that this is the result of an illegal abortion. Poor girl, I hope she will be alright.

23 August

Still lying on my stomach. The lady in the bed opposite me (Winnie Jones) is again recounting her bomb experience. She was having a bath at home, when the place had a direct hit. She was rescued by a fireman who wrapped her in a blanket and brought her here. She was covered in dirt and plaster debris – but miraculously the injury is mainly to her dignity.

Julie's parents came in this afternoon and are sitting at her bedside. They are so sad and bewildered, as they can see that their beloved daughter is dying. She is semi-conscious now. If only there was not such a stigma attached to being an unmarried mother – Julie would not be in this state. There is nothing that can be done. She is having morphia for pain, and she is

---

[*] Inflammation of the Fallopian tubes – in the days before antibiotics such infections were often fatal.

becoming weaker. Her mother cries and doesn't understand. If I ever have a daughter, I hope she will be able to talk to me.

[Later] I woke up in the early hours and the screens were round Julie's bed. She is dead.

In spite of bombings, leave in London promised a welcome convalescence for Mary after her illness.

15 September, London

Came up to London today to spend a few days with Pierre. Am fully recovered now, although still rather weak. It is bliss to be mobile again. It was extremely boring lying on my stomach for so long, nothing to do but read or listen to the wireless.

It was strange to be at the receiving end of my own profession. I was so well cared for, as are all the patients. The whole principle of our hospital service is that 'The patient comes first'. This duty is constantly drummed in to us. It was a happy ward and during air raids people kept up their spirits by singing 'Run Rabbit Run'.

Pierre met me at the station. He looked tired and ill, and told me that he had been on some abortive mission with De Gaulle somewhere overseas. The incident is over but he prefers not to talk about it. It must have been unpleasant.

We had lunch at Lyons Corner House in the Strand, went for a walk round the Serpentine and booked seats for the Leslie Henson Show in the evening.

There were lots of police, ARP and firemen around the outskirts of St Paul's Cathedral as we went by. Somebody said it was a delayed bomb. Hope they get it out safely. Jerry has been busy today. A Spitfire came down this morning as the train moved out of Tunbridge Wells. I could see the usual dogfight going on overhead.

The air-raid siren went off as we left the theatre and walked back to the hotel. It was a very dark night and I was glad not to be alone in the black-out. I held Pierre's hand tightly in the smoggy atmosphere which intensified the darkness and made me more conscious of the criss-crossing lights in the sky, as our boys searched for the German planes. There was one incident in which a Messerschmitt was caught in the searchlight and tried to wiggle away. There was a momentary quietness and the whole of London seemed to hold its breath – but it got away and Pierre lit a Gauloise and cursed in French.

We listened to the news when we reached the hotel. They say that we brought down one hundred and eighty-five of the enemy today as against thirty of ours. Pierre is jubilant and feels that this will stop Hitler's invasion. We can hear the swish and thud of bombs as we talk until the early hours. Will this war ever end? The All Clear sounds and I fall asleep.

16 September

Pierre and I decided to visit a friend of his who lives in the dockland area. He was visiting this friend last Saturday afternoon when there was a very heavy air raid. It was a lovely sunny afternoon and the two young men were walking down by the docks. Suddenly there was an air-raid warning and the distant drone of approaching aircraft. Pierre says that the German planes came up the river in waves, formations of between twenty and forty bombers escorted by an equal number of fighters. It was a day and night of horror for the people living and working there. Our fighter planes tried to intercept them, but the enemy did an enormous amount of damage on that sunny Saturday afternoon. Pierre went on to say that it was an awful experience, the dust and debris, the explosions and the screams. The firemen, ARP personnel, the police and the Salvation Army were marvellous. There were fires everywhere – a holocaust reaching up to the sky.

The All Clear sounded at dusk as the East End people surveyed the devastation – but they were not to have any rest. There was another warning and the enemy followed up his early advantage by dropping high-explosive bombs into the heart of the fires he had started in the afternoon.

We travelled by bus from the Strand most of the way to Tilbury. The city is in a mess, a huge crater in the Strand, debris everywhere, yet the buses, trains and taxis are running. There is a marvellous feeling of international camaraderie in London – everybody pulling together – and there is great friendliness. We talked with a young Polish airman on the bus. His English was very limited but we gathered that he and many other of his compatriots are training to fly Spitfires and Hurricanes.

Was amazed to see a couple of barrow-boys in the street as we neared the East End. There was a notice above one fruit barrow saying 'Hitler can't beat us' and 'Our oranges came through Musso's lake'. There were not many oranges left but Pierre bought one for me at the outrageous price of 2/9. The barrow-boy will be a millionaire soon if his stocks last.

We were walking along the road in the Tilbury area, when we heard the familiar and dreaded drone of planes again. The warning sounded and our fighters went up and chased them off. We all stood in the street and cheered, and then it happened, a straggler decided to drop his bombs anyway. We heard the thud as it dropped on a nearby factory. Pierre and I threw ourselves on the ground. There was a terrific bang – I waited and then opened my eyes. We were covered in something soft and the sky was full of fluff blowing about prettily in the breeze. My navy suit was covered in feathers, so was my hair. I looked at Pierre – we looked at each other sitting there in a street full of feathers. We laughed and all our feathered friends joined in – the local people who had been watching the dogfight. We were invited to a local house. It was once semi-detached but one of Hitler's bombs detached the other end. We all drank tea, and laughed at the absurdity of a direct hit on a pillow factory, nevertheless we were all glad that it was closed that day.

We went on to the local pub from there and had some beer and sandwiches. We were joined by Pierre's friend Jean soon afterwards, and several of the regulars chatted to us and commented on the day's events. They told us that the dockers and their families are angry with Hitler and angry too with a defence force which is ill equipped and unable to defend them. They feel that the LDF need better weapons and better training. That awful Saturday afternoon and Sunday morning has made them furious. They are strong family-minded people here, and the destruction of their homes, and the docks which provide their living, is very hard to bear. They are full of admiration for the Salvation Army, the 'Sallies' as they call them affectionately. The East End is a close community which fights for its own people.

Pierre and I returned to the West End about 6 p.m. We had a meal and hoped to go and see *Me and My Girl*, the Lupino Lane show, but all the seats were booked by the time we got there.

I must return to Tunbridge Wells tomorrow, so this is our last evening together possibly for some time. Pierre is still rather unhappy about the Pétain quisling set-up in France.* He is worried about his family too, as there is no communication.

We walked around London for an hour or two in the twilight. It was almost dark as we reached South Kensington. There was an alert and almost at once the drone of the bombers overhead, and the whee-ee of the bombs as they dropped around us. Pierre pulled me into South Kensington Tube Station. We went downstairs in the lift, still working but very crowded. An amazing sight greeted us after we had got out of the lift and turned the corner. There were hundreds of people settling down for the night, women knitting, children sleeping, others running around. They were lying on the platform covered with coats and old blankets and surrounded by thermos flasks and babies' bottles. They were of all age groups from the very young

* Philippe Pétain had become Premier of Vichy France in June and was seen as a traitor.

to the very old. The noise of the bombing was muffled down there and the people who were awake were remarkably cheerful.

Pierre and I sat down on the floor and talked and I tried to explain the meaning of some of the notices on the walls. 'Careless Talk Costs Lives', 'Chad' with the long nose peering over a fence* and 'Think of the Workers'.

It was nearly 2 a.m. before the All Clear sounded and we were able to return to the hotel. Another bad night for London. Shall be glad to return to the comparative peace of Tunbridge Wells but I shall miss Pierre.

∿

Back at the Kent and Sussex, fewer entries than usual here suggest that Mary was working especially hard, but she still took time to write sympathetically of her patients.

17 September, Kent and Sussex Hospital

Said 'Au Revoir' to Pierre. Hope to see him next month.

Reported to Matron who informed me that I am now back on Women's Medical on day duty. I wonder if Matrons ever realise the terror they strike in the hearts of young probationers. The work is very hard, and it is considered vulgar even to mention money in a profession obsessed with vocation, but I do wish that my 30/- a month would stretch further than it does, although we are fortunate to have free food and accommodation.

This Voluntary Hospital System is a good one. The patients are well cared for, and the Consultants give their time and expertise on a charity basis.† They earn their livelihood from the private patient.

---

* A graffiti character who came from the American 'Kilroy was Here', called Chad in Britain. Mary was probably referring to graffiti on the walls along with the propaganda posters.

† Before the creation of the National Health Service voluntary hospitals gave free care to patients who could not afford to pay.

The hierarchical set-up here is amazing. I made an awful bloomer once on Men's Surgical. There was an urgent telephone call for Mr Horder during his ward round. He was accompanied on this regal round by his usual retinue of deferential students, his House Surgeons and the Ward Sister. I excused myself to the great man, relayed the message and suddenly found myself in an awful row. Sister said icily 'See me in my office later, nurse.' I slunk off wondering what I had done wrong this time, but was soon to learn that junior nurses must never presume to talk to a consultant – messages must always be conveyed via Sister or Staff Nurse.

The patronising attitude of senior doctors towards patients always makes me angry. Women patients are particularly vulnerable. Miss Peggy Smith on my ward is a case in point. She is a sensitive, gentle little lady in her early fifties, timid to a degree and always over-anxious to please. She is also a very modest person and rather frightened of men.

I was in the ward this morning when the rather loud-voiced Consultant Physician did his round. On reaching Miss Smith, he ignored her presence, and started to tell the students about the case in florid medical language. He then threw back the bedding in order to uncover intimate areas of Peggy Smith without apology or explanation. The poor lady was in tears with embarrassment and humiliation and it took me ages to comfort her and try to restore her sense of human dignity. Why do people not insist that their own body is private property and not to be tampered with without consent?

I suppose it may be a deity thing – when we are ill we need somebody to believe in – but I personally would like that <u>somebody</u> to have some understanding and sensitivity.

29 September

Here I am back on Women's Medical Ward again. We had a young woman admitted this afternoon suffering from complete nervous and physical exhaustion. Katie Jones is twenty-one years old, rather pretty and frail with mousey-coloured hair, and a permanently anxious look in her blue eyes. Her husband is in the RAF Bomber Command and she works in a munitions factory. I feel quite protective of her because she is so timid and utterly worn out. Encouraged her to talk to me this evening after supper. Her work in the factory is extremely tiring. She told me about the women who have to be lifted off their benches at the end of the day, too exhausted to move. Katie found that she was too tired to eat, and was constantly worried about Tom, her young husband. The RAF are the heroes of today, but too much is expected of them. Tom has to go on and on flying and bombing and his wife suffers with him. She told me about the nightmares when she wakes screaming in the early hours. It is, I think, the worry about Tom that has reduced Katie to this sad state. She has been ordered sedatives and complete bed rest for a week.

1 October

This is a lovely ward, but extremely busy. We dash about all day and I am always hungry. There are times particularly in the fore-noon when I feel so faint from hunger that it is almost impossible to carry out my innumerable duties. Our food ration is totally inadequate – 1 oz cheese, 2 oz butter per week and one egg each fortnight, and of course our one orange each month. We tend to make up with bread – the National loaf is not bad, but once the butter ration is finished there is only dripping to put on the bread. It is hateful stuff, but better than starving. Serving the patients' lunches is a painful experience. It is exquisite agony to have to serve their food when one is so hungry.

26 October

Night duty on Men's Surgical. Many of the patients are victims of the recent Blitz in London. In the lonely hours of the night they tell me over and over again how awful the days and nights of bombing have been for them. Some have lost their homes and their relatives and are still in a state of severe shock. Harry Smith lost his wife and daughter in a raid and is here for the amputation of his left foot. He is remarkably cheerful. It will be difficult for Hitler to break the spirit of people such as Harry.

12 November

There are constant rumours of German invasion. The Home Guard (our erstwhile Local Defence Volunteers) are protecting our Kentish shores and it is alleged that a 'large number of German bodies' were washed ashore at Folkestone.

30 December, London, On leave

Decided to spend my nights off up here with Pierre. He booked a room for me at the Alexandra Hotel in Knightsbridge. In stark wartime London this is a most astonishing and unexpected place. The elderly porters wear royal blue livery, and the atmosphere is still Edwardian, a world of rigid uncomplicated values.

Pierre and I had tea in the lounge yesterday afternoon soon after my arrival from Tunbridge Wells. The other guests looked incredibly old, very British upper-class types, who talked in loud commanding voices.

Pierre looks the same as ever, such a gentle manner, and so much sadness in those deep brown eyes. We went for a walk after tea today and I was appalled by the destruction that has taken place in the October raids. St Clement Danes, that lovely church in the Strand, is almost completely ruined. Many famous landmarks have just disappeared.

London was peaceful, and we went on to dine at Simpson's in the Strand. We ate a delicious dinner of succulent chops and drank beer from silver tankards. It was rather splendid to watch the ceremonial cooking of the chops on a trolley alongside our table. The carpets were thick and luxurious, and somewhere in the background there was a record of a discreet Chopin Sonata. It was a place for romance and security – the war was forgotten as we talked about ourselves – always an interesting subject.

It was a clear frosty night as we stepped out of Simpson's. And we suddenly realised that there was a raid on the City. People were scurrying into the underground shelters, and there was the odd sharp command to 'put out that torch'. We could hear planes overhead but it was not until we walked across Westminster Bridge that we realised the full horror of the situation. The whole City was ablaze. It was like bright daylight and had we felt so inclined it would have been possible to read a newspaper. We could see the dome of St Paul's standing out against an awesome background of flame. There were hundreds of small incendiary bombs everywhere. Pierre threw his jacket over one that dropped near us and put it out at once. The Fire Brigade must have been trying to cope with fires elsewhere, for we did not see any firemen or fire-fighting equipment as we wended our way cautiously back to Knightsbridge. It was a strange night in London – quite unforgettable, the crackling heat of burning buildings, the uncanny quiet at times and the dull drone of the enemy planes above.

Tomorrow I return to Kent.

After a five-month silence Mary returned to her diary. Her time had been taken up with nursing duties and study for her examinations. The Blitz had been ravaging London since September 1940, and the war was having a greater impact on the Home Front with more restrictive rationing, conscription for women and government exhortations not to travel more than necessary. Mary was clearly

very much in need of an escape from duties when she travelled up to London again in May 1941, in spite of the risk of bombing.

9 May 1941, London

Life has been a hard slog of ward work and private study for the past few months. It is good to be away from the hospital for a while and to see Pierre again after such a long time. He is still very worried about his family and the recent news of Vichy collaboration with the Germans has increased his anxiety. He seems to take the downfall of France in a very personal way.

We went for a walk round the West End after lunch, and it was a shock for me to see London as it is now. After twenty months of war there is a smell of death and destruction every-where – blasted windows, clocks without hands, great mounds of yellow rubble. There is a poisonous tang of damp plaster and coal gas, a reminder that eighteen thousand Londoners have died here.

It was a lovely sunny spring afternoon and Hyde Park was full of daffodils. Pierre had booked a room for me at the Alex-andra where I stayed last year. As we walked through the streets we were amused by the posters and slogans. 'Don't be a food hog' and the new one which had pride of place, 'Britain can take it'. Another one we liked was outside a bomb-damaged church, 'If your knees knock together – kneel on them'.

We had afternoon tea at the Alexandra. The guests looked exactly the same as last year – elderly colonel types and their rather bossy and indomitable ladies.

Pierre had theatre tickets for the Haymarket and we went along to see Rex Harrison and his wife Lilli Palmer in *No Time for Comedy*. We both found it amusing and Pierre was in a more cheerful mood. As we walked back to the hotel the city streets came alive with a steady tramp of feet as, armed with bun-dles and bed-rolls, knitting and flasks of tea, people thronged towards their air-raid shelters.

There was no alert so far and we could hear the chorus of 'Oh Johnny, How You Can Love' rising from a pub cellar as we walked along the dusty streets.

11 May

It is a miracle that I am still alive. There are many people dead and dying. Last night was the most frightening of my whole life. Pierre had only just left me around midnight when there was an air-raid alert. There was a momentary feeling of trepidation when I wondered whether I should go to the underground shelter, but decided that I was too tired and that it would probably be only a few bombs on the docks as usual.

I walked along the corridor to Room 101 on the second floor and went to bed. It became so noisy after a while that I decided to get up and go downstairs.

The lounge was almost in complete darkness as I entered, just a small blue light burning dimly. There were I think about twenty people there – nobody spoke to me. I looked out of a window in the darkened corridor – there were fires everywhere and the sounds of crashing glass. I went back into the lounge and there were long sick minutes of silence that frayed the nerves and then it happened – a whining shuddering like an express train leaving a tunnel – the air shook with a volcanic rumbling, and a marble pillar in the centre of the room cracked like a tree trunk. In the maelstrom of dust, tumbling masonry and splintering woodwork, people were screaming. I may have screamed too – I do not know, but within seconds into the room there came a Niagara stream of plaster, dust, planking and chairs. The walls seemed to burst apart, raining light brackets, mirrors, clocks and chunks of ceiling. The centre of the floor where the pillar had stood burst apart and the debris thundered down to the basement. There was one terrible cry of terror from the shelterers beneath.

I realised that I should be helping people, not just standing there frozen with horror. I started by asking timidly if anybody was injured. Suddenly everybody started to talk at once. They were alright but they thought that one man had been blasted into the kitchen. I fought my way through the rubble and broken glass, and found a middle-aged man lying unconscious in a tangle of tablecloths and cutlery. There was nothing I could do but go out to find help. I stepped out onto the street. It was like broad daylight. Mayfair and most of the West End seemed to be on fire. Suddenly there were several men there carrying blue lamps – civil defence wardens. I told them about the man in the kitchen and the trapped people in the basement.

The ambulances arrived soon afterwards to take the injured to hospital. It was nearly 1 a.m. as the last person was put into the ambulance, the doors closed and they moved away.

I looked up at the front of the Alexandra. It was well lighted by the burning of Mayfair – and then I noticed to my astonishment that the fourth-floor bedrooms stood wide open to the moonlit park. There had obviously been a direct hit right through the hotel, splitting it in two halves.

I was watching all this in horror when a policeman came by carrying a long plank and some ropes and said, 'There is a family trapped up there, Miss'.

2 a.m. Some more casualties from the hotel were taken to St George's Hospital and I accompanied them to offer my services. It was utter chaos, the lighting had failed and surgeons were trying to work by torchlight. I helped with the setting up of blood transfusions and at 4.30 a.m. went outside for a breath of air. The All Clear had not yet sounded, but a strange hush had fallen on the scene. Across the park the guns were silent and the only sound was the muted blaze of a gas main burning in Park Lane.

I went back to the ward. It was awful – bed nudging bed and stretchers along the full length of the Nightingale-type ward. The nurses and doctors looked hollow-eyed with fatigue. They were still putting up blood transfusions and saline drips. I made tea for everybody.

Pierre found me at St George's around 5 a.m. He was horrified by the damage to the Alexandra and the enormous number of casualties from the whole area. I was dirty, covered in blood stains, and his face was black with smoke and there was a nasty burn on the back of his left hand, but we were happy to be alive and to be together.

We went round to see some friends of mine who own a pub. We were given a strong cognac, then a bath and some breakfast. Jean was kind enough to lend me one of her frocks as mine was in a terrible state. Jean and her husband, Charlie, had kept the bar open all night. They are lovely people, kind, generous and always willing to help others. Charlie was telling us that there are many callous people who take advantage of the Blitz and who deliberately 'move up west to do some nicking in the big stores'.

Pierre had spent the night helping to put out fires, or trying to help put out the incendiaries. The fire-fighting arrangements were a complete shambles. The water hydrants ran dry about 1 a.m. The river was low and no arrangements had been made for water carriers to be brought in to the city from outlying districts. Pierre tells me that the professional firemen are excellent at their job, given water and the right equipment. The real problem (apart from the shortage of water) appears to be the lack of training for the volunteer firemen and fire watchers.

5.25 a.m. The All Clear has just gone but the fires are still alight all over London.[*]

12 May, Kent and Sussex Hospital

It took me seven hours to reach here from London. There were delays all along the line. All the railway lines are disrupted. Feeling exhausted. I shall miss Pierre – but I must get down to

[*] Mary was not exaggerating when she called her survival 'a miracle'. The night of 10–11 May 1941 was the worst night of the London Blitz. At least twenty-four people died in the Alexandra Hotel.

studying for my Finals. Shall probably have to go back to Guy's
if the war is over soon.[*]

*Hard work kept Mary silent for over six months from the day of
her return to the Kent and Sussex. In spite of her hope that the war
might be 'over soon' now that the Americans had entered the conflict
as a response to the bombing of Pearl Harbor by the Japanese, the
further invasion of Hong Kong and other European colonies in Asia
in December 1941 escalated the scale of the war.*

11 December

The United States has declared war on Germany and Italy and
about time too. The Yanks have certainly taken their time. Their
dried egg and spam and Lend-Lease are most acceptable but
many people feel that they should have supported Britain at a
far earlier stage of the war.[†]

26 January 1942

The first American soldiers landed in Northern Ireland today.
The war will soon be over now that they are on our side.

3 March

Pierre is staying down here for a few days. We heard on the BBC
News that the RAF had bombed the Renault works in Paris.
The loss of this factory will be a serious blow to the Germans.

---

[*] If the war ended she would be moving back to Guy's Hospital in London, rather
than staying at the Kent and Sussex, since the move there had been part of Guy's
wartime evacuation precautions.

[†] Lend-Lease: a programme implemented in March 1941 whereby the United
States supplied Britain and other Allied countries with war materiel, but were not
directly involved in the war.

We went out to dinner at a hotel nearby. The food was awful but there was a good band. We danced and talked and the attractive lady vocalist sang 'The last time I saw Paris'.

Soon it was time for me to return to the Nurses' Home and it was as we walked back along the dark streets that Pierre told me that he would be returning to France in a few weeks. I did not ask the obvious questions, of how and why and where – but I have known for a long time that he was anxious to join his compatriots within the underground movement.

We said 'Au Revoir' but I wonder if I shall ever see him again.

21 August

Matron has asked me to go on night duty to special four Canadian soldiers in a small surgical side ward. They were transferred here yesterday and are reputed to be tough and unco-operative. Am feeling more than a little nervous. Their presence here is very hush-hush and must not be discussed outside the hospital.

Went on duty at 8 p.m. The Sergeant, McTavish, presumably of Scottish descent, is in his early thirties, the three private soldiers are in their twenties, and seem to be in a state of severe shock.

McTavish is in severe pain from shrapnel wounds of the left thigh. He is on M and B 693 in an effort to prevent and combat infection.* He is to go down tomorrow to have the deep-seated shrapnel removed.

His first words to me as I entered the ward were, 'Where is my bloody morphia?' I gave it to him without comment and he gradually relaxed as the pain decreased. I made him as comfortable as possible and introduced myself to the other patients. They were far from being in any way difficult or unco-operative. They were in a state of complete exhaustion and shock – too tired to talk. They just lay there looking at the ceiling. Their

---

* M and B (named for its developers May and Baker) 693 or variants, often referred to as sulpha drugs, were antibacterial medications.

physical injuries are not very serious, but I have never seen such total exhaustion as this. They are all Commandos, and the Sergeant said over and over again, 'It was bloody murder' and then fell asleep.

Had to awaken Sgt McTavish at 2 a.m. for his M and B tablets, they have to be administered four hourly and I feared his wrath at being disturbed. He took his tablets and then asked for a glass of beer. There wasn't any beer but he settled for a cup of tea instead. He was not too keen on the tea but he obviously wanted to talk.

I listened for nearly two hours while he told me about the incredible raid on Dieppe.* He told me about the dawn landing and the annihilation of practically the whole of the Canadian Commandos. He said 'We managed to negotiate safely through the enemy minefields and then came face to face with a gun battery. They mowed us down and as we retreated to the beach we ran into E-boats and flak ships'.

Sgt McTavish needed more morphia by now but he carried on talking and talking. It seemed to help him. He called the Dieppe raid 'the most murderously suicidal operation of the war so far'. His anger is very great and he is sad too for his dead comrades and for the mental horror that has been inflicted on *his* young soldiers.

This volatile and brave Canadian was sleeping like a baby when I came off duty. The other young men were quiet – too quiet.

24 August

Sgt McTavish is still in my care, but his three young soldiers have been transferred to a mental asylum for voluntary psychiatric treatment.

* On 19 August Mountbatten commanded Operation Jubilee. The infamous raid on Dieppe was a disaster: a destroyer and thirty-three landing craft were sunk, all the tanks that managed to get to shore were destroyed, and the Canadian infantry were trapped on the beach by heavy German defences, resulting in 4,000 casualties. Canadians felt that, as colonial troops, they were seen as expendable.

26 October

Working in Casualty day duty. Life here is very busy. There are long patient queues of people waiting for dressings and treatment. The same people and their families come back time and time again and we get to know them and their families quite well. They talk as we do the dressings. People are tired of this war. Food is in short supply and they are worried about husbands and sons in the Services.

I too am feeling tired. My State examinations are coming up soon and there is little time for study. I set my alarm clock for 4.30 a.m. and work on my notes and text books until it is time for breakfast at 6.30 a.m. All lectures are in our off-duty periods.

The patients are lovely, nothing else matters. It is good to meet people, and to be able to help them. Shall probably go on to take my State Fever examinations after I have (hopefully) gained my SRN certificate.

Two

'What a night!'

Fever nursing, Brook Hospital, Woolwich

Mary in her grey and scarlet Queen Alexandra uniform

Although the severe bombing of the 'Big Blitz' was over, intermittent raids continued and became more intense in the early months of 1944. Having passed her examinations, Mary was now a State Registered Nurse (SRN) and ready to begin further training in the specialist area of fevers. Before antibiotics, fever nurses were crucial to the care of patients suffering from any illness, often infectious or contagious, that resulted in a high fever. The Brook Hospital at Shooter's Hill, Woolwich in southeast London, where Mary underwent her fever training, had opened as a specialist Fever Hospital in 1896. During the war it became an Emergency Medical Scheme hospital and cared for air-raid victims as well as fever cases.

11 February 1943, Brook Hospital, Woolwich

Arrived here yesterday to commence fever training. This place is large and rambling. The Medical Superintendent's house is just inside the rather forbidding iron gates at the entrance to the hospital. Most of the wards are two storey with an outside iron staircase. These wards are old and depressing in appearance and could do with a coat of paint. There are several emergency huts scattered around the perimeter of this complex, all separated from each other by a covered passage way.

12 February

The MS [Medical Superintendent] Dr Breen and his wife invited me and the other new trainee SRNs to tea at their home this afternoon. He is a charming man, extremely tall and a great enthusiast for his speciality. He has written some excellent books on medical and nursing care for fevers. His wife too is a doctor, dark and petite with a very pleasant manner. They both seem to imbue a family feeling within this ugly complex of hospital buildings. They will act as our tutors in the year ahead.

Was surprised to learn that we have to go out on ambulance duty on a rota basis. This will be something quite new for me.

14 March, Night Duty

Night duty on Children's Whooping Cough Ward. It is quite impossible to sleep during the day, because the mobile ack-ack guns parade up and down outside my window. There are occasional air raids but they are totally irrelevant as the anti-aircraft bods seem to need continual practice all day long.

The noise of guns all day, and the coughing, vomiting and screaming of children all night is almost intolerable. My heart sinks as I climb the iron stairs and start another twelve-hour stint of coping alone with thirty-two sick children, comforting them and cleaning up the continual vomit and wet and dirty beds.

Most of these children come from the East End and are very under-nourished. Some of them are also chronic asthmatics and could easily choke to death on their own vomit during an asthma attack or a severe bout of whooping. The night is a long vigil of lonely anxiety and responsibility, and at the end of it I have to wash piles of vomit-ridden linen. Find it quite impossible to eat any breakfast.

26 March

Another noisy sleepless day. There was a new patient admitted last night – a six-month-old baby boy with whooping cough and gastro-enteritis. He is on barrier nursing, but as I am the only nurse here and there are thirty other children I am naturally worried about this baby and the awful possibility of gastro-enteritis spreading throughout the ward. Telephoned the office to say that I needed help, but I doubt if there will be any forthcoming. We are very short of nurses.

This dear little baby is very fragile and dehydrated. I give him drops of sterile water from a pipette every fifteen minutes. His nappy is bright green, a bad sign. I put it straight into the incinerator.

Baby John's temperature remained high, but he seemed to be a little better, as I tried to deal with all the other coughing and screaming children.

I was about half-way round the ward when he started whooping. He was extremely feverish and very distressed, almost black in the face, and then it happened – the one thing I dreaded – a severe convulsion. I must act at once otherwise there could be severe brain damage. I rushed into the sluice room – filled a sink with cold water and immersed him as gently as possible and without undressing him. I kept him there until the twitching and convulsions ceased and then undressed him, put on a clean nappy and laid him in the cot. I prayed hard that he would survive the shock and miraculously he did and I was able to give him some more boiled water.

It was now after midnight and most of the other children were still awake and screaming blue murder. It was nearly 2 a.m. before the rest of the children were settled. It was then that I heard the whine of the air-raid warning followed soon afterwards by a telephone call from the Porter's Lodge, to say that the night Superintendent had ordered the evacuation of all the children to the underground cellar beneath the downstairs ward. They would send a porter over to help me.

I was appalled. The majority of the children were in no fit condition to be moved. Baby John needed absolute quiet and there is a three-year-old girl Katie with broncho-pneumonia. I woke the older children first and told them what was happening. I put on all the lights, found extra blankets – it was a bitterly cold night outside and the children would have to be carried down the old iron staircase. I tried to get the children wrapped up warmly and made some soothing noises which were totally lost amidst the screaming cacophony of whooping and vomiting. The All Clear and the porter arrived simultaneously! It was a great relief to know that I could now make another attempt to settle the children for the rest of the night.

Baby John has rallied a little and has managed to retain the boiled water.

What a night! Exhausted.

28 March

Managed to get a little sleep today. Did not have to be on duty until 9 p.m. This is to make up for the fact that there is nobody to relieve me for the customary one-hour meal time during the night.

As I climbed those awful iron steps I kept my torch carefully angled downwards in order to comply with the black-out regulations. It was as I was nearing the top of the stairs that I saw them, big black furry rats – I was hypnotised with terror for a few dreadful seconds, while they stood their ground and looked at me. My knees were beginning to buckle when suddenly they scuttled away.

I reported the rats to the Day Staff Nurse, but she said that there was nothing that could be done. The food bins were not emptied very often because of the shortage of porters. She said, 'After all there is a war on'. This is a common excuse for every type of incompetence and inefficiency these days. There is no answer to it.

Baby John is rallying a little and has vomited less today. He is far less dehydrated. Katie is not so well and is in an oxygen tent. It is heartbreaking to see the suffering of this dear little girl, as she fights to get her breath. I gather that her mother visited her yesterday afternoon, but Staff Nurse Bell told me that this visit 'upset the child', and that <u>they</u> would not permit her to visit again. This attitude towards the mother upsets me very much. If I had a young child as seriously ill as Katie I would refuse to leave her, but the mothers are too easily bossed about by so-called medical opinion. Young children need their mothers and their presence can only be beneficial. All the children on this ward need time and love as well as expert care. I am only too well aware that it is impossible for me to provide all of these needs for so many children throughout the long dark night.

Four-year-old Jimmy said, 'Good-night sweetie pie' as I tucked him in for the night. They are all so lovely, and I feel distraught about my own inadequacy in coping with so many seriously ill children. This hospital is run by the LCC [London County Council] and I fear that the standards of nursing care are far below those of the Kent and Sussex.

Reported the presence of rats to the Porter's Lodge and asked them to do something about it – but they did not seem to consider it a very serious matter.

14 April

Katie died two days ago. Broncho-pneumonia in a debilitated child can be a killer. She did not have the strength to fight. Poor little girl. She was so young and so frightened. Her mother should have been with her, but medical and nursing opinion on this matter is appallingly intransigent. Many nurses see the ward as their domain and resent visiting by relatives.

Baby John is much improved now and sitting up in his cot. The enteritis has cleared up and the whooping cough is gradually improving. He gurgles and smiles as I give him his bottle. It is wonderful to see him looking so well.

17 April

The ack-ack guns are still trundling up and down the road but I am becoming accustomed to their awful noise and manage to get a little sleep.

The ward was in semi-darkness when I came on duty last night and the children seemed quieter. Jimmy said, 'Hello sweetie pie' as I went around the cots to look at the children, change the dirty beds and clean up the usual vomit.

As I approached baby John's cot I noticed the vague outline of a curved bottle in his mouth. He was very quiet so I switched on the light above his cot. There was a sudden scurrying of black fluffy shapes and I screamed and rushed for the telephone to ring Dr Breen. I was still hysterical as his quiet voice answered and I shouted 'A baby's face has been half-eaten by rats'. The children were howling when he arrived. He looked shocked and I kept saying 'The rats'. He said, 'There will have to be an inquest' and 'Pull yourself together, nurse, the child is dead'. He then added 'I will inform the parents' and I was grateful for that.

The cot was saturated with blood as I removed the little body and wrapped it in a sheet. A porter came along soon afterwards and took him away.

Jimmy climbed out of bed and sat on my lap as I cried quietly. He just said 'Sweetie pie' as he always does and that brought me to my senses and somehow or other I managed to get through the rest of the night.

It was nearly 7.30 a.m. when Dr Breen telephoned me again. (The day staff are due in at 8 a.m.) He said 'Last night's incident is top secret. Do not discuss this matter. It would be too distressing for the parents.' I replied weakly 'Yes Doctor.'

11 May

Still on night duty. Another children's ward, all types of diphtheria. There are twenty-nine patients all ages from one to twelve years. It is extremely hard work and I have one nursing orderly to help me, Mrs Campbell, who is quite marvellous, a middle-aged lady with grown-up children and a lifetime's experience in common sense.

All of these children are on complete bed rest. The child must lie flat without pillows and must be washed, fed and toileted in bed. The patient must be kept absolutely quiet and if there is any suggestion of heart failure the foot of the bed is raised on blocks to ensure the blood supply to the vital centres of the brain. The child is kept flat for two or three weeks, depending on his response to treatment. The primary treatment is the administration of serum as soon as possible. This neutralises toxaemia and arrests the spread of the fearsome membrane. The minimum dosage is about 8,000 units and each day the dose is roughly doubled – 100,000 units usually considered to be the maximum. In severe cases the serum is given intravenously and children require a larger dose than adults. No case of any severity, even in the absence of complications, is discharged before fifty-six days. Cultures prior to discharge are commenced as soon as the patient is up in blankets.

This is a dreadful illness with a distinctive sickly sweet smell – quite nauseating. These children look so pale and ill and are dreadfully bored. It is so hard for young children to lie still in bed day and night for weeks on end. I read stories to them whenever I can, and Mrs Campbell is a source of fun and entertainment.

There is one boy, Michael, in an artificial respirator, and he is totally isolated in a side ward. All but his head is enclosed in a metal box, within which a motor varies the pressure from normal to a vacuum every few seconds. The vacuum sucks out the elastic chest wall and thus expands the lungs which follow it and so fill themselves with air. Michael is a polio victim and without this respirator he would die.

James aged four in a cot near the door has had 100,000 units of serum. The membrane on his throat and larynx looks very nasty and he is extremely toxic. Have asked Mrs Breen (the House Physician) if he might be put on intravenous serum as he is having more and more progressive difficulty in swallowing.

Poor little James. He looks so ill.

12 May

Mary Kane is our runner tonight. She helped on my ward for about two hours which was most acceptable.

This is such a quiet ward. It is almost uncanny – twenty-nine children and hardly a sound. James is on intravenous serum but the membrane is still spreading. His pulse rate is increasing and he is becoming restless. Mrs Campbell and I have just fixed up a steam tent in the hope that it will help James to breathe more easily.

2 a.m. Telephoned [Mr Pakari] the Indian House Surgeon to say that James's condition has deteriorated and that he might need an urgent tracheotomy.

Mrs Campbell sat with James while I prepared for the stab operation. It had to be performed on the ward. The child was too ill to be moved.

I cleared the books etc. from the central ward table and placed the mobile screens around it. I laid James in a blanket tucked just below his shoulders. His arms were extended by his sides and the blanket wrapped tightly around him and secured with strong safety pins. I then placed him gently on the table and adjusted the sandbag under his shoulders so as to give the fullest extension to the neck. James's breathing was noisy and painful by now – the young dark-skinned surgeon looked at me and we both said 'There is no time to scrub up'.

I held James's head firmly and steadily in the mid-line and full extension. We both knew that unless the head was straight the surgeon might cut into the side of the trachea, instead of the centre. There was no time for a second stab. James was almost black in the face and in great distress.

Mr Pakari made his incision very rapidly. There was a blessed loud intake of air for James, and miraculously his colour became pink and to me quite beautiful. The trachea was open now and it was just a simple matter of inserting the dilators. With his left hand the surgeon introduced the tube and pilot, simultaneously withdrawing the dilators and quickly removing the pilot and securing the tapes around the neck.

We put James back in a warm cot and he fell asleep at once. We took away the steam tent. He was breathing normally for now. We must still be very careful of course and look for any recurrence of obstructive symptoms. This could arise from any blockage of the inner tube. We have to be particularly vigilant with young children as they are quite capable of pulling out the dilators.

14 May

James is marginally better. He had some more serum yesterday and we are all keeping our fingers crossed. The membrane, dirty yellow and foul smelling, is now extended across the posterior pharyngeal wall, across the palate and almost to the gums. His colour is improved nevertheless, and the pulse a little stronger.

The ward is again very quiet apart from the gentle hum of Michael's respirator. There are some planes about. Hope they are ours.

3 a.m. The air-raid warning sounded, followed by the usual order to evacuate the children. I contacted the Night Superintendent and asked for the windows here to be boarded up and reported that Michael and James were too ill to be moved and I would remain with them. I then ordered stretchers for all the older children. They must be spared any unnecessary movement.

It was nearly an hour later before the porters arrived to move the children to the shelter. The raid increased in intensity about 4.30 a.m. and there were some very loud bangs, some far too close for comfort. Was glad that the windows were boarded up.

James is on nasal feeding now and has been taking sips of fruit juice with glucose. It is so lovely to see some improvement in his condition. There is no further spread of the dreaded membrane.

The All Clear came at about 5.30 a.m. and the children were returned and tucked into bed.

It was soon after 6 a.m. when Mr Smith, the Head Porter, rang to say that the Medical Superintendent's house had a direct hit and Mrs Breen was dead. Mrs Campbell and I were stunned. She had been chatting to us last night, when she came round to see the children. Poor Dr Breen. They were a devoted couple.

Day Duty must have come as some relief to Mary. At least she was now spared the isolation of coping at night with little support. Her first stint was short-lived, however.

16 June

Back on day duty now and working in one of the sanatorium huts in the outer precinct of the hospital.

Have not been feeling well for several days – probably exhaustion due to lack of sleep. I have a sore throat and a fever and decided to inform Matron this evening. She was none too pleased. A sick nurse is anathema to every Matron.

Seen by the new House Physician after duty. He diagnosed tonsillitis and prescribed a few days' rest in the Nurses' Home.

20 June

Struggled out of bed to report to Home Sister this morning. Feel dreadfully ill – quite unable to walk. Seen by the doctor. He took a throat swab.

6 p.m. Feel awful. Lying flat on my back in a side ward off G Ward. Am not allowed to move or do anything for myself. The swab was positive. I have diphtheria.

2 August

Have been off sick for five weeks. It was dreadfully boring.

Now on duty on the TB ward. The Tuberculosis Sanatorium is comprised of a number of EMS [Emergency Medical Service]* huts on the perimeter of the hospital. These small wards are rather primitive and contain three iron beds each. There is a wide open doorway leading on to a wooden balcony and the beds are wheeled out there each morning and brought back each night. The doors are kept open day and night even throughout the coldest winter weather.

Most of these patients are on complete bed rest, and their pillows are fixed in armchair fashion which keeps them well propped up.

Was surprised to see how fit and bronzed everybody looked. My first introduction to the ward was hearing an American voice singing 'Oh what a beautiful morning'. Amos Cranshaw is a journalist who has been over here since 1940 and he told me that the song was from a show called *Oklahoma*. Amos has been here for nearly four months and is far more ill than he appears to be.

This man is in his early forties, rather thin with bright intelligent eyes. He talks a great deal and then suddenly becomes very tired. He has acute pulmonary TB and was admitted here following a severe haemorrhage. He is alone in this hut as we fear any outside infection could bring on another haemorrhage which might prove fatal. His cough is worse at night and his temperature shoots up each evening. He has severe night sweats.

I wear a face mask and a barrier gown which is kept in a cupboard outside his door. This is to protect him from any infections which I might have, and hopefully to protect me a little from the germs which he is constantly coughing up into

* The Emergency Medical Services had been established at the beginning of the war to cope with anticipated civilian casualties.

his sputum mug. Amos has a wife and two young children in Detroit but it is doubtful if he will ever see them. His X-ray plates are a sad sight. He is a cheerful, philosophical man who enjoys life, and has been totally involved for years in the business of telling the American people about wartime conditions over here. He has a wry cynical sense of humour and reminds me constantly that he knows the score. TB is rampant in Ireland and I am rather frightened of catching this foul disease. It is possible that my recent attack of diphtheria has intensified these fears.

There is a sixteen-year-old girl in the hut next door. Mary O'Brien is of Irish extraction and is quite startlingly attractive. She has high cheekbones, large grey eyes, a lovely complexion and long dark hair. She is also very emaciated and very ill indeed. Mary has acute pneumonic phthisis or galloping consumption. She was admitted here four days ago, transferred from another hospital where they had been treating her for pneumonia. She smiles weakly at me as I try to reduce her fever with cool sponging. She has swinging pyrexia which is always accompanied by drenching sweats. I change her bedding a dozen times a day.

Her anxious and loving parents visit her three times a week at visiting times. I find it quite heartbreaking and wonder why they are not permitted to visit more often. She will not live very long.

The adjoining hut on the other side is even more depressing. There are three children there, two girls and a boy of six years. The oldest girl, Jane, is ten years, the younger one, Mandy, is nine. The three children have TB meningitis. Their high-pitched screams are horrific. They are like terrified young animals. We give them sedatives for pain, but it never seems to help. I remember the <u>one line</u> in my text book relating to this awful disease which simply stated 'There is no treatment beyond meeting symptoms as they arise'.

8 August

Fever nursing is very demanding, time-consuming and more than a little frightening. We are very short of nurses, probably because so many of us seem to pick up infections from the patients, despite the rigorous rules of constantly changing gowns, caps and masks, and scrubbing up until our hands are red raw.

We had a new patient admitted in the early hours of this morning. She is on complete isolation and is extremely ill. Joan Baker's baby son was born ten days ago and she had returned from the maternity ward yesterday afternoon. She was taken ill suddenly in the night. Her temperature was 104 when she was admitted to us as an emergency and diagnosed as puerperal sepsis. She has a purulent vaginal discharge and an infection of the puerperal uterus. This is a terrifying illness for any woman. My mother died from it when I was three weeks old. Fortunately we have the sulphanilamide drugs these days, and they are an enormous help in fighting the infection. Joan is on M and B 693 and as much fluid as we can force her to drink. She is very restless and delirious, and we have to keep cot sides on her bed, as she is *non compos mentis*. This is in fact a type of puerperal insanity.

9 August

Poor Joan. Her condition is not improving and I have been assigned to special her.

Her mental symptoms are most difficult to cope with. Her husband came to visit her this afternoon and brought the baby as I thought it might help her. This was obviously a mistake. She screamed abuse at him and insisted that the baby was not her child. Mr Baker was in tears and it took me a long time to reassure him. He told me that she is a gentle quiet girl under normal situations.

Joan is refusing to drink now and threw a jug of lemonade at me this morning. She was apologetic afterwards and said that she did not throw it at me but at the 'black evil thing that sat on my shoulder'. She is hallucinating and I dare not turn my back for a moment as she is suicidal at times and very depressed. I keep her sitting up in Fowler's position as much as possible, but she frequently throws pillows at me. I laugh at this and she too sees the joke now. Am desperately trying to maintain a rapport with her.

12 August

Kenneth telephoned me last night and has invited me to have dinner with him tomorrow. We are to meet at Simpson's in the Strand. Kenneth is a radio officer with the Merchant Navy, also a poet of some sort. We met at a social function in Guy's Hospital almost a year ago and I have not seen him since.

Joan is much improved. She is far more rational today, but she seems to have obliterated her own macabre behaviour from her mind. She is a different girl, still very ill and feverish but far less depressed and anxious to see her husband and baby. The vaginal discharge too is less offensive and we all think that she is on the mend. Mary O'Brien died last night. She was so young and there was nothing we could do.

Amos is a little improved and has put on some weight. He has been receiving food parcels from his family in the States. Feeding our TB patients in wartime is extremely difficult. They need abundant good food, but with rationing this is impossible. We are hoping that Amos may be fit enough to return home in about six weeks' time.

13 August

This is the first day off I've had in weeks. It was such a luxury to lie in bed most of the morning. Breakfast was not worth getting up for – the usual chunks of bread and dripping and some foul dried egg mixture.

It was such a fine sunny afternoon that I decided to walk across the Common to the railway station. There were masses of gunner soldiers outside the Arsenal as I walked by and they whistled loudly as usual.

The city was hot and dusty – rubble everywhere. The devastation of London strikes me anew each time I go there.

Met Kenneth in the foyer of Simpson's. The luxury of the place amazed me as it did when I dined there with Pierre. There is the atmosphere of a luxurious church – with extremely polite vergers – a sort of hushed reverential air – as if one should speak in whispers. Kenneth has grown a black beard since I saw him last. It makes him look slightly sinister, which he is not, or maybe even interesting – which he is not.

I must not be bitchy about Kenneth. He is kind, considerate, generous, good looking and very dull. He has all the inhibitions of the product of a middle-class background and a minor public school. He denigrates his job which is an excellent and useful one, mainly because he is ashamed of the Merchant Navy tag. He writes reasonably good poetry – but not good enough.

We had an excellent roast dinner, served from a heated trolley, and the superb sauces were made by the chef as we watched. It was wonderful to be away from the hospital for a little while, and enjoy good food and good wine.

Kenneth must return to duty tomorrow, no doubt another Atlantic crossing. The transatlantic convoys are still vulnerable, too many U-boats around. He escorted me back to Woolwich Station and I promised him that I would take a taxi back to the Brook.

I had just waved good-bye to him when there was an air-raid warning. I telephoned for a taxi but there was no answer and the trams had stopped running as it was nearly midnight. There was nothing to be done but to walk back across the Common. It was a bright moonlight night. The anti-aircraft guns blasted forth as I ran as fast as I could past the Arsenal, across the park and on to the Common. The noise had intensified by then and I was terrified. There was the droning of planes overhead, the guns, the crackle of incendiary bombs and then periodically the loud explosion of a big one.

I was alone on the Common, and ran from the shelter of one tree to the next, crying with terror, my clothes tattered by brambles, my knees bleeding from throwing myself on the ground in an effort to avoid the shrapnel. There was flak all around me. It embedded itself in the trees as I lay on the ground quivering with terror. What a thoughtless fool I had been, no tin hat, no protection. I felt that Woolwich was the wildest, noisiest and most dangerous spot in the whole world as I struggled back to the hospital.

The raid was still on as I rang the gate bell for the Night Porter. He was horrified to see the state I was in, covered in blood and mud and unable to explain what had happened. He sent for Mr Pakari [the surgeon]. There was some shrapnel embedded in the upper part of my left arm, otherwise, miraculously, I was alright.

Mr Pakari kindly removed it under local anaesthetic – a nasty black piece. He promised that he would not tell anybody about this stupid incident and I know he will keep his word.

The All Clear sounded as I wended my weary way to bed.

19 September

We had a new patient admitted to one of the isolation huts last night. He was transferred to us from the Royal Herbert a few hundred yards down the road. Matron has assigned me to special him. He has cerebro-spinal fever and is a very sick man.

Pilot Officer John Hall is an Australian pilot in the RAF serving with 129 Squadron. He is twenty-three years old. It is broad daylight but I have put up the black-out curtains in the hut because of his severe intolerance to light. He has a high fever and intermittent bouts of vomiting. I talk to him in whispers because any loud noise causes an excruciating headache.

His neck and back muscles are contracted spasmodically so that his body when lying on his back is arched like a bow, and resting on his head and heels. This disease is often called spotted fever but so far no rash has appeared. Today a lumbar puncture was performed – the spinal fluid was turbid and under pressure. Sulphapyridine has been prescribed, to be given intramuscularly. He has become quite emaciated, yet I find it difficult to move him every two hours as I must do in order to prevent bed-sores. He is extremely irritable, poor man, and hates to be touched. It took me hours to pass a Ryles tube into his stomach for feeding.

He likes me to talk to him in a soft voice and as I can't think of anything much to say, I sit here reading extracts from Palgrave's *Golden Treasury*. This seems to help him relax. He obviously likes poetry.

24 September

John Hall is reacting well to his therapy and is now on oral fluids. The nasal tube has been removed. He talked to me this evening. He has been under the command of Douglas Bader, the legless flying ace.* He also talked about 'one of our greatest triumphs' – the raid on the dams at the Möhne Zee in May.†

It is wonderful to see how rapidly John is recovering. He is already putting on a little weight and the fever is subsiding.

* Bader's legs had been amputated following a crash in the RAF in 1931 when he was only twenty-one. In spite of this he continued flying and won numerous awards, including the DSO and DFC, the Croix de Guerre and the Légion d'Honneur.

† The Möhne Zee dam raid, led by Wing Commander Guy Gibson, was part of a raid on three German dams in May 1943, later made famous by the 1955 film, *The Dambusters*.

26 September

My patient is miraculously improved. Am very happy about this because John has had a hard time since he first came to England early last year. He had an incredible escape on his return from the raid on Dieppe. His plane had been hit, but somehow or other he managed to cross the Channel. He was 'half blinded and suffocated by smoke and fumes' and decided that he must crash the aircraft as he could not make base. His navigator reported that they were over open country and they both baled out at 3,000 feet. After only '50 seconds in the air' John landed in and bounced out of some high-tension wires and then found himself in a ploughed field. His navigator landed awkwardly and broke his leg. They were just beginning to congratulate themselves on their safe drop, when they were surrounded by an angry group of Sussex farmers wielding pitchforks and spades. The farmers thought they were Germans because of the navy blue RAF uniform. They were eventually identified and then the plane was found buried in a cornfield.

John is to get up tomorrow and he may be discharged in a week or two if his condition continues to improve. He is very amusing, but I still find it a little difficult to understand his Aussie slang.

Back on Night Duty, Mary was assigned to the 'dreaded Measles Ward', where she had to care for thirty-four children under the age of six on her own, showing how short-staffed civilian hospitals had become.

18 October

Back on night duty again. This time it is the dreaded Measles Ward. Thirty-four spotty children all sneezing and coughing and with permanently running noses. They are all under six years old and we have two babies in oxygen tents. I have a runner to help for about one hour each night – after that I'm on my own.

The anti-aircraft guns are still trundling up and down each day making a frightful racket. We still have air raids, but we seem to have become accustomed to them and their duration and intensity is less severe than last year.

Many of the children here come from the East End. Yesterday I was on ambulance duty stand-by and was awakened about 6 p.m. and informed that I must be ready to go out to Stepney to pick up some children with suspected measles.

The house was a tenement basement and the mother looked tired and hungry. The living conditions were appalling and it was obvious that she was beyond coping. She told me that her husband was in the army. There were four children and they all had measles. The baby, Josephine, was my main anxiety. She is only eight months old, looks emaciated and has a nasty dry cough. The oldest girl, Anna, is a thin nervous child covered in spots, but far more anxious about Josephine than herself. She kept asking me if Josie was alright. The two boys aged three and four respectively were also pretty miserable, so I rang the hospital and they advised me to bring them all in to A Ward.

They are all in adjoining beds here, and seem to be settling down well. The baby is in a steam tent and looks very fragile. I am almost frightened of touching her, because her breathing is so difficult. Her little body is so small and thin. Anna keeps getting out of bed and trotting over to the cot in order to keep a maternal eye on her little sister.

This ward is extremely hard, and the children require a great deal of careful nursing. They are feverish and miserable, cry almost continuously and some have developed bronchitis. The ward work is also complicated by the children's photophobia. They abhor light but we have to keep a constant lookout for conjunctivitis, which could lead to corneal ulcer and perhaps subsequent blindness.

The noise here is indescribable. It is sad to see so many miserable sick children. Talked to Anna this morning. Was horrified to learn that she looks after the others every night because 'Mam has to go out'. She added 'We get hungry sometimes'.

21 October

What a night this has been. The air-raid warning sounded at about 11 p.m. just as I had settled most of the children for the night. The telephone rang soon afterwards to say that I was 'to evacuate all the children to the shelter at once'. My reply was that it could be extremely dangerous to move them on such a cold night as this, and how was I to cope with the babies who were in oxygen and steam tents? The answer to that was that it could be <u>more</u> dangerous for <u>more</u> children if we stayed here.

I woke the older children first, told them what was happening and wrapped them in blankets. Tried to reassure them but they all howled dismally. I left the very sick babies until last and started to carry the older children down the outside iron staircase to the basement shelter. It was cold and dark outside and we were all terrified. The basement was a dreary place and there were other howling children there from another ward. These children had whooping cough, but the problems of cross-infection diminish when the alternative could be a bomb.

I struggled up and down that iron staircase at least twenty times before a porter came to help me. It was absolute pandemonium. I took baby James out of his oxygen tent, wrapped him up carefully and prayed that he would survive the upheaval.

Anna was screaming when I returned to the shelter because she could not find Josephine. I was bending over the baby's cot to pick her up when mercifully the All Clear sounded. I added another kettle of boiling water to increase the steam as Josephine was having difficulty breathing.

It was then a question of reversing the whole process, collecting the baby and returning him to his oxygen tent, and then carrying all the children back up the iron staircase again. The awful thing is that if Jerry returns we shall have to go through this whole routine all over again.

Feel exhausted this morning.

23 October

Another awful night. Josephine died at 2.30 a.m. It was broncho-pneumonia. Poor little mite. She did not have a chance.

I was worrying about what to say to Anna. She must be told the truth, but how was I to tell her? Her mother had not visited the children since their admission. She likes and trusts me. There is no one else to talk to her about this.

I took Anna in my arms and told her that her baby sister had gone to heaven and would not suffer any more. I just hugged her until her sobbing ceased and she fell asleep in my arms.

11 November

Was on ambulance duty last night. We were on our way to collect some children with scarlet fever, and were cruising along the West End after the All Clear when were stopped urgently by an air-raid warden who said there had been an incident at a nearby Tube shelter, and could we please help. He climbed into the back of the ambulance and we turned round to go back to the Underground. The warden led the way down to the subway and the driver and I followed. There was an uncanny rather sinister quietness and strange and unusual echoes. We reached the shelters, there were no apparent casualties, no blood, no screams. There were men, women and children there, some lying down, others sitting upright. There was food and knitting and blankets and thermos flasks, all the customary paraphernalia of shelter life.

We stared in amazement. It was absolutely quiet – and then Jock said 'Christ – they're dead'. We rushed from one group to the next – no sign of a pulse – they <u>were</u> all dead – men, women and children.

There were strange waves of quiet vibrations down there and then we began to understand. It must have been a bomb further along the line – no apparent physical injuries. The blast had killed them. We informed the police. There was nothing else for us to do.

We went on to collect the scarlet fevers but they turned out to be German measles and we felt that the mother could cope.

The streets of London were deserted as we drove back to Woolwich and that eerie whine of the air-raid alert started up yet again as we entered the main gate.

2 January 1944

Went dancing at the Rushgrove with Ricky. He is on leave from Egypt. Brought me some lemons.

We were caught in a raid on our way back here. It was a terrible experience – but rather dramatic. The sky was sprinkled with flares and the searchlights moved about the sky picking out the black shapes of the planes, and then we heard the shout 'Fire' and bang went the guns. The anti-aircraft guns and the shrapnel were far too close for comfort. We kept throwing ourselves on the ground and waiting for the bombs to drop. Were fortunate to have escaped unhurt. There were ambulance bells clanging everywhere as we made our way back to the Brook.

29 January

Had to do a fire watching stint last night. It was bitterly cold.

Received my application forms for the QAIMNSR [Queen Alexandra's Imperial Military Nursing Service Reserves].* Driscoll and I went to see *Phantom of the Opera*. She too has applied for the QAs.

---

* Mary was beginning the process of applying for active service.

14 March

My State Fever examinations at the Western Hospital. An awful feeling that I may have left out one of the compulsory questions.

27 March

We were having tea in the dining room when Driscoll came to say that there was an American on the telephone who wished to speak to me. Was rather intrigued as I do not know any Americans. I picked up the receiver and a voice said 'This is Michael' and as I sounded blank, he added 'Your brother'. I was speechless. I was eight years old when he left Ireland and we have not met since then. He is stationed in Chipping Campden and I am going down there next week to visit him. What does one say to a brother who is almost a complete stranger? Shall I recognise him?

Mary's brother Michael was one of thousands of American troops stationed in Britain as part of the build-up to the staging of a Second Front that would open with the invasion of Europe in June.

1 April, Chipping Campden, Gloucestershire

Michael met me at the delightful little railway station here. He is very tall and there is a strong family resemblance, so I recognised him at once.

He took me along to Walters' tea shop where he had booked a room for me. It is a lovely old Elizabethan house opposite the old Market Cross in the main street square.

Mrs Walters provided us with an excellent meal of new-laid eggs and home-made bread and scones. There is a lovely old inglenook fire-place, and beamed ceilings that make Michael bend his head as he enters the room. There was so much to talk about that we chatted until nearly 1 a.m.

2 April

Attended Mass with Michael and went back to the American camp afterwards. He introduced me to his CO and his friends. The Commanding Officer invited me to lunch there, adding 'You must stay to eat with us. Everybody comes along on Sunday after Church'.

The camp is situated on a patch of raised ground outside the village. Somebody said 'Chow coming up' and as I looked towards the village I saw a stream of people coming towards us. The whole village was coming up the hill, and all were dressed in their Sunday best.

It was a fine sunny spring morning, and trestle tables were carried outside, and everybody sat down on the wooden forms. These Yanks certainly have a good PX.* The food was good and plentiful, and the atmosphere informal, friendly and happy. The Americans may not be too popular in London or other parts of the country, but the villagers of Chipping Campden have taken them to their hearts.

3 April

Another beautiful day, and such bliss to be away from those awful ack-ack guns and to be able to sleep at night.

We cycled to Stratford-on-Avon and, like all Americans, Michael had to see the birthplace of William Shakespeare. Saw *A Midsummer Night's Dream* in the evening.

---

* The Post Exchange (PX) was a shop on the base that supplied items to the soldiers, usually American goods such as toiletries, candy, cigarettes, Coca-Cola and tinned foods that were not available in Britain.

5 April

Rode out to Broadway and walked up to the Tower. It was a fine clear day and we could see for miles around. It looked like a toy fairyland and so peaceful. The noise of Woolwich seems a million miles away.

8 April

Cycled to Stratford and took a boat on the river. Punting is quite an art. I fell in but managed to dry off quickly as the weather was warm and sunny. Went to the Shakespeare Theatre to see *Macbeth*. We found another lovely old pub in Mickleton on our way home.

Told Michael that I hoped to join the QAs. He is worried in case I have to go out to France when the Second Front is in operation. He too will no doubt be going over there. He is with a Signals outfit.

After her brief holiday with Michael, Mary returned to the Brook to confront her 'autocratic' Matron over her application to join the Queen Alexandra's.

9 April, Brook Hospital, Woolwich

Said good-bye to Michael and his friends and to Mrs Walters who has been so kind to me. Felt very sad at leaving all of them. It may be a long time before I see Michael again. It is awful to find a long-lost brother and then lose him again so quickly.

25 April

My first official interview at the Royal Herbert Military Hospital. There was a senior Matron and two male RAMC [Royal

Army Medical Corps] officers. Matron was very charming and suggested afterwards that I should tender my resignation at the Brook.

26 April

Handed in my formal resignation to Matron this morning. She kept me waiting outside the door for nearly an hour and then refused to accept the letter. She told me that she strongly disapproves of young nurses joining the Forces when civilian hospitals are so short staffed. She is an extremely autocratic woman. I tried to point out that I had completed my fever training, taken the examinations and that surely I was at liberty to resign if I wished. She refused to listen.

28 April

Decided that as Matron would not accept my resignation I must go and see the Medical Superintendent.

Dr Breen gave me an appointment at 2 p.m. He is a most pleasant and reasonable man. He assured me that he would 'talk to Matron' if I was sure that I wanted to leave. It was embarrassing for me to have put him in such a difficult situation.

29 April

Another interview from the QAs. This time at Sardinia House. They were more interested in my hobbies than my qualifications.

Had a very thorough medical at the Army Medical Centre in Croydon.

Driscoll left here today. She is to join the 108 Hospital in Naburn, Yorkshire. Shall miss her.

6 May

Matron has accepted my resignation! Leaving here on the 28th. She enclosed a memo to say that I am to go on night duty at once!

8 May

Back on whoopers ward again. Am not feeling too well. My face is swollen – probably a sinus infection. The hospital is a hotbed of infection. It is old, rat-infested, under-staffed and, in my opinion, a health hazard.

10 May

Received my call-up papers today. I am to join 101 General Hospital at Hatfield House, Herts.

It is rather exciting, but I feel too ill to appreciate it. I have acute sinusitis but must remain on duty as they are very short staffed. Have been prescribed M and B 693 but they merely make me feel nauseated.

Last night was awful. The children screamed and vomited most of the night and as I, too, felt quite ill it was all rather hellish.

27 May

An air raid in the early hours of the morning. The barrage was terrible. We took the children down to the shelter.

28 May

Left Brook this morning. Am going to spend a week with Michael in Chipping Campden. It will be marvellous to get away from Woolwich.

Three

Normandy and beyond

A proud officer of the British forces:
Mary in her QA uniform

Rumours of the Second Front abounded, but Mary and her fellow nurses began their training with no concrete knowledge of their future movements, though medical units had been preparing since the beginning of the year for their role in the Normandy landings. In spite of some trepidation on Mary's part about what the Second Front would mean, an aura of adventure dominated this preparation. Hatfield House, the home of the Salisbury family, had been turned into a military hospital and training depot.

5 June, Hatfield House, Hertfordshire

Arrived here last night having said good-bye to Michael in Chipping Campden. His last words were a cheerful, 'See you in France'. The countryside on the way up to London from the west looked green and peaceful. It was difficult to imagine what the Second Front would mean to us personally. My experience with the Dunkirk veterans had given me some indication of the horrors that might be in store.

Hatfield House is beautiful but rather frightening. People were dashing about all over the place looking busy, although the odd soldier in khaki battle dress had enough time to give me a friendly wolf whistle.

Found my way to the library eventually. There were three other girls all waiting there to see the Matron of our unit, Miss Sally Wade. There was a small dark girl with a sad intense expression who introduced herself as Aileen Baggs, an older woman, Wally, with a kind face and, to my amazement and delight, Driscoll from the Brook. She had been posted here from the 108 in Naburn. It was good to see her.

We sat in the library talking about our civilian hospital training days. Wally has been a Ward Sister, the others, like me, newly qualified and about twenty-two years old.

Miss Wade put in an appearance eventually. She is brusque, efficient, overweight, a no-nonsense type, but looks kind and motherly.

We slept on camp beds in the library. There was an uncanny silence. Felt fearful yet excited, rather lonely too. This is the start of a new way of life.

6 June

Dramatic news. The Allies have landed in Normandy. After breakfast we went to the library to listen to the BBC nine o'clock news read by Howard Marshall. He went on to say 'The combined landing operations comprised the whole area between Le Havre and Cherbourg, the main centre of attack being Caen'.*

Tremendous buzz of excitement, clusters of people talking about the news. Wondered if Michael would be sent over there. Baggs, who seems to know everyone, is convinced that we shall be on our way to Normandy in a few days.

7 June

We were given a list of our essential uniforms and equipment – such a long list.

Went to London with Driscoll to order uniform from Austin Reed. Headlines in all the papers about D-Day landings. The city has an air of bustle and excitement. There is talk everywhere of the Normandy landings. People are relieved that it has begun, and are waiting for another statement from Winston Churchill. Londoners look upon him as their saviour.

Had difficulty buying a trunk and other kit. Shopkeepers say

* Operation Overlord, the D-Day invasion, brought together 20,000 Allied troops, landing on the Normandy coast on 6 June 1944. After an initially successful landing, the Allied forces met with German resistance that resulted in heavy ground fighting and aerial bombardment in the area of Caen.

'Don't you know there is a war on?' and put anything in short supply under the counter for wealthy friends.

8 June

Lecture on army documents, very boring – each document has an identity number – they all work in triplicate. How did we ever manage to invade Normandy if the army is so full of red tape?

Our charming lecturer Major Sykes is extremely patient with us. He reminded me that it would be impossible to order hospital equipment or even special diets without a sure knowledge and understanding of the army numbers relating to this bumph.

Had a medical examination after lunch, also TAB, typhus and anti-tetanus injections. We must be going somewhere, Normandy likely.

9 June

We had a hilarious lecture on Saluting and General Army Protocol. It was extremely difficult to take it all very seriously, particularly as we were wearing cotton frocks and sandals. Our sergeant instructor was rather put out I fear.

Driscoll, Wally and I went for a walk round the lake. The grounds here are very beautiful.

10 June

Indoor uniform arrived this morning. It is very attractive – a simple grey dress – scarlet cape and white organdy head-dress – two lovely shining pips on the shoulder and our own QA badge.

Feel better today. Am in the QAs at last.

11 June

Still waiting and shopping – a feeling of anti-climax. Spent
the day in London trying to find a trunk and dodging doodlebugs. These buzz bombs are quite terrifying and in London
one tries to keep underground as much as possible. Had a very
narrow escape near Victoria Station. I was on my way to the
Tube when I heard the ominous buzz. I ran and listened as I
ran because the moment they stop buzzing they drop. It is an
alarming situation – everybody running for the shelter before
the awful thing drops. I had just reached the entrance to the
Underground when it dropped and blew up. I could hear the
ambulance bells ringing as I descended the stairs. Londoners
are remarkably phlegmatic and carry on with their normal lives
in between dodging the doodlebugs.

14 June

Our new outdoor uniforms and equipment arrived this morning – very exciting. We are busy packing trunks and valises.
There are fascinating pieces of equipment such as a canvas bowl
on a tripod, a canvas bucket, a Tilley lamp and even a collaps-
ible canvas bath. We had great fun trying out this latter piece
of equipment. Wally, Driscoll and I put it on the bathroom
floor, filled it with water, and unfortunately I lost the toss and
had to be the guinea pig. It was useless, so dreadfully wobbly
and swishy. The others held on to the sides while I tried to get
in, the result was disaster and water everywhere. We were so
convulsed with laughter that we did not hear the knock on the
bathroom door. I grabbed a towel and opened the door to Miss
Wade! She was furious. 'What were we doing? Why was there
water everywhere, and what had happened to the piece of army
equipment, i.e. the canvas bath?'

I tried to explain between giggles that it was a serious scien-
tific experiment in order to find out if the said piece of equipment

was satisfactory. Miss Wade then said, surprisingly, 'Is it?' and
we said in unison 'NO'.

15 June, Bognor Regis

Should have headed this 'Somewhere in Southern England' but
this is a very private diary.

We left Hatfield at 11.25 a.m. and arrived here about 5.30
p.m. It has been a bright sunny day and all fourteen of us girls
travelled in an open-backed 15-cwt vehicle. The road signs were
blocked out all along the route (to discourage Nazi invaders)
and we looked out on to a war-torn southern England.

We stopped occasionally in various towns en route. There
were troops and armoured vehicles everywhere and I was
amused to see how quickly the wolf whistle was transformed
into a smart salute when the soldiers noted our two pips!

We are billeted in an empty house here, backing on to the
beach. This was once a family home, but there are no civilians in
this street now, no furniture, no beds, just a few battered-looking toys scattered around.

The beach is covered with rolls of barbed wire and warning
notices to 'Beware of Mines'.

We are sleeping on the floor here tonight. Our first taste of
the discomforts of war.

16 June

Miss Wade gave us our new address this morning. It is 101
British General Hospital BLA [British Liberation Army]. My
personal army number is P/322412.

We are ready to move off at 0700 hours tomorrow.

17 June, Southampton

We left Bognor at 9 a.m. arriving here at our marshalling area at 12.30 p.m. Here is an astonishingly luxurious American Army transit camp, situated in the middle of a forest outside Southampton. The lush foliage of the trees provides the most perfect camouflage.

Wally, Driscoll and I are sharing a tent – but what a tent! There are comfortable camp beds, a table and chairs and electric light. There are showers too, with masses of hot water. What an idyllic place.

The Americans are delighted to entertain us. We are the first women to be in transit here, and the generosity of our hosts is amazing.

They have showered us with presents from their PX, chocolate, chewing gum and tins of fruit. There is one rather attractive young man called Steve who appears to have taken on the role of my personal batman. He wanted to give me a lovely pair of silk stockings, which I had to refuse reluctantly, mainly because I have a suspicion that they might not be very useful in Normandy.

18 June

We waved good-bye to our American friends this morning and we girls were all clutching addresses stretching from Maryland to Ohio. We were on our way to the port wearing tin hats and full battle dress.

We were given our iron rations box as we rolled along. It says 'To be used in Emergency only'. Everybody is subdued. The security of the transit camp and the nice Americans are behind us. Where do we go from here?

The sea was calm and beautiful as we went aboard HMS *Duke of Lancaster* – a lovely evening.

We all clambered aboard and were greeted cheerfully by the

sailors. We found a comfortable spot on the deck, removed our kit bags and sat down on top of the valises. We haven't seen our trunks, but Driscoll tells me that a few of the MOs are looking after them and the hospital equipment on our sister ship.

We ate some of the precious chocolate given to us by the Yanks and just sat and waited. I am reading *Mein Kampf*, which always makes Wally snort with anger. She calls me a fifth columnist.

19 June, Somewhere in Normandy

We sailed out of Southampton docks about 11.30 p.m. last night. It was great to be on our way at last, very exciting. We assembled in Matron's cabin afterwards in order to be briefed. We were fully kitted out, battle dress, tin hats, kit bags, rattling billycans. We were told (as if we did not know) that we were on our way to Normandy, and would be met by a landing craft, which would take us and our equipment ashore. We are to 'stand by and wait for further orders'. The sailors kept bringing cups of tea from the galley and appeared astonished by our temerity in entering this man's world. Tried to look cool and nonchalant but lapped up the obvious admiration.

It was a beautiful moonlight night with a calm sea. The hush was uncanny as we moved, almost silently, through the water – voices were muted – Driscoll was sleeping. I was too excited to sleep. There was fear and anticipation. What will it be like over there?

My reverie was interrupted by voices giving sharp orders. A sailor shouted 'Red Alert'. A mine had been sighted. The engines were cut and again there was silence. Driscoll awoke and asked if we would be blown up. Other girls joined us and Matron came along and ordered us to go below. I clutched my rosary beads and prayed as I had never prayed before.

We stayed below for what seemed like hours without movement. The tension was terrible, and then suddenly the engines purred again and we were on our way. The weather was deteriorating by then and I felt very sea-sick. Somebody took me along to the Captain's cabin where Miss Wade was talking to one of the officers. I just heard him say 'it glided by', we obviously had a near miss. Miss Wade took one look at me (I felt awful), poured out a large tot of rum and made me drink it. 'We have no time to be sea-sick, Sister' she said coolly. My brave new QA image had been shattered by wave after wave of nausea. She found me a bunk to lie on, and soon I felt too intoxicated to care about anything except sleep.

Woke up a few hours later, felt a little better and went up on deck. The seas were mountainous. It must have been a force 9 gale or so it seemed to me, if not to the sailors. A helpful sailor offered me tea, which I refused, and observed that we might have difficulty in transferring to the landing craft if the wind did not die down. There was plenty of bustle and activity by now. We were nearing the French coast and were due to meet the landing craft in an hour.

We had a final briefing with Miss Wade and a rather handsome young Naval Officer. They explained how we were to be deposited on the beach at Graye-sur-Mer. We were ordered to assemble on deck, fully kitted and wearing our Mae Wests* – we were told to put all the personal valises together. The sailors would look after them. Our hands must be free.

I went up on deck to see an astonishing sight. The girls squealed with amazement and terror. It was like Guy Fawkes' night. There was the noise of aircraft and brilliant multi-coloured flares, which the sailors called 'flaming onions' dropping from the sky, all around us, lighting up our ship and the flat, dark shape of the landing craft about five hundred yards away.

There were flares dropping everywhere, and the whine of tracer bullets some little distance away. A passing sailor said, 'Jerry is busy tonight'. The elements too were busy, the churning

---

* The bulky life jackets named after the buxom actress.

sea slamming against the sides of the ship and soaking us with spray. The roar of the waves, the rat-tat-tat of not-too-distant gunfire and the fireworks created an atmosphere of panoramic unreality. It was strangely exciting, the type of excitement associated with fear of the unknown.

We waited and watched on deck while the *Duke of Lancaster* hove-to. The landing craft was drawing a little nearer as the ship tried to head up into the wind. As the engines cut back I heard an explosion and to our horror a ship blew up some little distance away. It was a horrific sight. About 4 a.m.: The landing craft was attempting to draw alongside of us with very little success. Each time the LC drew near the ship, a huge wave tore them apart. It looked distinctly alarming from where I stood looking over the edge of the deck and down on to the craft way below.

The sailors had attached a scrambling net to the side of the ship and in theory we were to descend in agile fashion down this net, while the sailors on this side helped us over the edge. The men on the landing craft were ready to catch us as we jumped aboard. That was the theory, but the heavy seas made the synchronisation of these events highly unlikely. The wearing of a Mae West, although essential in such weather, would increase our girth and make the effort of climbing down the scrambling net very difficult. It might have been easier if we were all eight months pregnant.

Our strange silhouetted shapes were lit up periodically by the flares as we stood there in fear and trepidation as to who should go first. I volunteered not out of bravery but because of feeling sea-sick again, anything to get off that ship!

I was all right while the sailor lowered me over the edge of the deck, and while I could feel his strong arms, then I was on my own. Voices from above and below said 'Hold on carefully and do not look down'. I kept going down with the Mae West bulk constantly pushing me away from the too-mobile scrambling net. I thought I was almost there when a voice behind me said, 'Hold on until the exact moment I say and then jump backwards'. They assured me that they would catch me at the right moment, but it must be right. I was soaked in spray by now, cold, wet and frightened, but when someone shouted 'Now' I fell straight back into waiting arms.

The relief was instantaneous and my spirits rose as I encouraged Driscoll and Wally who came down next. The sailors on the landing craft were a very jolly bunch, full of jokes and laughter. We were the first English women who had literally fallen into their arms in Normandy!

Matron was the last to come down, which she did without too much loss of dignity. We watched all the activity around us, as the landing craft crept towards Graye-sur-Mer. When we got there the tide was in and we had to sit and wait until it ebbed before going ashore. Chatted to the sailors. Some of them had landed the D-Day troops and told us about their experiences. We got ashore eventually and are now sleeping on stretchers on the floor of an old barn alongside the beach.

I am too tired to write any more and listen to the screaming shells in the distance before going to sleep.

19 June, 9 p.m.

Writing this in an apple orchard somewhere in Normandy, sitting on the grass outside my tent. We left Graye-sur-Mer about twelve hours ago. This has been such a long day and so much as happened that I feel disorientated. It would be lovely to be alone for a little while just to think, but we have strict orders not to leave the camp. There is constant activity, and too many people and always so much noise. The fighting must be quite close.

My first look at the Normandy beach came when I woke up this morning about 8 a.m. Cpl 'Taffy' Jones brought me a foul cup of sweet tea and flashed a nice gummy smile. He and the other RAMC orderlies have been with us since Hatfield

House and Taffy in particular takes a paternal interest in us girls. He is fat and cuddly and anxious to look after us. He is also a rather endearing coward and rushes for shelter each time there is a loud bang, which means most of the time here. We ate some of our emergency rations for breakfast. I had some very bitter dark chocolate, but extremely welcome. The emergency was our united hunger. We were starving and the cooks appeared to have mislaid the bully beef rations.

The beach was a deserted battlefield in the daylight; smashed amphibious vehicles, the remains of concrete embattlements, a paradise of scrap metal, tin hats, broken rifles etc. It was easy to visualise the bitter battles that had been fought there less than two weeks before.

We clambered aboard a 3-tonner open lorry after breakfast and set out inland. I asked where we were going and Matron said, 'A Cathedral city near the fighting line'. It must be Bayeux. I wondered idly as we drove along if the famous tapestry was still there or if Goering had confiscated it as he had done (so we are told) with so many works of art in France.

It was a warm sunny morning and my first impressions of Normandy as we left the coast were of clouds of dust, a flat countryside, straight poplar trees standing like sentries on the skyline and the sound of ack-ack guns and screaming shells. The roads, trees and fields here are covered in a mantle of white dust. It is in our hair and eyes and sticks to our damp battle dress. I feel dirty and hot and dream of a cool shower as we move along.

I was not prepared for the sights that greeted us as we neared Bayeux. The parting of clouds of dust revealed huge tanks on the side of the road, black from burning, dozens of them with the dead crews hanging half in and half out of the turrets and escape hatches. There was mile after mile of destroyed armoured cars, trucks of all kinds, and always the dust, heat and stench of decaying maggot-ridden bodies. There were dead cattle in the fields.

We met up with our Pioneer Corps escort at Bayeux. The Cathedral is mercifully undamaged and the city is surprisingly intact. There could not have been very heavy fighting here. The shutters are up on the shop windows and the place looks deserted apart from some troops in battle dress wandering about, many of them Free French soldiers. We stopped in Bayeux for about an hour, and Driscoll told me that General De Gaulle had been in Bayeux a couple of days before and had to introduce himself to a city which knew him by name but had never seen his photograph.

We left Bayeux and eventually went off the long straight road leading to Caen, leaving some of the appalling dust behind, and arrived in an orchard. There is not any sign of farming activity here although there is a dilapidated farm and disused barn nearby. This particular orchard produces the type of small apples that end up as the highly potent Calvados. It is a low lying dust bowl, not flat enough for pitching tents. How is this to be transformed into a field hospital? We are sitting on the grass chatting and worrying about the non-arrival of our trunks, and drinking some of Taffy's awful Compo* tea.

A great deal of hospital equipment is still missing so the erection of the hospital tents must wait. The living tents are erected and the kitchen and food areas organised. We can at least eat and sleep.

20 June

There is a R/C Padre attached to our unit. Heard Mass in a tent and received Holy Communion.

The water supply is nearly two kilometres away. The resourceful Pioneer Corps have found some water barrels in the disused barn, and now we have a special water tent. All drinking water must be boiled of course.

* 'Compo' or Composite Rations were the emergency rations issued to soldiers and intended to last 24 hours. The tea was premixed with sugar and milk.

Heard some tragic news this morning. The explosion which we noticed before landing at Graye-sur-Mer involved our sister ship. Two of our medical officers are reported missing and we have lost some valuable hospital equipment, also the trunks containing our dress uniform and indoor dress and scarlet cape. Our Medical Commanding Officer is a Canadian, Lt Col John Cordwell, a tall ascetic-looking man in his early thirties with a rather aloof manner. He seems forbidding, but I do not yet know him very well. He is a go getter and set off this morning with another officer to try and dig up the extra equipment we need. We are particularly short of theatre instruments and gas and oxygen cylinders.

The RAMC orderlies are a motley bunch, some, like Taffy Jones, are from Wales and others are cockneys. The cockneys are cheerful and just get on with the job. They have many roles to play: batman to the medical officers and nursing Sisters, general factotum in the hospital, cooks, stretcher bearers, ward helpers, etc.

The Pioneer Corps are our Armed Guards, rifles at the ready, standing on the edge of our compound. They are delightfully unmilitary, rather untidy, soldiers. Many are basically conscientious objectors. They are multi-nationals from all walks of life, some very well educated and with useful specialist skills. There is an officer with an unpronounceable name whom I call 'Chezzy'. He has told me a little of the background of some of these men. Many were refugees from Germany before the war. Chezzy speaks fluent English and German, also Polish and Russian. I think he is a Polish Jew, loves music and is a professional pianist in civilian life. He is short and dark with a big nose and the most beautiful deep brown eyes. Chezzy has so much warmth and personality that it knocks me over. Why are ugly men often more attractive than the handsome ones?

Our large hospital tents are now erected, also the operating theatre (a bell tent) thanks to Chezzy and his men.

There was some rapid gunfire this evening in the vicinity of the farmhouse. A Pioneer Corps Corporal found the sniper. He cannot be more than fifteen years old. He was wounded in the leg and ironically became our first casualty! Fritz told Chezzy when he was interviewed that he had been ordered to stay behind to 'fight for the Fatherland'. The wound in his leg is superficial – a flesh wound. Fritz is very high and mighty, the product of Hitler Youth I suppose, but he did not refuse the food we offered. He was ravenous.

The Pioneer Corps completed our new canvas latrines today. There is alarmingly little privacy. Driscoll and I are reducing our fluid intake in order to minimise the embarrassment of being escorted to the latrines by an armed guard (Matron's orders because of the snipers). There are some terrible jokes about 'pot' shots.

The weather is still very fine and sunny.

21 June

Worked hard all morning making beds and getting the wards organised.

An RAF Officer drove by in a jeep this morning with an invitation to us Sisters to an RAF dance in Cruelly. We do not know whether Matron will permit this as Cruelly is close to the front.

The sterilising equipment on the wards is almost non-existent, positively archaic. I am sure Florence Nightingale was better off in the Crimea. We have to put syringes and needles, dressings, forceps, etc. in spirit. This is a terrible fire hazard particularly under canvas. We have primus stoves for boiling dressing bowls and heating drinks. I have been practising on one today and find it unpredictable, unreliable and dangerous unless one is very careful. It needs the most patient pumping and cajoling to get it to work. I am terrified that it is going to explode. Hope I get used to it. We have no alternative.

Matron eventually agreed to us going to the RAF dance but

we must be accompanied by our own armed escort from the Pioneer Corps. Chezzy decided to accompany us. It was almost dark when we reached Cruelly, so I did not see a great deal of the area, there is quite a lot of mortar damage here and there I gather. The gunfire and noise of screaming shells goes on most of the time. Our armed escort took us into a building where a band was playing Victor Sylvester music. The RAF had put on a lovely spread for us, cold chicken, hard-boiled eggs, etc. I was a little suspicious of their origin and wondered if the chicken and eggs had been nicked from a farm by some enterprising airman. Anyway it was delicious chicken, I was in a good mood, and felt that Normandy owed us the odd chicken. Were we not the liberators?

The boys in blue looked very dashing, particularly Fighter Command with their long moustaches and top tunic button undone (memories of the Battle of Britain). Such studied nonchalance, very impressive. They had to work very hard to impress us as there were at least ten of them to each one of us. It is quite exciting to be surrounded by so many men who obviously feel the need for female company. They spoiled us beautifully and we danced and laughed with all of them. Transient fleeting friendships are a part of the war. There is never time to get to know anybody, and for some there may not be a tomorrow.

We danced until 2 a.m. and Chezzy decided that we must go back to camp. We piled into the truck; I was pleasantly happy despite the noise and bombardment and we sang songs like the 'Siegfried Line' all the way home. A soldier with a gun asked for the password as we entered camp. He apologised when he recognised us and said, 'There are snipers about'.

23 June

There was a great deal of bustle everywhere this morning. The word has got round that 101 British General Hospital is in business, and we are expecting our first casualties today.

Two of our first patients are Germans, picked up by a Canadian officer in a jeep. One is a frightened young boy about the same age as Fritz our sniper friend. Fritz is still hobbling around with a stick, tending to exaggerate his leg injury. He is quite cocky now that he knows we are not going to poison or shoot him. He was delighted to see a young compatriot and they chatted away to each other in German. Jan, the new young man, also has a leg injury. He tried to run away from the Canadian who was out scouting for snipers and was promptly shot in the foot. Looks as if it might need to go in plaster.

The other German is a man in his thirties with a kind, sensitive face. His name is Hans and he has a wife and two children in Frankfurt. I do not know what he was doing wandering round roads in Normandy, probably a deserter. He is delighted to be with us and apart from malnutrition and some superficial cuts and bruises, he seems to be OK. We cannot chuck him out to starve and there are not any POW camps here, so he will probably do odd jobs on the wards or around the camp to earn his keep. Hans is quite unlike the jack-booted Hun whom we had anticipated. He is polite and timid and makes me feel that he is one of the many pawns in this game of war. Propaganda is a big word in wartime. We deduce that good propaganda is whatever makes us hate the enemy or 'Narzis' as Winston Churchill calls them.

At 4 p.m. 101 British General Hospital had three patients – all German. I was going off duty at 5 p.m. when the ambulances rolled in, three in rapid succession. It is now midnight and I have come off for a rest but may have to go back on the ward later if any further convoys of wounded come in.

Most of our casualties come from the area around the Odon and Orne where there was heavy fighting as a result of Monty's efforts to get his armour on the open ground south of Caen. Some of the first men were from the Reconnaissance Regiment Welsh Division. There were at least fourteen severe gunshot wounds and some will need leg amputations. They were all laid out on their stretchers on the floor as we systematically examined them. The RAMC orderlies examined their identity discs, verified identification and put the information down on a luggage label attached to a tunic button. The QA Sisters examined each man carefully, referring any urgent cases to Col Cordwell or Lt Kelvin or Capt Phillips, his junior medical officers. Miss Wade worked with us and her experience was a great help. Chezzy and some of the Pioneer Corps boys helped to undress the less urgently serious cases, shell shock etc., and get them into bed. The ward was filled with the voices of the valleys. One young man, Dai Evans, puzzled me. I thought he was in a coma, he appeared so deeply unconscious. His friend lying alongside said, 'Don't worry Sister bach, Dai drunk half a pint of Calvados, thinking it was NAAFI beer, and got slung in an ambulance with us lot'. Poor Dai! He will have a terrible headache tomorrow before he is despatched back to his unit.

We have a mixed bag on the ward now, Germans, Welsh, some Canadians, a few cockneys, several Poles, one or two Free French soldiers, a civilian member of the Maquis, shot while escaping from somewhere, one Latvian and two Americans. Chezzy and his men are of enormous help in interpreting Polish, German and even Latvian for us. It took many hours to clean them all up, put on temporary dressings and give them food and drink. The ones who were shocked through loss of blood were put on a plasma intravenous drip. There will be a long operating list tomorrow.

24 June

Went on duty at 8 a.m. Grateful not to have been called in the night. Am in charge of thirty-five men. It is daunting to see so many intravenous drips, trolleys with bloody dressings everywhere. Taffy is trying to boil water for tea on a primus stove, which is being temperamental as usual.

Dai Evans is up and ready to go back to his unit. Poor boy, he is a great source of amusement to his friends. Hans and Fritz are helping Taffy to take round the tea, some people are moaning with pain, others chatting cheerfully, relieved to be away from the fighting.

Hans brings me a cup of tea as I sit at my desk to read the night report. My mind wanders for a while as I think of this ward and my charges. This multi-national microcosm of a Europe at war is interesting and sad. A badly wounded cockney says 'thanks mate' to Hans as he gives him his tea and fixes his pillows. Why are they all tolerant of each other inside this canvas tent, and killing each other outside? The Germans will eventually go back to a POW camp in England, our severely wounded will go to hospital in England as soon as an air-lift is available. The others we shall patch up as best we can and send them back to Monty on the front to fight again.

Spent the morning doing dressings, giving injections and fixing plasma drips. Col Cordwell made a ward round, and told me that the operating list would have to be postponed until tomorrow. We are waiting for equipment, which should arrive today. At the end of this round my ward treatment book contained enough work for at least six SRNs. I was the only Sister in my Section, but some of the RAMC orderlies had previous experience in military hospitals in England. This situation needed new methods of working if these patients were to receive the treatment which Col Cordwell and I considered they needed. There were special diets, special medication, special dressings for all of them. Impossible for one Sister, a few medical orderlies and one or two keen but clueless Pioneer Corps boys who had volunteered their services. The problem of communication because of language barriers was also time consuming. Chezzy has duties other than unofficial interpreter!

In my training days in a civilian hospital it was considered good policy not to tell the patient anything, just to fob them off by saying 'It's alright dear'. Consultants were only a little lesser personage than God, and Matron ruled the roost.

It is very different here. I decided that all the conscious patients should be given a detailed list of their own treatment, diet and medications and asked to remind the day and night staff at the right time and to nag them if necessary. I hope this works, for with so much to do it would be impossible for me to keep track of everybody's therapy. I can now concentrate on the seriously ill cases who are unable to help themselves. I call it patient participation but I dare not imagine what Matron will say when she finds out.

25 June

Saw Col Cordwell at breakfast and he asked if I would assist him in theatre today as many of the cases are from my ward. My heart sank, I hate theatre work and am not too keen on Col Cordwell. I respect his ability but he is very intolerant and I am not too efficient in theatre.

Went along to check over the instruments after breakfast. This tent is very different to our aseptic well-equipped civilian operating theatres. Fortunately there is a good light (run off a dynamo in the field outside).

There were several repairs of gunshot wounds on the list. I boiled all the necessary instruments, including a bone saw should an amputation be necessary, and prepared the table and anaesthetic trolley. Determined not to incur Col Cordwell's wrath by any incompetence on my part.

Dashed back to the ward to give pre-medication to the next operation case. They had already been written up in the notes by Lt Kelvin who is today's anaesthetist. The men looked incongruously ethereal in their white operation gowns open at the back, long white socks and silly little white caps. They provoked great merriment in the ward. They signed the consent forms and I warned them that should it be found necessary to amputate a leg, it would be done today. They were resigned to leaving this decision to the surgeon. There were six cases on the list, all of them extensive repairs to gunshot wounds; some were abdominals, which took a long time.

The heat in the tent was heavy and oppressive and the flies were very worrying, the possible carriers of infection. I stood there for nearly six hours silently handing Col Cordwell the instruments at the right moment. He never spoke and I had to watch carefully to mop his brow periodically. Lt Kelvin too was silent as he watched over his anaesthetised patients.

We were all exhausted by 4 p.m. and went to sit on the grass outside to drink a cup of tea kindly provided by Taffy.

The two worst cases were still to come and we feared that both of these young men would lose a leg. One, Private James, is only twenty years old. It is frightening to contemplate the future effects on these men, but there is no hope of repair when there is extensive damage such as theirs.

They both lost a leg and my own personal sadness for them was intermingled with exhaustion, and the nauseating job of clearing up the blood-stained theatre afterwards, and carrying away the legs to an incinerator and watching until they were completely burned.

Went back to the ward to check on the post-operative medication and treatment and write the report for the night staff.

Too tired to eat any supper.

26 June

Good news this morning, some replacement uniform and underclothes arrived from England including ghastly khaki knickers. These pants are hilarious, huge and elasticated at the waist and legs, but we could hardly have expected army supplies to have equipped us with glamorous cami-knickers. It will be blissful to feel clean. My battle dress is dirty and blood-stained. Hot water is such a luxury. We are becoming anxious about hygiene in general, particularly as some of the girls have developed a mild dysentery. We are so short of Sisters that we cannot afford to have anybody off sick.

Yesterday's operation cases are doing fine. They are very cheerful, no signs of gangrene so far. The first sign is the smell and we are constantly alert to this. Hans is a great help in the ward. Private James keeps asking him to remove the bed-clothes from his non-existent leg. There is a cradle over the stump and this young man feels that the leg is still there. He does not want to feel the reality of the situation and Hans is sensitively aware of this, despite the language barrier between them.

We had another convoy of casualties this afternoon. Twelve more serious cases for my ward including a very badly shell-shocked young officer, Lt Martin, twenty years old, newly passed out from Sandhurst, no apparent physical injuries, but completely withdrawn and unable to communicate as he has lost the power of speech. I gave him a pencil and pad but he will only write down his name, rank and number. This young man needs far more time than we can give him. He needs seda-tion, reassurance and speech therapy. It is heart-warming to see how the other ranks react to this young officer, even the ones who say they hate all officers. Their interest and warmth will be his best therapy here. His hands shake all the time, and the 'up' patients feed him like a baby; even our two young tearaways Fritz and Jan chat away to him in German. We do not even know if he understands German.

27 June

We had another very serious case of gunshot wounds and blind-ness brought in today. Len was brought here by jeep and carried in to us by a friend in his unit, the Royal Rifles. He, too, is very shocked, but talks on and on interminably and cheerfully about his incredible experiences. He has a nice voice, and the warmth of his personality comes over as he talks. He completely ignores the appalling state he is in. The British are renowned for the stiff upper-lip, but this is ridiculous. He stinks to high heaven, and tells his story to Taffy and me as we endeavour to cut him out of his filthy, smelly, blood-stained uniform.

Len is a Normandy veteran, one of the shock troops who arrived at Leon-sur-Mer in the early hours of the morning of D-Day, complete with a folding bicycle on his back. His first memory of Normandy was of being dragged up onto the beach and landing face downwards next to a dead German soldier. He had been knocked over by a wave as he jumped off the landing craft and was unable to swim because of the weight he was carrying. He eventually made it to Cazalet Wood but his Wheels unit was sadly depleted by then.* He and the remnants of his unit got dug in there and apparently 'all hell was let loose' around them. They were surrounded by minefields and the shelling went on day and night. Their battle for survival went on for two weeks. They kept their heads down and stole eggs from farmhouses at night. They were completely cut off from the rest of their unit and were unable to make any contact. Len and his friends eventually got out of their predicament in Cazalet and joined up with Monty's men somewhere round the Odon and Orne area.

It was here that Len's real troubles began. During a particularly tough battle he dived into what he believed was a slit trench but it turned out to be a German latrine. While sitting there a massive shell landed nearby. The impact blinded him completely and although he is too shocked to realise it yet, most of his right leg has been blown off. His face is completely blackened from impacted shrapnel.

Len talks on as we bandage the remains of his leg. It is a terrible mess. He tells us how he forced himself to crawl out of the latrine and under a tank. He banged on the underside and

* Len may have been a Commando; each unit had a platoon that landed carrying fold-up bicycles for transport.

shouted above the noise until someone with an English voice found him. He then helped this other soldier to put a make-shift tourniquet on his thigh as he was losing so much blood. He then remembers being strapped on to the top of a jeep and being driven over the agonising bumps on the road. As if this were not enough, a screaming shell blew the jeep over, on its way here, with Len still strapped on top. The jeep was righted and incredibly Len is still with us. The bleeding has stopped now, but Len is weak although still talking bravely. I fix him up with intravenous plasma and give him a shot of morphine. He will need sleep to prepare for major surgery in the morning.

I get off duty at 1 a.m. and am too tired to sleep. Wearing my tin hat in bed as there is a great deal of shrapnel flying around!

28 June

On duty at 6 a.m. Len looks very ill – yesterday's cheerful chatter is over. Endeavoured to prepare him for theatre. It is impossible to remove the black shrapnel embedded in his face. Discover that he has some broken ribs. His breathing is difficult. I inform Lt Kelvin as he is the anaesthetist on duty. Len will need to see an eye surgeon as soon as he is over today's operation.

The new wonder drug penicillin* is a great help in the fight to save the lives of young men like Len. This is the first time that I have seen this antibiotic in action. It is not yet in use in the civilian hospitals. It seems to be particularly good in pre-venting gangrene infections in gunshot wounds.

---

* In 1940–41 a team at the Dunn School of Pathology at Oxford University had begun developing the new antibiotic drug penicillin for use in humans, but had been unable to find a strategy for making it in large quantities. British pharma-ceutical companies were either too busy or uninterested, so the British approached American companies. By 1943 the development of penicillin had become second only in priority to the nuclear weapons programme in the United States and over the next year Pfizer developed a mass-production process. By June 1944 there was enough to treat every soldier in the Allied advance, but its use was still strictly limited to the military.

Lt Martin seems to be a little less withdrawn this morning. He smiled at me as I held his hand and talked to him. He looks so bronzed and fit, but he is a very sick boy. Col Cordwell disagrees with me and thinks that he is swinging the lead [malingering]. John Cordwell is kind and competent in dealing with the physically injured. Why can he not see that the mind of this sensitive man has been shattered by the horrors he has seen here in Normandy? I wish we could get him back to England for psychiatric treatment.

Len is subdued as I give him his pre-medication. The anxiety of his blindness and the pain of respiration is quite enough without the added fear of major surgery and amputation. The other patients sense his fear and try to cheer him up. He tries to respond but by now it is time for Taffy and the other orderlies to fetch a stretcher and take him across to the theatre.

It was just at this point that Jerry, utterly disregarding the Red Cross on the roof of our tent hospital, decided to strafe us. The Luftwaffe planes swooped low and then were away. The two orderlies having seen a bomb drop harmlessly on the ground, panicked. They dropped Len and his intravenous bottle of plasma and ran. Col Cordwell heard Len shout, came out of the operating tent on his hands and knees wearing his gown and mask, saw what had happened and went back in for his revolver. There was shrapnel from the ack-ack guns flying around but the CO found the men and forced them at gun point to pick up the stretcher and bring Len in to have his anaesthetic (very necessary by now). These orderlies should be put on a charge but I doubt if they will. We are too short of personnel.

Lt Martin was very distressed by the strafing incident and we had a lot of trouble trying to get him out from under his bed. The bombs dropped wide – miraculously no injuries.

29 June

Driscoll was Theatre Sister this morning. Len had his leg sawn off above the knee. The anaesthetic was difficult because of his fractured ribs and difficulty in breathing. Col Cordwell was just going to sew up the flaps of the stump when the Luftwaffe came over again, so he was bandaged up quickly, and returned to me on the ward. I continued with the plasma, and gave him morphine for the pain. He, too, feels pain in the non-existent leg.

The ward was a shambles by now, and I had ordered all the patients to wear tin hats as shrapnel was coming through the canvas roof.

This is very unlike the usual well-ordered military hospital with patients sitting to attention before Colonel's inspection and with all bed wheels and pillow case flaps facing away from the door!

Miss Wade did a ward round this afternoon and turned a blind eye to the chaos. We do all we can to make the boys as happy as possible.

2 July

The rains have come to our low-lying Normandy orchard, and yesterday's stifling dust has become today's sticky mud.

Went to see the Quartermaster Sergeant about some Wellington boots. Yes, he has some in stock – incredible – but he reminds me pessimistically that he may not have any to fit me and adds triumphantly that under ordinary normal conditions I would have to submit a requisition form in triplicate! Anyway I have got my Wellies, bliss not to be sloshing around in the mud!

Still raining this evening, most of us are in Wellies now and look more like farmers than surgeons and nurses. The ward work is aggravated by this mud. We battle to keep it outside and there are constant cries of 'Wipe your feet'. There is a heavy green tarpaulin on the floor.

The patients, or most of them, play a game called housey-housey for hours. It is noisy and cheerful and hilariously funny because of the language barriers. It is amusing to see the amount of concentration given to their cards by Fritz and the other Germans. Pierre, our French underground casualty, is particularly quick to fill in his card, despite the shakiness of his English.

The players have hand-printed cards containing sixteen numbers ranging from one to one hundred. The numbers are shouted out by a caller, each number combined with a rhyming phrase, and the one to fill in the card first and shout 'housey-housey' wins. This must be a traditional army game as I have not heard of it before.

It is lovely to see how the players try to involve the shocked ones like Lt Martin with encouraging remarks of 'Have a go mate'; pulling rank is not on here. They are all patients, rank and nationality do not count. I suppose this makes us neutral territory.

The mud has entered our sleeping tent. Driscoll and I found it oozing all over the floor when we came off duty tonight. That will teach us not to chuck our books and belongings on the floor. We take off our Wellies very carefully and prop them up beside the camp bed. It would be awful to have to get into a boot full of mud in the morning. Our Tilley lamp is a great comfort.

4 July

Letter from Michael. He writes from Pont-l'Abbé. The Americans have cut off the Cherbourg Peninsula. The GIs appear to be making more progress than us. The French civilians are in a bad way. Pierre fears that the Germans will blow up the docks and all communications before leaving Cherbourg. His friends in the Maquis are active there.

Len had an eye operation today. We shall not know if it is successful or not until the bandages are removed in six days. He is completely helpless, poor boy. His head held rigid between sandbags. He must not be allowed to move a muscle. I have asked Lt Martin to take care of feeding him. He shakes far less now, and Len is good for him because of his constant cheerfulness. I could never run this ward without the lovely spirit of warm friendliness which exists between all of us. They like to tease me and I like to encourage their involvement with each other.

Hans and his two young friends are going back to a POW camp in England in a few days. It comes as a shock to realise they are the enemy. We never think of them as such, now that we know them. The fifteen-year-old boys are just young and foolish.

The mud is still with us and today we had some disgruntled visitors out from England. War photographers from the magazine *Picture Post*. They took formal photographs outside our hospital tent and less formal ones as we worked. They were unable to hide their irritation at the sight of their muddied boots and were in terror of dropping their precious cameras. It was unkind to laugh at their discomfiture.

5 July

We had a convoy of young Canadian casualties brought in this morning. I was called for duty at 3 a.m. and was appalled at seeing their condition when I entered the ward.

There were stretchers all down the middle of the tent, there were charred bodies everywhere, some were quiet and dying, others screaming with pain, all with severe burns.

Everybody had to help, up patients, orderlies and Sisters off duty, Pioneer Corps soldiers, and all available medical officers.

Their bodies were black, their appearance horrific. We gave them morphia and more morphia and watched helplessly as they died. We moved the dead out of the ward and got on with trying to save the living. They were all so young and frightened.

The extra beds were put up, and we cut off the remnants of their uniform and gently laid them on their beds. Coverings were not possible because they could not tolerate anything touching their bodies. We tried to replace fluid loss with intravenous plasma and saline, and were glad of the human heat generated by the overcrowded ward. They were so cold. We gave them penicillin in the hope of preventing infections, but we are very conscious of the fact that this is the worst type of condition to deal with in our inadequate surroundings and with so little equipment.

A young officer, Jock McCabe, one of the few able to speak, told me what happened. There was bitter fighting somewhere near Carpiquet aerodrome. The Canadians wear a darker shade of khaki uniform to ours, similar to the Germans. Our troops attacked them with flame throwers, thinking that they were an enemy target. Such is the stupidity and futility of war.

We did everything possible for these young men, but nineteen in all are dead. Spent the afternoon in the depressing task of trying to identify the dead, filling their labelled details and laying them out.

Their average age was twenty years. They had so much living to do. Feel tired and depressed.

9 July

Felt too ill and tired to write this for a few days. Len had his bandages removed this morning. He can identify objects with his left eye although there is a great deal of blurring. It is good news. Everybody is happy for him. He will need more eye surgery, but will probably go back to Moorfields.[*]

Jock McCabe is a little better and reacting to penicillin. The other boys with burns are not so good. The smell is terrible. We carry on with intravenous fluids.

---

[*] Moorfields in London remains the largest specialist eye hospital in the world.

Said good-bye to Hans and his two young friends as they go back to a POW camp in England.

A new Sister arrived this evening to replace Wally. Her name is Mary Kane* and she is tall, dark and attractive. She is also remarkably clean. We are envious of her cool competent appearance. She looks too fastidious for our muddy tent hospital.

18 July

It is much quieter here now, less noise at night and less shrapnel. We had a small convoy of patients in today. On the way to Falaise our troops captured a German hospital and released some British prisoners. The stretcher wounded, English and German, filled one ambulance, the other German cases had to walk.

Col Cordwell was very impressed by the skill of the German surgeons. Our boys said that they had been well treated, but complained that the Germans did not have pretty nurses like us!

Len and some of our Canadian burns left us today. Len to go to Moorfields, and the Canadians to the famous skin-grafting unit at East Grinstead. They promised to write.

20 July

Matron was upset at breakfast this morning. Fortunately not our fault; *Picture Post* was the culprit. It had published photographs of us at work, some of which were reproduced in *The Times* and *Morning Telegraph* under the invidious caption of First ATS [Auxiliary Territorial Service – women's branch of the British Army] in Normandy. Sally was incensed on our behalf and bustled off to write stiff letters to *The Times* and the War Office.†

---

* This appears to be a different Mary Kane to the nurse mentioned at the Brook Fever Hospital in Woolwich.

† Matron is probably angry about the misnomer. She wouldn't want her nurses to be erroneously identified as members of the ATS, which had a completely unfounded negative reputation.

We had another small convoy in today, mainly gunshot wounds. They tell me that there is still great fighting along the Orne River. They are using heavy tanks to clear the minefields.

We had an invitation to a dinner and dance in Bayeux from the Royal Navy. Hope I can get off duty.

21 July

I was doing a duty in the reception tent this morning when I saw a bedraggled group of soldiers arriving. The smell came first. They were German prisoners without an escort. Some were wounded and they were all very tired, dirty, hungry and frightened. I sent for Chezzy to act as interpreter. They are a small pocket of resistance troops who had been captured on the road to Falaise, had been relieved of their weapons, turned around and pointed back to us. The war is moving on fast. This situation could not have arisen a week ago.

We sorted them out, gave any necessary treatment, fed them, deloused them and made the usual arrangement for them to go to POW camps in England. The wounded are now on the ward. Chezzy is keeping the others under guard. They are too tired to be any kind of threat.

Came off the ward at 9 p.m. They were still playing housey-housey and I could hear their shouts as I walked across to my tent. The rain has stopped. The silence is uncanny. There is a strange feeling of change and movement in the air – a rather unsettled feeling.

2 August

We are not quite so busy on the wards now as many of the patients have been evacuated to England. This is the first day off I've had for several weeks. The sun was shining and I decided to walk to Bayeux. The Cathedral is beautiful. There is a lovely tapestry there but I am told that it is not the original, just a copy. Apparently the authentic article is safely hidden away in Paris.* The city is still very dirty, looks neglected and sad. There are many abandoned army vehicles and a motley crowd of soldiers of different nationalities just wandering up and down the streets looking rather lost. The dust too has returned with the sunshine and has settled on the trees and roads. Was given a lift back to the hospital in a jeep – extremely bumpy! The roads are terrible. The occupants were Canadian officers and they gave me a ticket for a Noël Coward (live) show in Bayeux on 7 August. It is entitled *Stars in Battledress* and should be amusing.

7 August

Had masses of letters from England today and feel far more cheerful. A new batch of Sisters arrived this morning and amongst them to my amazement was Joyce Bale. I had not seen Joyce since our training days at Tunbridge Wells in 1942. Managed to wangle a ticket for her to see the Noël Coward show. We had a marvellous time. The hall was packed with troops. We were the only women in battle dress there and several of the performers commented on our presence during their act. We were overwhelmed with offers to bring us back to camp but opted to come home with Chezzy and Lt Kelvin.

9 August

Joyce, Mary Kane and I were invited to a Naval Officers' dance near Graye-sur-Mer. It was fabulous. We all had a terrific time – lots of lovely food and handsome British and American officers. We danced until our feet were dropping off and it was almost dawn when we returned to camp! I met a delightful Sub-Lieutenant who came back with us and insisted upon giving me his duffle coat as I was a little chilly. His name is David

* The famous Bayeux Tapestry was coveted by the Nazis; the original was stored in a vault of the Louvre museum in Paris during the war.

and we talked about the poems of Rupert Brooke. We both felt rather sad and tragically romantic as we said good-bye and promised to write.

There is a reported breakthrough at Caen today. Several convoys of new patients.

11 August

Went to an RAF dance this evening – somewhere near Caen. Bolt and Driscoll came with me. We were greeted by the CO, a Wing Commander. He was extremely pleasant, lonely and rather boring. He pestered me the whole evening by refusing to leave my side. It was not on to be rude to our host so I had to grin and bear it while the others were having a great time with masses of young RAF types to dance with. Came back with Chezzy and his driver Cpl James.

16 August

Bill, one of the Canadians I met last week, took me out for a drive to Cruelly. The devastation is terrible and we could hear the loud crackle of gunfire as usual. What an awful waste of life and property all this is and so much destruction, and yet there is a feeling of constant chance and excitement. I should, I know, hate it all – and the human suffering is appalling – but I must admit to enjoying the excitement.

20 August

We had several casualties brought in last night – many are Canadians. Was talking to Lance, a colonel in a Canadian regiment, and he assured me that despite the influx of new casualties and the constant rat-tat-tat of gunfire, the battle of Normandy is over. Patients tell me that Monty has outwitted the Germans, but why are we all still here when I know that

Michael is well on his way to Germany with General Patton's Army? The news sheet that is pinned to the outside of the hospital tent is totally unreliable. We do not know what is going on.

23 August

Went on duty at 1 p.m. to hear the patients singing (with different accents) 'The last time I saw Paris'. Dashed out to look at our apple tree bulletin and it read: PARIS FREE. The patients shouted and cheered with glee. It was surprising how many bottles were unearthed from lockers. I turned a blind eye and joined them in a celebration drink. Everybody was happy and there was very little work done this afternoon.

Another dance in Courseilles this evening – another celebration of the freedom of Paris. Met a crazy Irishman from Roscommon, a bomber pilot with the RAF. Paddy is a most unconventional character, a wild man of the bogs. He has all the traditional dislike of the Irish for the British yet like thousands of other Irishmen he has joined them in this fight against Hitler. He is the only man I've ever met in the British forces who is drawing an extra shilling a day because he speaks Gaelic – but can one believe Paddy?*

24 August

On the news bulletin ARMISTICE WITH RUMANIA. Letters from Kenneth, Peter and Fred today.

---

* It is difficult to estimate how many Irish men and women served in the British forces during the war. Many, like Mary, were living in Britain when they joined up. One source gives 165,000 Irish men and women service members' next-of-kin addresses in 1944.

29 August

Kenneth arrived unexpectedly today. He looked impeccable in his naval uniform and was flatteringly pleased to see me. We went along to see Miss Wade in order to beg some time off for me to see him. Was given three hours off, 2–5, so we went for a drive in his borrowed jeep. We went along to Tilly. It is completely razed to the ground, just a few scrawny looking chickens wandering about. Where are the people? There are so many questions here and never any answers. 'Careless talk costs lives' we are told, but no talk and no information creates anxiety and uneasiness. Kenneth has just come over from London. He tells me that despite rationing the people are in good morale. He is rather pompous really and refused to tell me much about his work. Have known him for about two years now, but I still don't know him. He rejoined his ship this evening and gave me a bottle of vintage champagne as a parting gift. Wonder when I shall find an occasion big enough to live up to this extravagant luxury.

31 August

We have a new MO from England. Captain Jack Wyper is tall, dark and not very handsome. He is a Scot with a rather bossy manner, probably in order to hide his nervousness. I think I shall like him when he relaxes and becomes normal. He has been specialising in gynaecology in England, so there is bound to be a certain amount of culture shock for him here!

3 September

Our news sheet states 'Brussels Liberated by Guards Armoured Division' – more rejoicing – the war will soon be over. The weather here has turned cold now. It is particularly cold in my tent at night. How I long for the pleasure of a hot shower. A new American Canvas Hospital has arrived here. They have all mod cons of course – incredibly well organised – rather late in the day as all the action here is dying down now.

5 September

A day off. Bill took me out for a drive in his jeep. We had lunch at his Mess outside Caen. The Canadians are a nice bunch – but they are tired of Normandy and want to move on. We drove through Caen despite the innumerable warnings about snipers. It is in an appalling state. There is nothing left standing – just masses of rubble and an uncanny quiet between spasmodic bursts of gunfire. This whole city will need to be rebuilt after the war. We drove on to Deauville. This was once a very fashionable seaside resort. It is still quite attractive. Deauville and Trouville run into each other. There are very few people around – it looks as if everybody had left in a great hurry.

We went in to Rouen for dinner. The venue was a surprise to me, a lovely old monastery set in beautiful grounds on the outskirts of the city. There were several Rhodesian and Canadian officers billeted there, some special detachment, all very hush-hush! The Father Superior was a most delightful host and spoke perfect English. He entertained us to the most marvellous meal. There was soup thick with lots of vegetables and croutons – followed by steak, mushrooms and a green salad and accompanied by a marvellous bottle of old wine. It was such a joy to eat real food again after months of army bully beef and stodge. The conversation was sparkling and amusing. Bill is rather a dear, we've had a marvellous day and it is now well after midnight.

7 September

Went to visit Joyce who is now here with 106 BGH. She is a little disappointed to have missed the early days here in

Normandy. She tells me that they are opening a QA Club shortly near the 106. It will no doubt have hot showers – the bliss of anticipation. Another new MO arrived here today, Captain Stoker. He is very pleased but rather astonished by our unconventional methods of surgery and post-operative nursing. We have all learned a great deal here, mainly by trial and error. Necessity has created a great deal of inventiveness.

10 September

Heard this morning that the 101 is moving, probably to Brussels – great excitement. The patients are to be evacuated and sent back to England in a week's time. We are sad at the thought of saying good-bye to the patients, particularly the few who have been with us since those hectic early days. It is raining again and there is mud everywhere. We are back to wearing our Wellies.

12 September

We have started to pack up the medical equipment. Chezzy, Captain Wyper and Captain Stoker are helping us. It is very boring packing surgical instruments etc. Captain Wyper is good fun. He has a marvellous poker-faced dry wit, which is very entertaining. He doesn't seem to hit it off very well with Richard Kelvin.

Went along to see the new QA Club this afternoon following the old railway track. Met Joyce and some of the other girls. We had a lovely gossip over some excellent coffee and then the big moment arrived – my first hot shower since leaving England. What absolute bliss too to wash my hair in hot water. It is quite long now. Suppose I shall have to cut it before going to Brussels.

16 September

Still packing and doing routine ward work. Went to see *Fanny by Gaslight* with Captain Wyper in a funny little fleapit in Bayeux. It was packed with troops, whistling and stamping their feet. It was quite a good film, but anything would seem good after so many months without celluloid entertainment. There was an impromptu party in Captain Wyper's tent afterwards. It was his birthday and more and more people arrived as the night wore on. The tent was literally bursting at the seams and everyone was in a cheerful mood. There was an amusing Frenchman called Pierre – a native of Bayeux and a prominent member of the Maquis. He was drinking from a large bottle of Calvados and kept singing 'Normandie ma Normandie'. Somebody remembered that the theatre tent was now empty, so we all decided to go along there to dance. It was pitch dark and wet as we scrambled across the field and Pierre had to be pulled out of a ditch on several occasions. We danced all night in the bell tent where I had spent so many anxious hours helping with ops in the early days here. It still smells of anaesthetic. We had boiled eggs and bread and cheese for breakfast and afterwards some of us went on duty and back to the boring business of packing.

18 September

It is still raining and mud and slush everywhere. Went to tea at the QA Club with Richard Kelvin. Richard is dark, attractive and Jewish in appearance – quite clever and a very talented musician. He has an intense personality, which can be rather exhausting. He is not too popular with the other MOs probably because he is a Jew. Hitler obviously is not the only one who dislikes Jews. It must be his religion and culture that makes him unpopular as he is a pleasant fellow. I wonder if there will ever come a time when people are accepted as they are regardless of race, colour or culture. My Irish accent is still looked upon with suspicion by some people!

We met two American medical officers at the Club and they invited us back to their Mess for a party. We had lots of lovely food, plenty of hot water – such luxury. The whole hospital is very well equipped – but no patients! How absurd to come here at this stage of the Normandy campaign. We could have done with their help two months ago. The American Sisters are charming, but I was not too pleased when one extremely smart lady lieutenant described my rather battered battle dress as 'cute'. The Americans drove us back to camp at about 2 a.m. or at least they attempted to do so. The jeep got stuck in a ditch in the pouring rain. There was a farm nearby and I went to look for a spade to dig ourselves out. The rain rattled on the galvanised roof as I poked around in the dark and then suddenly there was an angry gaggle of geese hissing at me loudly. I ran back to the jeep with the geese in hot pursuit. We got out of the ditch eventually and arrived back here at about 4.30 a.m., looking more than a little bedraggled and covered in mud.

19 September

Went to ENSA [Entertainments National Service Association] variety show in Bayeux with Richard. It was quite amusing, Feeling very tired today and bored with packing.

20 September

Went to Bayeux to have my hair shampooed and set. Was enjoying the luxury of having my hair dried and in rollers when the electricity was cut off. (This happened to me once before.) It was pouring with rain as I started to walk back to camp feeling thoroughly browned off! But fortunately Lance, my Canadian friend, came by and gave me a lift. He asked what I had been doing in Bayeux and I said having a coiffure! My hair was dripping wet – somehow I don't think he believed me!

21 September

Went to our unit dance. The band was excellent and I danced with lots of lovely men. Richard was absurdly jealous. We went back to his tent afterwards and I made coffee on the old primus stove as usual. We are not permitted to visit MOs in their tents. It is against the rules – but I have never been interested in rules unless there is a good reason for them.

23 September

We are on 8-hour standby and will be leaving here tomorrow. It was sad to see the last of our patients leave. It is the end of an extraordinary part of my life. Richard and I went to the QA Club this afternoon, walking along the old railway line in an attempt to avoid the mud. It is still raining. We had tea there and met some friends. He is frightfully keen on me but I am only marginally interested. We both know this and recognise that this will probably be our last evening together in this cosy little tent. It was great fun while it lasted – but life will be different for both of us in Brussels.

Four

'Rushed off our feet'
Belgium

A photograph from this time shows Mary
enjoying a rare opportunity to be out of uniform

Belgium had been invaded by German forces in early May 1940 and forced to capitulate before the end of the month. It was liberated by British forces in early September 1944. Mary's transfer to the university town of Louvain about 16 miles from Brussels, shows that the Allied medical teams were establishing hospitals in concert with the military movement north.

24 September, en route for Brussels and Louvain

Left Normandy at 7 a.m. – travelling in open trucks. It was bitterly cold in the early morning and we shivered and chattered in our greatcoats as we trundled along the familiar bumpy roads. As I looked back I caught a last glimpse of the poplar trees standing like sentries on the horizon. It may be a long time before I see Normandy again. It has been a dramatic, poignant and very vivid part of my life. I hope that life will return to normal soon for the farmers here, but the devastation is appalling. We move on, but the people of Normandy must stay behind and clean up the mess.

We reached the staging camp at Poix at 2.30 p.m. We had some lunch and then looked around. It was a former SS barracks and we were delighted with all the mod cons. Indoor lavatories were a great joy – no trudging across muddy fields to spend a penny! The SS quite obviously lived in style here – but they must have left in a hurry as there were German uniforms lying around and plenty of tinned food in the larder. There were German magazines too, mostly the type with unclothed ladies looking nonchalant in impossible positions!

While looking through a desk in my cubicle I came across some maps. There was one of particular interest, a detailed map of Southern England, showing the proposed areas for invasion. The place-name spelling was not too accurate but otherwise it was explicit. It was quite a shock to see how close England had been to invasion. I gave the map to Miss Wade and asked if I might possibly have it returned after the powers that be had inspected it.

25 September, 101 BGH, Louvain

We set off from Poix at 0700 hours. We drove through Flanders Fields. Was disappointed not to see any poppies. The area looked cold, flat and lonely. It is awful to think of the number of men who died there in that war. The Belgian countryside looks quite prosperous, practically no damage as far as I could see from the back of a lorry.

Spoke to Richard once or twice on the journey when we stopped for a tea break. He is Officer I/C [in charge of] luggage and equipment and he seems to be taking his duties rather seriously. He is very pompous sometimes.

We were all very excited as we reached the outskirts of Brussels. It was tremendous fun as our cavalcade entered the city. Everybody waved and shouted to us in welcome. We were the first British Army ladies whom they had seen since the liberation. There were lots of troops everywhere, particularly in the area of the Gare du Nord. They were of all nationalities and all who saw us girls were quite astonishingly enthusiastic. It would have been lovely to stay in this beautiful city but we had to press on to our camp. Our final destination was the Sacré Coeur Convent on top of the hill in the pretty university town of Louvain. We were tired, dirty and hungry but the Mother Superior made us all feel most welcome. She spoke to us in French not Flemish, which was a blessing and food was ordered and provided, and we were all shown to our tiny private cells for the night. This little bed is narrow and uncomfortable, but I am too tired to think of anything but sleep.

26 September

This convent is beautiful but the sanitation is non-existent. Miss Wade is looking decidedly worried. How are we to convert this erstwhile home of a closed order of nuns and make it habitable and suitable for war-injured men?

There appears to be only one indoor lavatory and the plumbing of that is unpredictable. What can we use for a sluice-room and the disposal of dirty dressings? The War Office must be mad to send us here. Still, 'ours not to reason why' etc.

Spent the morning helping to convert the dining room into an operating theatre. The absence of piped water is a major headache.

Went down the hill into the town with Robin Driscoll. Our eyes were popping at the sight of shops with fruit and vegetables. Bought loads of grapes. They were very expensive but I could not resist their black glossy juiciness. I missed fruit very much in Normandy. Vitamin C tablets are not much of a substitute for the real thing. Driscoll and I had lots of fun trying on cosmetics. Madame was most tolerant and helpful. We bought lipsticks and some Chanel No. 5. Blissful!

28 September

We are busy preparing the wards with the kind help of the nuns. There is one dear little fat nun who has attached herself to me. Her name is Soeur Marie-Anselma. She is rosy-cheeked, plump, always smiling and speaks only Flemish. She has helped me to put up the beds this morning and twitters away happily although I do not understand a word. I think the nuns are delighted to have us. Their lives in a closed order must be incredibly boring. It is surprising to see how well they communicate despite the language barrier. Taffy and the other orderlies send them into restrained fits of giggles. Men have not been a part of their lives.

29 September

Went to Brussels with Richard this afternoon. We had tea at the Atlanta. It is exciting here. So many people – a feeling of excited anticipation. Richard talked to me about his family in Germany. They are orthodox Jews. He is very concerned, particularly about his parents. There are rumours of ill-treatment of Jews there. We know so little of what is happening elsewhere.

30 September

We are still preparing wards with the help of the nuns. They are charming and happy and will be helping us with the nursing once the patients arrive. We are also opening wards in St Pierre in the town. It is an annexe to the Sacré Coeur situated near the university.

The architecture here is most impressive. Went for a walk round the town and the Bocage with Connie. The Bocage area is lovely and there are some pretty churches notably the Eglise St Michel. The sun was shining and we wandered around the Heverlee area and admired the delightful stone grotto.

We met one of our new MOs, Capt Phillips, and he offered to take us out to see the Waterloo battleground. He is a tall, dark, rather serious young man – a skin specialist in civilian life. We drove out of Louvain in his jeep. The countryside is rather flat and uninteresting. We went on to Argenteuil. This is a nicely wooded area near Tervuren. Everything looked so peaceful that it was difficult to imagine the famous battle where Napoleon met his match at the hands of Wellington in 1815. There is a small castle and museum there. It was interesting to see so many relics of another war. On our way back we drove through the beautiful forest of Soignes. We arrived back at the Sacré Coeur just in time for dinner. Wore my dress uniform for the first time since we left England. It was good to get out of my dirty battle dress. It would have been better still to be able to have a nice hot bath and get into a slinky evening dress. How lovely it will be to wear a pretty gown again.

1 October

Am now working at St Pierre, the small convent annexe. Connie is also down here and some young nuns including Soeur Marie-Anselma. There is a convoy of patients arriving tomorrow. Some will come here, the others will go to the main convent building. St Pierre is quite small. We have three wards prepared at present. The sanitation too is much better than at the Sacré Coeur and best of all there is a bathroom with running hot water. It is absolute bliss, my first hot bath in three months.

We have our meals with the MOs and there is an easy relaxed atmosphere. Miss Wade visited us today and tells me that I shall be in charge of K1, a thirty-bedded ward. It will be nice to have patients again. Capt Phillips is MO here.

2 October

We are back in business. A convoy of patients arrived today. They have come from somewhere up the line. I had the ward prepared for surgical cases – but instead we have thirty men with skin diseases and psychiatric problems. It is certainly an unexpected turn of events, but it should be interesting. Capt Phillips is pleased as this is partly his speciality. I have Taffy as orderly and Soeur Marie-Anselma as an assistant. Taffy is wary and suspicious of the chubby little nun. I suppose it is his Welsh Chapel anti-Catholic background. Marie-Anselma presented me with a string of beautiful mother-of-pearl rosary beads this morning. It is a charming gift and I am very touched. She was going off happily to give another one to Taffy but I persuaded her not to, as tactfully as one can without speaking a word of Flemish. I gather that Marie-Anselma has had some nursing experience. She would be a great help if we can manage to overcome the language barrier. I miss Chezzy, my favourite interpreter. He promised to write. Hope he and all his Pioneer Corps are alright.

Capt Phillips and I did a ward round together. This is a very different situation to our gunshot wards in Normandy. It is very difficult to decide which men are genuinely sick and need treatment and which ones are swinging the lead. Capt Phillips is most conscientious and has prescribed all kinds of skin treatments. His favourite idea is to remove all scabs with sterile forceps and paint the area with gentian violet. Marie-Anselma loves this treatment, particularly the gentian violet bit. She must be a frustrated Matisse.

I feel very sorry for the shell shocked, anxiety-state boys. They shake constantly and they too have skin troubles, but I doubt if the source of their troubles will be cured by painting with gentian violet.

3 October

We had a Colonel's inspection this morning. The new CO is a regular army man and a stickler for bull. The wheels of the beds must stand to attention facing away from the door, as must also the openings of the pillow cases! The up patients had to stand by their beds to attention and bed patients had to lie rigid in order not to make the bed-clothes look untidy. This is a new experience for me, this extraordinary obsession with army rules, particularly the tidiness. Was amazed to see how the soldiers from the Guards Division reacted. They are unbelievably disciplined – never seem to relax. Sgt Hall of the Coldstream Guards lies to attention in bed to swallow his pills at the double. I was politely reprimanded by the CO for putting a cradle over a patient's bed. Pte Williams has a severe eczema of his legs and the bed-clothes were irritating him. Was told that cradles were unmilitary!

4 October

The CO and Miss Wade came along to the ward this morning to inform me that the skin patients were to be evacuated within two hours and we were to be ready for new casualties at 1400 hours. It was a frightful panic, last-minute treatments – packing up gear, farewells. We were just getting to know these boys. Am hoping that some of them at least will be sent back to the UK for further treatment, particularly the shell shocks.

Soeur Marie-Anselma is a tornado of energy, cleaning up the sluice and treatment room, making beds, etc. Taffy and the other orderly are exhausted. We are expecting surgical cases and the ward has to be spotless.

The first ambulance arrived at 1400 hours: fifteen men who looked very ill indeed and extremely dirty. We laid them on stretchers in the corridor to find out their particulars and recent drugs etc. and also to establish priority for urgent treatment.

After 15 minutes another convoy arrived. Twelve more blood-stained battle-weary boys, some of them still wearing the red beret of the Paratroopers. The rest of the day has been hectically busy. Capt Phillips, Taffy Jones, Marie-Anselma and the other nuns were magnificent.

I made a quick check of the men who were in obvious pain and bleeding badly, also the ones in a state of shock. Capt Phillips helped us to get the worst cases undressed and into bed – some were given intravenous plasma at once, others blood transfusions as soon as we could identify the group. (We have a small blood bank here.) Some of them had come from Casualty Clearing Stations near Nijmegen, others from a hospital in Arnhem. Some of them had no medical notes of any kind, just an identity disc and the name, date and time of any administered drug written on their forehead. I have not come across this practice before – not even in Normandy. The casualties in Arnhem and Nijmegen must have been enormous if the MOs and orderlies did not have time to write any notes or attach labels.

Have just crawled off duty at 2 a.m. The patients are cleaned up, undressed (we had to cut off their clothing) and in bed. There are six blood transfusions and thirteen blood plasmas on the go. Hope Connie can manage for the rest of the night. She has two good orderlies.

5 October

The patients are a lovely cheerful crowd – so delighted to be out of the ghastly horror of Arnhem and Nijmegen.* Lt Brian Stephenson is in the first bed on the left inside the ward door. He has gunshot wounds of the stomach and is still on blood transfusions. The wound re-opened on the bumpy ambulance ride down here and he lost a great deal of blood. He is with the 1st Airborne Reconnaissance Squadron and landed in Arnhem on 17 September. He is feeling a little better today but is obviously in a state of nervous shock – quick puffing of cigarettes and a great need to talk about the horror of what he calls 'The Cauldron'. Arnhem he tells me was a shambles, utter chaos, no communications and thousands of men from the 1st Airborne Division are dead. There was constant street fighting for eight days – houses burning and constant mortar stonking [artillery bombardment]. He was wounded after eight days of hell, no food just some fruit from the Dutch civilians – very little water and no sleep. Men were running around screaming, trying to find any escape. He was taken to a Dutch hospital behind the German lines. He had two abdominal operations performed by a German surgeon and he was well cared for by Dutch nurses.

* The Allied advance was being slowed by well-armed and organised German troops in the Netherlands and Rhineland. To overcome this, Montgomery planned Operation Market Garden, an advance that began on 17 September 1944. The whole operation went badly wrong, resulting in the chaos of the Battle of Arnhem. By 26 September, the Germans had taken nearly 6,000 prisoners and the Allies had lost almost 15,000 troops.

Brian will be alright physically once the wound has healed but I think it will be a long time before he gets over the shock of Arnhem. Connie tells me that he has to be constantly sedated at night to stop him screaming in terror. He is only twenty-two years old.

Sgt Mullins also from the 1st Airborne has had an horrific experience, but seems to be recovering in an amazing way. He is, I think, just happy and surprised to be alive. He was crawling along in the street fighting at Arnhem when he came face to face with a German self-propelled gun. He said 'I thought I was a gonner but suddenly the anti-tank gunner, a big bloke, leaned out, picked me up bodily and stuck me across the chassis beneath the barrel of the gun. The cheeky bastard then tracked back safely and my mates on either side of the road could not throw the Gammon bombs [hand grenades] they had removed from their belts'. Later he said 'I was thrown on the side of the road where my mates picked me up and I was taken to the First Aid Station'.

Sgt Mullins was 'patched up' as he put it and went back to the street fighting again. On the eighth day of Arnhem he 'copped this lot'. This 'lot' is an amputated left leg and gunshot wounds of the shoulder. He described that awful eighth day at Arnhem as chaotic fighting, groans and shrieks of pain, heavy gunfire, the dead lying all around us. The wounded screaming for water and stretcher bearers, machine guns everywhere, trapped between German infantry with mortars behind and half-track tanks in front. It was also 'belting' rain and 'we had no sleep or much food for days'. This sergeant, too, was taken to the St Elizabeth Hospital at Arnhem and from there has come down the line to us.

6 October

The Arnhem boys were still talking about their shocking experiences when I went on duty this morning. They were delighted to see me, someone to listen to them at last. They talk and talk and I encourage them to do so. Soeur Marie-Anselma stands patiently listening while doing dressings etc. She looks so sympathetic and understanding, they do not know or care that she doesn't understand a word they are saying.

Private Jim Peall is only eighteen years old and still very shell shocked. He can't speak, just stammers and shakes, but today for the first time he said one sentence: 'There was blood coming out of my mate's mouth'.

These boys are very resentful of the RAF. Capt Wilkens of the Royal Engineers said 'The only time we saw the bloody RAF they were dropping supplies behind the German lines'. A dead German soldier had Woodbines and other British goodies in his pocket. Capt Wilkens has gunshot wounds of the chest and has difficulty in breathing but that doesn't stop him swearing about the RAF – and 'anyway where was the bloody 2nd Army and where was HQ and the top brass?'

He did have a few kind words to say about the Dutch civilians and, incongruous as it may seem, he was genuinely sad about their beautiful homes and the destruction of 'lovely antique furniture' which was used for barricading doors and windows during the street fighting. The Dutch civilians, including women and children, spent the whole time in the cellars. It was too dangerous to come out. He was wounded while trying to attack a pill box near the bridge with a grenade. He threw the thing and then there was a momentary pause before 'all hell was let loose'. There was a tremendous explosion, which shook the ground on both banks of the river, and splinters of wood and glass shot through the air. 'We did not know at the time but in the sheds by the bridge there were dumps of ammunition, and these exploded in a series of deafening roars as tracer bullets shot out towards the high steel arch of the bridge. It was like bloody Guy Fawkes' night. We waited for the bridge to collapse, but everything went quiet, the smoke cleared and the bridge was still there. I was standing gawping at all this when a bloody sniper picked me out and I copped this lot'. What an incredible experience!

Feeling exhausted tonight – but I am on call all night as Connie is off sick. Should not be writing this diary. It is against regulations, and we are constantly reminded to 'Save Paper' and 'Help the War Effort'. I probably write this because I resent having my private letters censored.

7 October

Heard today that our commissioned officer patients are to be removed to the Sacré Coeur to an officer ward there. We shall miss them all but particularly Brian Stephenson.

One of our quietest patients talked to me today as I dressed his wounds. Sgt Melbourne is a tough, cool, experienced soldier, a veteran who fought with the 2nd Battalion in North Africa. He was one of the first to land in Arnhem on that Sunday. The lack of co-ordination and discipline was very hard for him to tolerate. 'The RAF did not know what they were up to'. They dropped 5 tons of ammunition and food on a Dutch farm, which was in German hands within the hour. He told me that there were 'no orders from anybody and we were shelling each other in the dark'. Sgt Melbourne had the bright idea of a cry which they could recognise. It was, he told me, the astonishing shout 'Whoa Mahomet'. He first heard the Arabs call this out in North Africa. The Germans were unable to copy it – or perhaps too mystified! Sgt Melbourne, a round-faced solid farmer from the West Country, went through hell in Arnhem and on the fifth day of the street fighting he lost both hands and his left eye.

My heart aches for this kindly man so solid, strong and reliable. Will he ever be able to work on his farm again? He has a wife and two young children at home. What is his future to be? He talked to me quietly about how his mates dragged him into the cellar of his battalion HQ. He told me they were working 'up to their elbows in blood'. The Padre took Sgt Melbourne to the hospital occupied by the Germans. He stuck a Red Cross flag on the front of the jeep and drove right up to the German guard shouting 'This man needs attention at once'. He was taken into the hospital, given morphia and later underwent surgery. The Padre was allowed to go back to his post. Sgt Melbourne went on to say 'I was well cared for, there were a few British POW MOs, a few German surgeons, Dutch nurses and young nuns like you have here'. This sergeant is being seen by an ophthalmologist tomorrow. He has been having trouble with his good eye.

Soeur Marie-Anselma is proving a great help on the ward. She is kind, sympathetic and tireless. The language barrier is transcended by simple human kindness.

8 October

We have some Polish patients at present, some from the Polish Airborne Brigade. One, whom we call Bruno, as we can't pronounce his name, reminds me of Chezzy. He can slip so easily from one language to another, and is full of compliments and endearments to me in every language. His blarney* is particularly endearing because he is in severe pain quite a lot of the time. He has had his left leg amputated but the stump has become infected and does not appear to be reacting to penicillin. He has a lively extrovert personality and is very popular in the ward. He, too, has a horror story to tell about his landing in Arnhem. He said that they were 'under attack by Messerschmitts and ground forces and many of the glider-borne units who did manage to land were taken for Germans and attacked by the British'. Bruno tells me that it was an impossible and appalling situation. 'We panicked and managed to find a Dutch farm where we holed in for the night'. Bruno eventually attached himself to a British unit where he was met by a dirty

* An Irish term for good conversation and storytelling.

bearded sergeant who thrust a rifle and two grenades into his hands and said 'Well, get stuck in then'.

9 October

The boys here talk constantly about Arnhem and Nijmegen. I was surprised to hear about the many who had deserted to the Germans and the fighting between officers and men.* Brian Stephenson corroborated this. He tells me 'Fear was everywhere'. Men's nerves were completely shattered by the constant barrage of guns – the lack of sleep, food and water and the quantities of Benzedrine tablets† they consumed in order to keep awake. Brian is still in a state of nervous shock and as yet unfit to be moved to the officers' ward at the Sacré Coeur. His abdominal wound is gradually healing, but he still smokes too much and is very jumpy and nervous. This afternoon he told me about the German psychological warfare. Each night the loudspeakers crackled and a German voice with overtones of 'Lili Marlene' in the background said 'Tommies. It is better you should give yourselves up. Your General is our prisoner and the rest of the Division has surrendered. If you do not, you will die. Are you hungry? Would you like to share the food the RAF has dropped to us? Think of your wives and children.'

There was fear in Brian's voice as he spoke of the German tiger tanks, like 'prehistoric monsters as their great guns swing from side to side breathing fire'. He said 'One kept on thinking where is the RAF? Where is the 2nd Army?'

Corporal Hughes in the next bed to Brian is a lively young

* It is impossible to verify or deny the charge of desertion. It may be that those who surrendered to the Germans or disappeared after being cut off from their units in the fighting were considered 'deserters'. Later accounts certainly confirm the German use of messages transmitted over loudspeaker to encourage surrender as described by Mary's patients.

† The stimulant Benzedrine (amphetamine) was given as a ration to the troops to help them stay alert when they had to go long periods without sleep. It was also used by medical personnel so they could work long hours to treat casualties.

lad from the north with the South Staffordshire Regiment. He has gunshot wounds of the shoulder. He tells me that it was almost impossible to make a distinction between the German and British lines. During the street fighting one day he crawled over to a house which a few hours before had been occupied 'by some blokes in the RASC [Royal Army Service Corps]. There was a cellar full of tinned fruit and stuff there and I was after it for my lot'. He jumped in through the window and landed smack in the lap of a German who was squatting on the floor. 'The Jerry was as surprised as I was and as I was jumping out of the window, he laughed and said "Auf Wiedersehen".'

10 October

We have about twelve soldiers from the Guards Armoured Division. I never cease to be astonished by their discipline and personal tidiness. They were wounded at an assault across the Waal [River] at Nijmegen. They are reluctant to talk about their experiences and treat me not so much as a Nursing Sister but a superior officer. These boys seem to be ram-rod stiff even in bed. They never discuss or argue about any treatment, just accept it. They are, I am sure, excellent soldiers, but what are they like as human beings? What type of training is it that makes the Guards different to other soldiers?

We have a nice American here at present. Sgt Ellman was wounded in a battle on the outskirts of Eindhoven. He has a charming southern drawl and a very warm personality. He has invited me to visit his home in Texas after the war and shown me photographs of Mom and Pop and his kid sister. I receive so many invitations such as this. It is rather sad really. We make these boys well just so that they can return to Nijmegen and Eindhoven to begin fighting all over again. The tempo of life is so urgent and swift in wartime and the characters transitory. Men and women come into orbit and then slip out of one's life never to be seen again. One wonders, have they been killed or just posted to another theatre of war? It is impossible to make lasting relationships. Life is a brain-scrambling rush that must get so many duties performed each and every day.

11 October

Letter from Michael. He is well and with General Patton's Army 'somewhere attempting to cross the Rhine into Germany'.

Our shell shock cases are recovering very slowly – some are unable to feed themselves. They keep shaking and gibbering and puffing away at cigarettes. You can see the fear in their eyes. Soeur Marie-Anselma is excellent with these boys – so kind and patient. Sgt Louis Hagen had shell shock and gunshot wounds of the arm on admission. He is recovering now and is gradually beginning to talk to us about his experiences in Arnhem. Louis is a Dutch German-speaking Jew with dark hair, a thin sensitive face and the most beautiful brown eyes. He has a soft voice and a gentle manner, which makes him a great favourite with me. He talked this evening while I was doing his dressing about the retreat of the 1st Airborne Division from Arnhem and the crossing of the river there. He said that 'the survivors, many of them wounded, stumbled through the darkness down to the river. The current was swift and they could not see the bank on the other side. All of those unable to walk had been ordered to stay behind. They were bloody wrecks of men from the Casualty Clearing Stations.'

As Louis approached the river he saw bodies lying all along the path. There were feverish pleading eyes looking up at him from the darkness of the meadow, arms frenziedly clutching his legs. He said 'I dragged limp bodies along towards the beach. I ran round and round close to hysteria until someone came up from the river and in an authoritative voice ordered me to leave the wounded where they were'. Louis said 'I vomited over and over again, and the screams and mortar fire went on. I got into a boat. The heavy gunfire went on as we tried to cross. Several men jumped into the water fully clothed and tried to swim with Sten guns across their backs. They could be seen frantically struggling to disentangle themselves from their straps and laces before sinking. Others dived in half naked (like me) and most of us got across and staggered dripping and covered in mud to houses on the far bank. We wrapped ourselves in anything we could find'.

Louis survived all of that only to be picked off by a sniper while fighting with the 2nd Army a few days later. Poor Louis. He apologised for making me listen to this sad story. War is not for gentle, artistic, sensitive people such as Louis. I could cry for all of them, but what use are tears?*

Noted that some of the boys who have shell shock are also suffering from double vision. It may be the prolonged use of Benzedrine.

12 October

We are all working a twelve-hour day, but so far I have not been called during the night. Am amazed by the incredible endurance of some of our young soldiers. Private Hughes, an eighteen-year-old Welshman with amputation of the left leg, is a case in point. He copped this in Arnhem. He tells me that the average amount of sleep they had during the Arnhem cauldron was two and three hours in twenty-four. The men 'looked as exhausted as if they had been sea-sick for a week'. He was wounded in the street fighting and taken to a dressing station. The place was hit by a phosphorous bomb soon after he got there and then everything went up in smoke. He said that there weren't enough stretchers and 'most of us were trundled out in wheelbarrows'. He tells me that a Dutch nurse and two orderlies were killed there. The injured were then taken to another

---

* Louis Hagen would later write a book about his experiences, but interestingly did not acknowledge his shock and played down his arm wound and his time in hospital.

dressing station and somebody went round with little packets of sulphonamide and morphia. Later he too was taken to St Elizabeth's Hospital where he was looked after by girls of the Women's Wehrmacht Army and some Dutch nurses.

Our officer patients are still here awaiting transfer. One of them is a Polish Liaison Officer and extremely useful to me in helping his men understand their medication and treatment. Capt Zwolewski has gunshot wounds of the chest. He landed with the unfortunate Airborne Polish Division in Arnhem and did a marvellous job convincing our men that they were Polish not German. He is an experienced soldier and tells me that Arnhem was in fact a gentleman's battle despite all the slaughter and suffering. The Germans were helpful in allowing the Allied wounded into their hospital. He speaks German fluently and was once despatched to the German HQ carrying a Red Cross flag. He talked his way past the guard on duty and was shown in to see the German officer in charge. He demanded a two-hour truce to get the wounded moved out of the fighting zone. The officer, a 'decent chap', granted this and astonishingly gave Zwolenski a bottle of brandy and some sandwiches! He then asked the German officer if he might have some of the food and medical supplies that were dropped by the RAF. He was then escorted to a store room and shown the contents of recently dropped panniers. They contained soap, red berets and stationery. The Germans were amused. Zwolenski was not. There was 'soap for men without water' he muttered angrily. This officer too was picked off by a sniper a few days later. 'They were everywhere – waging a war of nerves'. There were soldiers crying with fear and exhaustion crawling to the German lines to give themselves up and others too scared to come out of their trenches. 'It was an extraordinary battle' he tells me. The hospital in German hands was guarded by one nervous German soldier. The wounded walked in for treatment, others were on stretchers or wheelbarrows. The walking wounded were often allowed to go back to their unit after treatment.

13 October

Our officers were transferred to the Sacré Coeur today. We shall miss them but we need the beds desperately. There are convoys of wounded coming in almost every day from the front, which seems to be around Nijmegen and Eindhoven areas. The ward is very busy. We are understaffed and rushed off our feet. It is a desperate race to get the dressings etc. completed each day. There is also the anxiety of ward tidiness. The Colonel's inspection this morning was something of a disaster! I forgot to turn <u>all</u> the bed wheels away from the door, the pillow case openings were also looking the wrong way and then the most wicked crime of all, I had put cradles over the amputees to prevent the bed-clothes touching the stumps. I was also reprimanded for fixing the pillows armchair fashion. I hate this army bull. We did not have to put up with this type of nonsense in Normandy.

I had an afternoon off today (two hours). Capt Phillips took me in to Brussels. We had coffee and some gorgeous cakes at Madame Funck's. There are not any obvious signs of food shortage here.

Was amazed to see many Belgian girls wearing coats made from blue hospital blankets. Felt rather irritated as we are short of blankets for the patients – now I know why! They are obviously being sold on the black market by ex-patients or orderlies.

16 October

The nuns here are an enormous help to me, particularly Marie-Anselma. It must be extremely difficult for her to cope with the nursing duties here – some of which are very intimate and difficult. The patients are on the whole very grateful for everything we do for them and it is rather endearing to note how they restrain their more colourful army language when we are around. On the other hand they do tend to vent their feelings on poor old Taffy Jones, who is very good natured but constantly running around like a scalded cat.

Have been trying to teach Marie-Anselma English and she is learning quite quickly. She loves to practise this new art and tries it out on the patients. The results are hilarious. The look of blank astonishment on a patient's face after a treatment with our little nun is very funny. I sometimes wonder how she and the nuns will cope with going back to their old routine in a closed order after all this is over.

Went to a party given by the MOs at the Sacré Coeur. Danced most of the evening with Richard and John Phillips.

19 October

The last few days have been very busy as I am starting a forty-eight-hour leave in Brussels tomorrow – my first leave since joining the QAs. Connie is now off night duty and will take over from me. It is fortunate that she knows the patients already but nevertheless there is a great deal of handing over to be done. The men have promised to be good and co-operative. I wonder. These nosy patients of mine are far more interested in <u>whom</u> I am spending my forty-eight hours with rather than where!

20 October, Hôtel Splendide, Brussels

Arrived here at 3 p.m. There was a telephone message from Lance, one of my Canadian friends from Normandy days, inviting me to the Canadian Officers' Club for dinner and a dance tomorrow evening. He must have contacted me through Miss Wade. Feeling very tired.

21 October

This place really is rather splendid. I have a room en suite and the bathroom is quite fabulous – very ornate – a marble bath. This is such a luxury – time to bath and wash my hair at leisure. Lance and Jerry, a friend of his, picked me up at 6 p.m. and drove me to their Club. This place is very plush and ornate. There were Canadian voices everywhere. We had a super dinner and then went upstairs to the ballroom. There were several Belgian girls in evening dress. They looked so lovely that I felt a momentary pang of envy. Anyway it was short lived. The Canadians made a great fuss of me, and champagne flowed freely. There were crystal chandeliers, happy voices, laughter, tinkling glasses, a world so far removed from my ward and the horrors of Arnhem and Nijmegen.

I was dancing with Jerry when a voice said, 'May I have this dance?' I looked at him and listened to the slow drawling voice. He seemed interesting, not one of the 'Do you come here often?' types. We sat down and he walked across the room to order champagne. He was tall and lanky with dark hair. His movement as he walked across the large room to the bar was totally relaxed and indolent. There was a strange feeling of power behind the cool lazy appearance. We drank a bottle of champagne and talked for hours. He is a strangely perceptive man. We had a wonderful time until Lance came to take me back to my hotel.

22 October

Vernon telephoned me at the crack of dawn and said that he would be round with a jeep in ten minutes. He was, and we remained quiet as he drove out to Laeken. He is stopping at the Atlanta and after a long walk we drove back there for luncheon. The food was fabulous and accompanied by champagne and <u>real</u> coffee. Went for a walk in the Botanical Gardens later, and we looked around the city generally. I did not see or notice anything very much except this tall, lanky, funny man with the slow voice. He talked about his life in Canada, the loneliness, the remoteness from civilisation, the hard physical work which he enjoys. He is so much at ease, yet has a perceptive and forceful intellect. What will this war do to him? He returns to the front tomorrow. Will he survive? We went back to his room at the Atlanta later. He ordered champagne, cognac and sandwiches. There is a curfew in Brussels but we walked hand in hand through the empty streets at 2 a.m. back to the Hôtel Splendide. Brussels was quite strange and lonely. I felt that way too.

23 October, 101 BGH, Louvain

Vernon telephoned. He must return to Nijmegen at 1000 hours. I hate good-byes. If only we could have had a few more days together. Feeling very miserable. Lance brought me back here this evening. He is rather nice and sad to see me so unhappy. There was a letter from Peter awaiting me. He is now serving in Burma.

24 October

The patients were delighted to see me back but it is hard to return to their cheerful and flirtatious banter. Connie is staying on for a few days to help me, until she goes on her forty-eighthour leave. She is such a lovely cheerful person (from Cardiff) and good fun. People are being exceptionally kind. Hope I am not looking too unhappy.

28 October

We are still receiving casualties from the Nijmegen area. Louis Hagen and some of the more serious cases from the Arnhem battle are being sent to the UK. We have quite a few Americans in the ward at present.

Had a letter from Kenneth enclosing a book of his poetry dedicated to me. Feel very flattered. They are good.

No letter from Vernon. Hope he is OK.

5 November

Capt Phillips keeps inviting me to go out with him. It is rather awkward as we have to work closely together on duty. Went to the cinema with him this evening. It was a ghastly propaganda film, so unrealistic. We went on to Madame Funck's afterwards. He likes the place and the food is good. We met a friend of his, Lt Gray (Guards Armoured Division). He joined us for a drink after dinner. Did not like him. He seems frightfully arrogant and loud voiced – so full of his own self-importance. He was trying to give an impression of self-confidence and failed dismally as far as I was concerned.

Wonder if I shall ever see Vernon again.

10 November

Went to Mass at the Sacré Coeur this morning. It is a beautiful little chapel – so serene – a happy atmosphere. Feel strangely comforted.

When I went back on duty, Lt Gray was waiting in my office. He has been pestering me to go out with him and will not take my no for an answer. I think he finds it hard to understand that any girl can find him anything other than totally irresistible. Was able to tell him that I would be on duty until 1000 hours and after that would be going straight to bed <u>alone</u>.

16 December

Letter from Michael. He is somewhere along the Siegfried Line.* (Can't imagine how that managed to get through the censor's red ink.) He is having a hard time. It is extremely cold with lots of snow and it is difficult to obtain supplies. His main concern seems to be for the morale of his friends in the unit. He tells me that he refused to have his name put forward for a commission. He writes 'I mean to survive this and it would be almost impossible to do that as a junior officer with this outfit. The man who must give an order to go over the top gets a shot in the back'.

Colonel's inspection again today and I managed to have all the bed wheels and pillow case openings facing the same way. The CO saluted and said 'Carry on Sister'. What can he mean? Received a lovely letter from Vernon.

18 December

The news is rather alarming. Nancy Munro heard on the Forces programme that the Germans have penetrated 16 miles inside Belgium. We think that their objective might be Antwerp. This situation puts our hospital far too close to the front for comfort. The bombers stream over Louvain every day. We are still having casualties from the Remagen area. No further letters from Vernon.

Called to a staff meeting at the Sacré Coeur at 1800 hours. We are to start evacuating the seriously ill patients tomorrow. Some are to be airlifted back to the UK, others will go back down the line. Nobody knows what is to happen to us.

---

* Siegfried Line (German term: Westwall): an almost continuous line running from Switzerland to Antwerp. The first major offensive against this line began on 29 September 1944. In October and early November this was followed by the Battle for Hürtgen Forest. Allied advances took Metz and Strasbourg but were halted on 16 December when the Germans launched an offensive in the Ardennes (the Battle of the Bulge).

A great deal depends upon the military situation.* I informed the patients and staff. Tomorrow the beds must be emptied. Up patients will be returned to their units.

19 December

A very sad day – saying good-bye to the men whom we have grown to like so much. Soeur Marie-Anselma was in tears all day. We all stood on the steps outside the beautiful Eglise St Michel and waved until all the ambulances were out of sight. I wonder if we will ever see any of them again. We were almost like a family in our ward – but families break up eventually. It is almost impossible to have any continuity of friendships in this war – people come and go. Felt very depressed as we went inside to tidy up the empty ward and clear up the mess. They were so noisy and demanding and cheerful. I do miss them.

The CO came round this evening to say that we are confined to barracks until further notice. Listened to the news. The Germans have broken through the American defences and are within 4 miles of the Meuse.

23 December

Hurrah. We are no longer confined to barracks. Sharing a room with Connie and Nancy. The last few days have been rather tense. We listened to the roar of our bombers going over each day. They said on the news this morning that the Germans have been pushed back.† We are staying on here and presumably we will be opening up the wards in a few days.

Received a lovely letter from Vernon. He has, I think, been having a hard time. Went to an American officers' party in

* The potential outcome of the Battle of the Bulge.

† On 23 December bad weather cleared, allowing air support, which stalled the German advance, though the situation was still unstable. The fighting continued and the Germans did not fall back until early January 1945.

Brussels. It was too noisy and there were too many drunks. Feeling very lonely.

24 December

Christmas Eve. Went to the RAMC Sergeants' dance at Heverlee. Richard and John were there. Danced with both of them most of the evening. Richard was reminiscing rather dangerously about Normandy days. He is being posted back to the UK shortly and John is being promoted and will be joining the 108 in Brussels. There is a strange feeling of insecurity and change. Hope the war will be over soon.

25 December

We had a marvellous Christmas dinner and dance at the Hôtel de Ville. The food and wine was excellent and we were waited upon and fussed over by the MOs and orderlies. There was terrific hilarity, lots of music and singing – records of 'Lili Marlene' and Vera Lynn. Danced with Bill, a new MO out from the UK. He is a typical rookie in the sense of having an extraordinary enthusiasm for experiencing the war. He can't wait to get to the front and work in a Casualty Clearing Station. We danced tangos, waltzes and foxtrots to the tunes of Victor Sylvester and in between he told me the story of his life. He is English middle-class to the core, the son of a country family doctor, and the product of a minor public school, Cambridge and Guy's medical training school. He loves rugby and gives an outward impression of almost arrogant self-confidence, but somehow I feel that he is rather frightened inside. We danced and drank champagne until 5 a.m. It was great fun.

27 December

Went to an RA [Royal Artillery] officers' party in Brussels. Met a very attractive and extremely charming man in his early thirties. Major Tim Sykes is the type of man who makes a girl feel that she is the most interesting and fascinating woman whom he has ever met. It is all a line of course, but it is very hard to resist someone who really listens to what you have to say and appears to be genuinely interested. He has a great warmth of personality and an unconventionality of manner. I feel that I can be myself with him. We talked until 4 a.m.

31 December

The last day of 1944. This has been an eventful year for me and a sad one for many people. I hear that we shall be opening up the wards again early in the New Year.

Tim sent two of his officers to collect me in a jeep. The dinner dance was quite a glittering affair, excellent food, champagne, music and laughter. It was rather exciting and Tim was most attentive. There were several Belgian girls in evening dress. Some were very attractive. I noticed that two girls were wearing wigs and another had a headscarf worn turban fashion. I wondered if these girls had also attended the glittering dinner dances of the Wehrmacht when they were here. I once saw a girl being chased through the streets of Brussels by a crowd of women. They cut off all her hair. It is the retribution for collaborators. Anyway everybody seemed to be enjoying themselves tonight and very noisily. Tim was the host at this party but he still found time to make me feel a most honoured guest. At midnight we all sang 'Auld Lang Syne'. I wondered what 1945 would hold in store for me. Tim brought me home at 4 a.m. – a wonderful night.

2 January 1945

Went to a unit dinner dance at the Allied Officers' Club in Brussels. Had a wonderful time. Bill was there, also Tim and Richard Kelvin. Tim was in a very flirtatious mood much to the annoyance of the other two. I was in great demand which was extremely pleasant. We all danced and talked and drank champagne until 4 a.m. Social life is very exciting at the moment.

5 January

Went out to dinner with Tim in Diest. It was a marvellous place and the meal (French cuisine) was superb. Tim has known the proprietor since before the war. He was very amusing as usual and teased me about Bill. Arrived back here at 3 a.m.

6 January

The ward is filling up again with casualties and there are several Americans and Canadians amongst them. I am always fearful of finding Michael or Vernon amongst the injured. We have an international ward once again, no hierarchy, no barriers even of language, just the unwritten language of human caring, epitomised by dear little Soeur Marie-Anselma. She is so gentle and kind. We all work hard at the job of repairing bodies so that they will be fit enough to go back to the front and fight all over again.

Tim came along to the ward this afternoon and waited patiently in the office until I finished duty at 5 p.m. We went into Brussels and saw *The Merry Widow*. Had dinner at the Officers' Club afterwards. He gave me a lovely pair of sheer silk stockings. It is bliss just to look at such lovely feminine things. I do miss pretty frocks. Anyway the war may soon be over. We drove back to St Pierre at 2 a.m. Tim is married. I do like him but do not like the situation.

13 January

Went to a dance at the American Officers' Club in Tirlemont with Victor, one of my ex-patients. Victor was a Nijmegen casualty last year. He is an extremely large Texan, with an easy relaxed manner and a delightful southern drawl. He is so tall that he makes every room he enters seem small. I feel very protected while I'm with him and feel that I can talk about anything. Told him about Tim and his advice was 'forget the guy'. We had a very pleasant and totally relaxed evening.

16 January

The casualties are rolling in again, many from the La Roche and Ardennes area. There is much talk of snow and lack of supplies, white camouflage in the snow, and the sheer hardship of living conditions, quite apart from bombardment by the Boche. Many of these boys are battle weary. It has been a hard slog all along the way.

Letter from Michael including a snap of himself and his friends taken in the snowy Ardennes. The hardship there is terrible.

23 January

The convoys of wounded are coming down the line to us every day. We're short of Sisters and Connie's illness has made things even more difficult. She is recuperating at the Convalescent Home in Waterloo. Poor Connie. Night duty did not do her health much good. She has a tendency to bronchitis and the combination of hard work and a cold winter has been too much for her.

We have a constant succession of new MOs who do not know the patients. We are rushed off our feet all day. It is a battle to find the time to write the reports and to fill in the wretched in-triplicate forms in order to obtain essential drugs and equipment.

There is one new element amongst our casualties this year – battle weariness. There is far less gaiety and *joie de vivre*. These men want to go home to their wives and families. They are tired after all the bloody battles of Normandy, Arnhem and Nijmegen.

27 January

Am sharing a room with Nancy Munro and Kathleen Aitken. There are always problems about sharing a room. Some are tidy, some are not, some are noisy, others quiet. Today I have the room to myself. Am in bed with laryngitis and a heavy cold. Nancy brought me a light lunch and an aspirin gargle. Richard has sent me some flowers and Bill a lovely basket of fruit – delicious. It is only today that I finally realised how tired I am.

28 January

My voice has gone completely and I am still in bed. Richard, Bill and Capt Knox came to visit me. They are all rather darlings and Richard kissed me for 'old times' sake'. Am lucky to have such lovely friends. Soeur Marie-Anselma brought me tea and some cake. Feel very guilty as the ward is so busy.

1 February

Back on duty again. My cold is better but the laryngitis continues much to everybody's amusement. I've had to write out treatment instructions for all the orderlies, and all special patients. I've found it extremely useful to give each patient a written statement of all their medication, diet and treatments. They can then remind the orderlies if medication is late or not forthcoming. Am also pleased to see how delighted the men are to be given information about their own case history and treatment. It gives them a feeling of involvement and helps me to prevent mistakes on my ward.

10 February

Am now on night duty on my ward. Connie has taken over from me on day duty. Taffy Jones is my orderly and he too knows the patients, but I miss Marie-Anselma and the other nuns. We have all become such good friends. It is very busy tonight, and apart from the cups of tea which Taffy provides, we have no time for any other sustenance.

The ward takes on a ghostly atmosphere at night. There are innumerable drips to be watched and there has to be constant vigilance for the unexpected haemorrhage from a wound. Smells are important. It is vital to be able to smell the early stages of gangrene as this could mean an emergency amputation.

The men, too, are more insecure at night. They worry about their families at home and every spare moment is spent listening to their problems and providing endless cups of tea. One of the patients presented me with a sketch of myself which he did last night as I sat at the table in the middle of the ward with a red cloth draped over the light. I like it. The QA uniform is excellent. The flowing white organdie head dress, little red cape with two pips on the shoulder and the plain grey dress, but my face – well – that is too angelic by half!

12 February

The convoys are still coming in. We are very busy. Soeur Marie-Anselma is to ask Mother Superior if she may join me on night duty.

15 February

My birthday. Twenty-four today. Awful thought. Am getting so old. Letters from my family in Ireland, also Kenneth and Ricky. Kenneth is somewhere on the high seas, Ricky in Egypt.

Feeling very tired. It is difficult to keep up with all the treatments. Several of the patients scream in the night as they re-live some of their appalling experiences. It is difficult to sleep during the day. There is so much noise and many of my friends call round not realising I am on nights.

18 February

Went out to dinner at the Officers' Club in Louvain with Peggy Lloyd and an officer patient. Had to be back for duty at 8 p.m. Eric Brook (Peggy's friend) is a pilot officer in the RAF. He is in Bomber Command and was shot down and wounded in Arnhem. Another busy night. Exhausted.

25 February

Last night should have been my night off. Bill and Eric Brook came along to the Mess at 6 p.m. to collect me and Peggy. Eric invited us to the RAF Officers' Club in Brussels. We were joined for dinner by a rather interesting man, a Squadron Leader Young, and we all went on to a party afterwards at his Mess. It was great fun. They brought me back just after midnight and there was a message waiting for me to say that I must go on duty at once as a new convoy had come in. My bed had never looked so inviting as I changed into my grey and scarlet uniform.

There was absolute chaos on the ward. All the lights were on – stretchers on the floor and Taffy Jones and Soeur Marie-Anselma rushing around in circles. Driscoll was trying to run both her own ward and mine. Bill put on a white coat and joined me as we tried to bring some order into the situation and deal with the most seriously injured cases first.

Most of them had come down from the Siegfried Line area, near Goch. Many of them were Scottish troops of the Canadian First Army. We had to cut their battle dresses off their bodies and the stench of blood and vomit was overwhelming. We did not sit down until 0800 hours when the day staff came on duty to take over. I then sat down to write a detailed report on each patient and put all their notes and records in order. I handed over to Connie at 1100 hours and literally staggered off duty.

8 March

Went out to dinner with Bill and Eric. Had a lovely if rather battered-looking letter from Vernon. Hope he survives this 'lot' on the Rhine Bridgehead. Am coming off night duty on the 12th. Went into Brussels to make reservations for my nights off. We have been extremely busy on the ward for weeks now.

13 March, Brussels

Started my nights off in Brussels. Have a very nice room at the Hôtel Splendide. It is sheer bliss to sleep at night again and to have a room of one's own. Spent most of the afternoon luxuriating in a lovely hot bath. Met Bill at the Plaza at 7 p.m. We both had a little too much to drink and got lost on our way back to the hotel. We were amused to see so many haute couture versions of our blue hospital blankets being worn on the streets here. Actually I am not that amused. There is such a shortage of blankets for the patients that I have to plead for them from the Quartermaster Sergeant.

14 March

Bill has managed to wangle a day off and arrived here for morning coffee. We went exploring the city and then had lunch at the Allied Officers' Club. Bill is rather nice but his apparent self-confidence makes it more difficult to get to know him. His reactions are those of a typical 'middle-class' educated young medical officer. What would he be like without the veneer of this composure?

15 March

Bill has a forty-eight-hour pass so we can have another day together. We went exploring again. This is a lovely city – some beautiful architecture. Afterwards we went to a tea dance at the Plaza. There is something delightfully depraved about dancing in the middle of the afternoon, particularly when there is a war on.

16 March, Louvain

Bill and I were rather subdued as we drove back to Louvain. He dropped me outside St Pierre and went on to his Mess at the Sacré Coeur. I was on duty at 1200 hours.

There were two letters from Ricky and one from my Auntie in Ireland. My native land seems very far away.

17 March

Many memories of Ireland and St Patrick's Day. The ceilidhs of my childhood and the 'wearing of the green'. The patients sang 'When Irish Eyes are Smiling' when I went on duty, most embarrassing! Soldiers on active service are all extremely senti-mental – hence the popularity of Vera Lynn and such songs as 'We'll Meet Again' and 'Lili Marlene', a favourite of both the

Germans and the Allies. It is not surprising that emotions and sentiments are intensified when every situation is constantly changing. Lovers, friends, even duties are here today and gone tomorrow.

Went to the local Officers' Club with Bill for dinner. There were several nostalgic Irish tunes being played by the band. There is remarkably little resentment or even comment on Ireland's neutrality during this war. There were of course dark mutterings from Churchill in the early days, particularly his fears that the Germans might well find well-lit Irish ports very useful. Anyway there are so many Irishmen in the British Services that most people have forgotten that they are volunteers and that this is not their fight.

We were joined at dinner by Paddy, a Major in the Royal Artillery. He asked if he could join us with such pleasantness and a beguiling brogue that we could not resist. He and three other officers are going back up the 240* to Germany in the morning. His friends joined us later and we drank masses of champagne and Irish coffee. Paddy was a little put out to find that the waiter was adding Scotch to the coffee and cream and not our own Jameson's.

We had a hilarious evening and I ached with laughing so much. The wit was such as I have not experienced since leaving my native shores. Paddy is a great raconteur with the endearing ability of laughing at himself. He has rather wild-looking red hair and is very tall and skinny with that rather strong jaw line and stubborn chin that is often typical of Irish physiognomy. His eyes are blue and full of devilment. His mother must have had an awful time when he was a small boy. He is a very experienced soldier and has fought in North Africa and Normandy. He reminds me of a young Bernard Shaw – creating vitality and controversy wherever he goes. His attitude to life is that to a thinking man life is a comedy, to the feeling man it is a tragedy. We talked and talked until all the champagne was finished and

* The 240 was the road route to Berlin.

the coffee pot was empty. It was fun to be with people who made one feel very much alive. Paddy made me feel at ease in his company. Nothing shocks him any more and yet one senses great compassion and tenderness in this wild Irishman. We all said good-bye on the steps of Eglise St Michel. I hope to see Paddy again and I wish him well.

23 March

Went to an excellent ENSA concert here in Louvain. We entertained the artistes here in our Mess afterwards, including Dale Smith the famous baritone. He is a nice man, not at all pompous. He was amused by my patients' interpretation of the letters ENSA: 'Every night something awful.'

24 March

Heard on the Home Service news that we have crossed the Rhine and are advancing from Remagen, also that General Patton's Army have broken through in the Oppenheim area.

28 March

Went out to dinner with Bill at the Club. He looks rather tired. The wards are still very busy and we are all working a twelve-hour day. He was talking to me about the nuns at the Sacré Coeur. He has the conventional Englishman's suspicion of nuns and particularly an erstwhile closed order, but he is now completely won over by their ability, kindness and charm. He has an enormous respect for the Mother Superior. She is a charming lady who is coping magnificently with unsophisticated young nuns, and an Allied Invasion into her peaceful and ordered world. I, too, have often watched her during Mass at the Sacré Coeur and wondered at her outer tranquillity while dealing with an extraordinary situation such as this.

2 April

Went to an ENSA ballet in Louvain with Bill. It was very good and we thoroughly enjoyed it. We met some of the dancers and invited them to dinner at the Club afterwards. We were joined by some Canadian officers. The accent always reminds me of Vernon.

7 April

Peggy invited me to go with her to the Officers' Club for dinner on a blind date – one of her ex-patients and a friend of his. I was rather reluctant but Bill was on duty, so why not? The meal was a disaster, or at least my date was. He was loud-voiced and definitely the worse for drink. I excused myself and hid in the Ladies' Room until his befuddled brain had accepted the fact that I did not want his company. I was sitting there rather forlornly when Wally came in. Wally is a practical little soul, a friend from Normandy days and older than the rest of us. She decided to rescue my ruined evening by smuggling me upstairs to the ballroom, where we could sit behind a fake palm tree and drink coffee. We sneaked upstairs unobserved, and as I entered the door behind her I noticed a young subaltern with blue eyes and a shock of unruly blond hair sitting on the sofa. He looked slightly rumpled.

Wally and I sat at a table and ordered coffee. We watched the dancing until a Scottish reel was played by the band. I could not resist this. Had I not won cups at the Feis in Ireland for jigs, reels and hornpipes? I joined in the reel and it was great fun. I went back to Wally feeling utterly exhausted and then this blond young man stood up and asked shyly if I would like to dance. I would have preferred to get my breath back but something about his eyes made it impossible to say no. The dance was a Victor Sylvester foxtrot – slow, slow, quick, quick, slow – one of my favourites. I love to dance and like to do it well. This young man with one pip on his shoulder was hopeless. He had no sense of rhythm. He fell over my feet and we got in a terrible mess. I thought the best thing would be to sit down and give him some coffee. He told me his name was Malcolm.

9 April

Bill picked me up after duty and we drove to the Allied Officers' Club for dinner. He leaves for the UK tomorrow. It is so sudden – we were just beginning to get to know each other. We were both subdued during dinner and afterwards over coffee we talked about the work we share and the whole stupid futility of this war. He assured me that we shall meet in London on my UK leave. I always seem to be saying good-bye to men whom I might have loved had there been more time.

10 April

Saw Wally at breakfast this morning. She seems very anxious to befriend the two young subalterns, Malcolm and John. Suggested that she might like to invite them both to our ATS dance tonight. I could try and teach Malcolm to dance.

The ATS dance was great fun. I enjoyed it. Malcolm may not have a sense of rhythm but he does have a lovely sense of humour.

11 April

Had a lovely bunch of spring flowers and a note from Bill. He is on his way back to the UK now. I shall miss him. Wally dragged me out to the Club as I was feeling miserable. Malcolm was there and we talked for ages. He is an aspiring artist, rather shy and so refreshingly young and uncomplicated.

13 April

There was a note from Tim Sykes. He called round while I was out.

Went for a walk round Louvain with Malcolm and dined at the Club afterwards. He is extremely nice, but very young, almost four years younger than me. I feel quite ancient at times, have seen too much suffering yet would not want to have missed any of the life I have lived so far.

14 April

Half day off. Malcolm and I went for a walk on the hillside outside the town. We met a lovely little dog who looked hungry, so we fed it with issue chocolate. It followed us up the hill until we sat down to look back down at the view. Malcolm's black beret was upside down on the grass and I noticed that his initials were exactly the same as mine: M. E. M.

15 April

There are signs of spring here now and hopes too for an early end to the war – still no news of Michael or Vernon. Felt rather depressed as I came off duty but was cheered to find Malcolm waiting for me. He was wearing the black beret of the 53rd Reconnaissance. It was a lovely moonlight night and we wandered around the gardens sniffing the lilac and all the other lovely smells of early spring. We watched the reflection of the moonlight on the water as it flowed under the bridge, and there were glow worms shining on the ground as we walked across the dewy grass. He is very relaxing to be with and so understanding. In many ways he is far more mature than his years. Time went by as we talked and it was nearly 2 a.m. when I got to bed.

17 April

Went along to the Club this evening. Malcolm was there and obviously delighted to see me. We had dinner together and then went for a walk. As I turned to go up the steps of St Pierre he said that he loved me and asked me to marry him. I was stunned. We have only known each other for fourteen days! He did not want an answer at once, so I went to bed feeling slightly dazed.

22 April

Malcolm and I went to the international football match in Brussels. It seems funny to be watching a football match while there is a war on. It was a good game, England v. Belgium, the result a nil-all draw.

We went on to the Allied Officers' Club afterwards and then walked back in the pouring rain. It was 2 a.m. when we returned to St Pierre. Hope it is not hurtful to Malcolm, but I need more time to get to know him and consider his proposal.

23 April

My day off. Malcolm came along to say that he has been posted to Germany. He will be acting as Officer I/C POW train. It came as a sudden shock to realise how much I would miss him. I now know that I love him and will marry him. We spent most of the day making wild extravagant plans about our future.

26 April

The last few days have been miserable without Malcolm. Told Richard and he is generously happy for my happiness. Wally, too, knows about us and is a great comfort.

We have had a new convoy of patients in from Germany.

They tell me that Nuremberg is captured and our troops are advancing rapidly.

27 April

Malcolm came back from Germany unexpectedly with a convoy of POWs for a camp in Brussels. It was wonderful to be with him again. He should have returned on the 7.30 p.m. train but it went out just as we arrived at the Gare du Nord. We came back here to the Club for dinner and sat in the lounge talking and drinking coffee. He finds the sullen, depressed and dirty POWs rather distressing. Many of them are very young and very frightened. They are convinced they are to be shot. He stayed here for the night and slept in an empty bed in my ward. He left early this morning.

1 May

Wally has been posted to Belsen.* She is one of the last of our original Normandy crowd. Will miss her friendship and common sense. Hope she will not find it too painful in Belsen.

2 May

Berlin has fallen to the Russians. The war will be over soon. Malcolm arrived back with another cargo of POWs. Our rapid advancement in Germany is creating a problem. The Germans are so frightened of the Russians they are demanding to be

* At Bergen-Belsen concentration camp in northwestern Germany, 70,000 prisoners, including Russian POWs, died of starvation and disease. On 15 April 1945 the British 11th Armoured Division liberated the camp, and Number 11 Field Ambulance and Number 32 Casualty Clearing Station with eight QAs and a senior Sister began tackling the vast medical problem. As the camp was cleared, the 163rd Field Ambulance, six Red Cross teams, the 29th British General Hospital and ninety-seven volunteer medical students moved into the compound and hospital to care for survivors.

taken prisoners by the British and the Americans. Poor M looks so tired. Stayed here for the night.

4 May

Listened to the news this morning. Northwest Germany and Holland have surrendered to General Montgomery. There are rumours that Hitler is dead. Mussolini has been caught and hanged – a horrible photograph in the paper. This European war should be over quite soon. We are still busy on the ward.

6 May

Malcolm arrived late last night looking tired and dirty. He had a bath here and we went out to dinner at the Club afterwards. We talked until nearly 2 a.m. about our future and his present job of ferrying POWs from Germany to Brussels. He and his friend Jeff with a small handful of soldiers pick up these prisoners from temporary camps (usually a fenced-in compound without any facilities). Yesterday they brought back 1,500 prisoners, many of them with dysentery. These men, some as young as fifteen years old, others in their sixties, are pathetically frightened, docile and demoralised. One young boy was in tears and begged to be shot 'for the Fatherland'. The POW train is of the type used for transporting cattle in peacetime. It is open in all weathers and the Germans are packed in with a pail in the corner for a lavatory. M finds all this rather horrific and spends most of the time on top of a ladder over-looking the trucks – writing poetry to me.

7 May

There is a tremendous excitement here today. Germany has surrendered unconditionally and we are all waiting breathlessly for Mr Churchill to announce the end of war in Europe.

How dramatic that speech will be. Have just been watching the Belgian people in the street below this window. They are running about and talking to each other excitedly in little groups. There are flags flying from every window and church bells are ringing. The last All Clear has just died down mournfully in the distance. This is a great day for them also. It is such a short time ago since the Gestapo patrolled along the streets where the flags are now flying so gaily. Wish M were here with me. We could go out in the country, walk through the fields and sit down quietly and try to realise fully how much this means – no more waste of life – no more casualties, no more horror and destruction. How wonderful to think of walking through the streets of London with the lights shining everywhere, to look into the dark depths of the Thames and to realise that the dark days of the Blitz, the V1 and the V2 are really over.

We must not forget the war with Japan of course. Wonder if M and I will be posted to SEAC [South-East Asia Command].

8 May

Victory in Europe Day. Mr Churchill announces peace. Germany is beaten. According to the radio there is great excitement in London.

The patients are delighted and are making plans for their return to Civvy Street. Went to the Club for dinner. Richard was there and several people whom I know. We drank champagne and danced until the early hours. Richard is rather browned off about his posting. He wanted to go to Germany, was posted back to the UK temporarily and re-posted back here again. The ways of the mighty War Office are strangely mysterious.

The following poem has been inspired by the proclamation of peace and is strictly for the privacy of this diary.

Peace

There's movement, colour, gaiety
wheeling around us.
Life is whirled back again from war
and swift death, groans and gore,
destruction. All are ended. Our loss
is not forgotten, though green moss with time
the healer shall grow o'er our pain.
Yet through war we live to gain.
The clouds of life, the scent of flowers will heal our hurt.

All this is ours.
The scent of new mown hay, the cow's warm milk,
the water's cool caress, the feel of silk, the sheen of hair,
and purpose for to carry on and live anew,
with faith drawn from war's abyss and unshared still
by those we miss.

Five

Aftermath

Mary and 'the young subaltern' Malcolm

Although the war in Europe was officially over, there was no let-up for Mary, with many patients suffering from war-related illnesses, as well as physical and psychological injuries.

11 May 1945, 101 BGH, Louvain

Malcolm's birthday. He arrived at lunch time and I managed to get the rest of the day off. We went to tea at the home of some Belgian friends of mine. Had a lovely English tea. The décor is beautiful – particularly admired the wall tapestries. The majority of homes in Brussels have come through the war remarkably unscathed.

We had dinner with Jeff at the Allied Officers' Club and hitch hiked back here. M must return to Germany tomorrow and as I am going on leave on the 15th, we shall not see each other for some time. It will be awful to be apart for so long.

14 May, Palace Hotel, Brussels

This place is very luxurious. My leave begins tomorrow. Met an old friend and ex-patient in the Plaza – Squadron Leader Young. He has offered to run me over to Croydon tomorrow, 'quite unofficial you know, old girl'. Jim Young was telling me about the inconceivable destruction of some of the German cities. He says that the Germans have 'a panic fear of being handed over to the Russians and are very anxious to be conciliatory to us'.

∾

It seems Mary had not been home to Ireland since July 1940. She returned five years later, not only engaged to be married to an Englishman but carrying the weight of her years of war work.

15 May, Dublin

This is my first long leave since joining the army – very excited. Jim Young drove me to Brussels' aerodrome. We boarded a Dakota and set off at 1000 hours arriving in Croydon at 11.45 a.m. It was my first trip in an aeroplane and I was bubbling with excitement and fear. The journey was only slightly marred by the discomfort of sitting amongst luggage and petrol cans and feeling rather air-sick. There was a fabulous view of London and the Thames as we flew over. It was rather foggy in Croydon but we landed without any problems.

We had a meal there and, much to my amazement, Jim then rang Dublin for permission to land there. It seemed rather hazardous to me but he reminded me that the war was over. Anyway he managed to obtain permission and we flew over to Dublin. It was rather foggy there and I was given the terrifying task of looking out for the runway and talking him down. Somehow I managed it despite air-sickness and bashed shins from petrol cans, and the noise of those bumps as we hit terra firma was music to my ears.

Dublin was as friendly and lovely as ever. We had dinner and went on a pub crawl along O'Connell Street. There is very little walking to be done in a pub crawl in Dublin.

16 May, Galway

Jim saw me off on the train to Galway this morning. Wonder if I shall ever see him again. He is a good friend, whom I have known since the days at Bayeux and Caen.

The train chugged away happily on its leisurely way to Woodlawn, stopping at every station and with a nonchalant disregard for time schedules and any such nonsense. It was very relaxing if one was not in any hurry and I was just happy to see the green fields of Ireland again. It seems like a million miles away from the war zone – cows grazing in the fields, and everybody knew everybody else all along the line. They even stopped <u>between</u> stations to pick up stray passengers. It was raining, a lovely, pleasant, 'soft' day as the Irish say.

We puffed into Woodlawn Station nearly two hours late and I saw Auntie waiting at the gate with the ass and trap. It was wonderful to see her and I couldn't wait to tell her all about M. The sun came out as we jogged on home through the familiar villages, greeting everyone we met on the way.

There were several neighbours at the house when we got there, all bringing me small presents, home-made 'barm-brack'* etc. It is good to be home.

21 May

Auntie and I went to Killasolan to see Daddy and Paddy. The house was deserted when we got there. They were out working in the fields. Daddy did not seem very happy about my forth-coming marriage. The English have never been his favourite race of people and he worries about the difference in our religion and culture.

22 May

Fixed a puncture in my old bicycle and cycled to the fair in Mountbellew.

The cheeky and witty cheapjacks were still shouting their wares at the fair and there were burly farmers slapping the behinds of cattle and paying the bob that seals the bargain for a sale, before going in to the snug in Fahley's Hotel to finalise the deal and drink gallons of porter.

The asses and carts wait outside and occasionally somebody remembers the patient animal and brings out a nosebag of oats for him. The ass is a great animal of Ireland – a member of the family. On market day he usually finds his own way home, with

---

* An Irish yeast bread enriched with plenty of dried fruit.

his master sleeping it off in the cart amidst the bags of oats and flour.

Mountbellew is always noisy and happy on market day.

23 May

My leave ends tomorrow. It has been wonderful, meeting old friends, seeing the people I love, drinking innumerable cups of tea (weaker than it used to be) and talking to Auntie. She is such a lovely person and just says 'Acushla [dear one] I want you to be happy'. She is very hospitable and there is always a Céad Míle Fáilte for everybody who comes to the door, whether he be priest or tinker.

I may be going away from this world of my childhood but I shall always remember it.

25 May, London

Sailed to Holyhead this morning. The crossing was extremely rough. Met Bob Murison, an RAF pilot, on the boat. He has been a POW at the Curragh in Kildare. He came down in Dublin early in 1944 and appears to have had a very cushy time there. He was allowed to do just as he pleased in Dublin, providing he wore civilian clothes. He told me that there were several Luftwaffe pilots there also, 'terribly good chaps'. He implied that the German aviators had deliberately landed in Ireland in order to 'get out of the bloody war'. I was certainly surprised to hear German spoken in Clery's yesterday afternoon.

28 May, Louvain

Flew back to Brussels this morning. Reached St Pierre at 0200 hours. There were masses of letters awaiting me, from Malcolm and others.

There was a distressing letter from Wally. She is completely shocked by the conditions in Belsen. It is impossible to cope with the extreme cases of starvation. In order to survive they must eat only minute quantities of food at first; they die if they are given too much. The patients are in a very serious mental state, quite unable to comprehend the vital necessity of gradually building up their strength. They go to the kitchens and steal food and are then found dead hours later. Typhus is rampant and the stench is appalling. She goes on to say that the sight of 'dead and starving children is the hardest to bear'.

29 May

Back on A Ward. There are several rumours circulating re postings to Burma and India. Heard this evening that I am on the list for India.

The uncertainty and variety of army life has always intrigued me, and before meeting Malcolm I would have been wildly excited at the prospect of the voyage and the idea of seeing the sub-continent, but now I can only think that it might mean a separation of three years. I must send him a telegram or signal message as soon as I know something definite.

Shall hate leaving Louvain. The Club where I first met M, the boulevards that we know so well and the bridge where we stood and watched the water sparkling in the moonlight. We must come back here one day.

4 June

The powers that be must have forgotten me and my posting. People keep looking at me suspiciously and saying foolishly 'Haven't you gone yet?' Am determined not to unpack again regardless of how scruffy I may look.

We are having a farewell dance for Matron this evening. Miss Wade is retiring to live in a cottage in Devon. I can't imagine her living in the country. She loves to be the centre of attention and to be able to display her impressive rows of medals. She has been an excellent Matron, particularly in Normandy, but she is very much the regular type.

5 June

Went for a walk in the country this evening. There was a glorious sunset. The golden glow superimposed on a duck-egg blue sky with cumulus clouds, looking unearthly and frighteningly beautiful. It leaves one with such a feeling of helplessness and sadness to see such beauty and yet be unable to describe and capture it. I miss M. It is a strange feeling to be in love, a mixture of sadness and joy. Sometimes I feel as if I were walking on clouds, a decidedly euphoric state.

6 June

The 101 is going back to England en route for the Far East. It looks as if I shall remain with this unit now.

Went along to the Club this evening. Involved in an argument with some arrogant young subalterns about Irish politics. Found myself angrily defending Eamon de Valera.* Can't imagine why, except that everybody else was running him down and describing Ireland as a 'hotbed of Nazism'. They described an incident in Dublin in a very biased way. It was all associated with peace celebrations. I happened to be in Dublin a couple of days after and heard the true story from a reliable source. Somebody decided rather tactlessly to take down the Irish flag from Trinity College and hoist the Union Jack instead. It would

* Ireland's neutrality during the war was contentious. Churchill had been angry at de Valera, head of the Irish government, for not letting Britain use Irish ports and some in Ireland saw neutrality as isolationism, while de Valera and the majority of the Irish population saw it as necessary to their survival. However, when de Valera followed diplomatic protocol and sent his condolences to the German ambassador on Hitler's death, many saw that as a step too far.

have been acceptable if both flags were flying, but the removal of the green, white and gold filled some of my countrymen with a hilarious type of indignation. They threw a few stones at the windows of the College, made a few bonfires and created a good deal of noise before retiring to the nearest pub to talk about it all. On the whole nobody took much notice, that type of incident is a common occurrence in Dublin. It was grossly exaggerated by the Press.

7 June

We are starting to evacuate the patients and are not taking any admissions. The latest official news is that the unit is returning to the UK in about ten days and re-mobilising for Burma. It will mean at least a few months in England while we obtain tropical kit and have lectures on tropical diseases etc. I've had my demobilisation number today, 56, whatever that means. I signed on for the duration of the war, but in the Medical Corps that really means the duration of the emergency, which is a different matter. It can't last for more than two or three years anyway.

Am writing this in bed and was looking out of the window a few minutes ago, and watched a little old man going along the street lighting the gas lamps. It seemed strangely symbolical.

8 June

This has been a beautiful sunny day. I pushed the patients out into the grounds, much to their consternation, they would far prefer to remain in the stuffy ward.

Soeur Marie-Anselma brought me a lovely basket of straw-berries when she came on duty. She really is a sweet person. She knows I love fruit. We are very good friends despite all my abortive efforts to teach her to speak English.

We have a nice crowd of patients at present – most of whom

will be leaving us in a few days. They have all had a long hard war and are very interested in the coming General Election in the UK. Hope the new Government, whatever Party, will ensure a decent future for these men. They deserve it.

9 June

Another beautiful day. Went boating on Lake Leopold with Richard. It was great fun. We are still busy packing and evacuating the patients. It gives me quite a pang of sadness to see my ward almost empty and without the usual shouts as they play housey-housey. I shall miss St Pierre. We have all worked very hard at making the patients happy and comfortable.

Have been packed now for nearly two weeks and have reached the stage of having to wash and iron my uniform in off-duty time. It is rather awkward, but not nearly so awkward as it would be to make any attempt to undo my trunk and valise. Must have collected an awful lot of oddments en route with the BLA [British Liberation Army].[*]

Had a letter from Michael today. He is stationed in a small town called Apolda not far from Buchenwald.[†] He was one of the first Americans to reach there. It was a terrible shock. He is due for seventy-two hours' leave and is hoping to come to Brussels on the 12th. Have written to M to see if he can possibly come here at the same time. I would like him to meet this brother of mine. He is great fun, about 6 foot 3 inches tall, looks like an American, speaks like a Yank but is 99 per cent Irish. He is my favourite brother although he still treats me as if I were nine years old, and spoils me hopelessly.

---

[*] The British Liberation Army (BLA) was made up of the 21st Army Group: the British and Canadian armies who had landed in Normandy and liberated France, Belgium and the Netherlands.

[†] At Buchenwald concentration camp near Weimar, Germany, approximately 56,565 prisoners died from disease, starvation and executions.

12 June

We are still here. I've got one military patient on A Ward. The poor man looks completely lost in a large ward where the emptiness almost shrieks at you.

We evacuated the others this morning. It was terribly amusing to see everybody including our dear little nuns dashing around wildly and getting things incredibly muddled. The patients who were supposed to be on stretchers were walking about casually, and others who were quite reasonably fit were being joyfully carried on stretchers along the corridors by our over-enthusiastic Flemish-speaking workers. I gave up!

There is still a considerable amount of equipment to be packed and everybody seems to be getting in everybody else's way. It is great fun. I love the excitement of moving and packing. The Quartermaster, who appears to know everything, told me today that we shall be here for at least two or three weeks yet. That's the army!

Michael should be arriving here today but it is now 8 p.m. and he has not appeared. Am beginning to feel rather browned off. It is pouring with rain and I've been watching the reflections of the gas lights on the wet cobbles, and the people rushing by with umbrellas and turned-up coat collars. It always gives me a comforting feeling to watch the rain through a window. It is almost as nice as tramping along in the mud through a downpour and enjoying being miserable and wet, because you know that soon you will be home to the comfort of a warm fire and dry clothes.

13 June

Michael did not turn up. Feel very disappointed.

Had a most unfortunate experience this morning. I trod on Matron's dentures. She was talking to me in the corridor on her way to see the dentist apparently, anyway she dropped this small parcel and in an effort to pick it up, I accidentally stepped on it. She was furious at first, but in a little while her sense of humour emerged and we both laughed. I accompanied her to see Major Chisholm (the dentist) in order to explain my nefarious conduct in the affair. Fortunately she has a spare set to carry on eating with!

It is late now and all the girls are in bed. This place is filled with the noisy stillness of a building that has unaccustomed quietness. The Mess is really eerie – the doors squeak and there is a mouse in the cupboard who is making so much noise that he must be eating the plate as well as the cheese. These white-tiled walls and uncurtained windows give the room a dreary appearance, and yet it is a friendly room. I have been happy here.

15 June

Malcolm arrived on a twenty-four-hour leave. Am ecstatic with happiness – so lovely to see his dear smiling face and the look of amusement in his eyes. He has been posted to Düsseldorf. We had dinner in Brussels with Jeff. He is staying here on the ward tonight.

16 June

Gave Malcolm breakfast in bed, in the large empty ward. We went in to Brussels and had lunch at the Plaza and afterwards went out to Tervuren. The woods were beautiful. Came back for tea at the Officers' Club in the Rue d'Arlow. M had to catch the 7.10 p.m. train to his new posting but we arrived there just in time to see it go out.

I felt dreadful and was convinced that he would be court-martialled for being AWOL. We dashed outside, grabbed a taxi and shouted in my best French 'Follow that train to Malines'. The taxi driver drove like crazy, only to watch the train go out

<u>again.</u> We paid the taxi driver 600 francs and he went back to Brussels leaving us to ruminate on our problems. We talked to the Stationmaster who said that the city train going up to Germany that night was an Express at 11 p.m. and it did <u>not</u> stop in Malines. We asked if there was an RE [Royal Engineers] Officer on the premises and went along to see him and after some gentle persuasion and a certain amount of pulling rank, he promised to stop the train just long enough for my darling to jump aboard!

Felt thoroughly exhausted in the taxi ride back to Brussels (another 600 francs!).

17 June

This has been a dreadful morning. Was dragged out of bed at 6 a.m. in order to attend a Court of Inquiry, relating to some deficiencies in ward stock. Have never known anything so pompous and absurd. We were all forced to sit on hard chairs for over an hour while the CO demanded an explanation for the disappearance of four medicine cloths and one bedpan. (The mind boggles!) The rest of the morning was spent checking and re-checking piles of sheets and blue blankets. It is rather late in the day to be worrying about the blue blankets. They were keeping Belgian ladies warm throughout last winter.

We are moving up to the other Mess at the Sacré Coeur tomorrow, and it will mean sleeping on camp beds again.

Michael's leave must have been cancelled, because so far he has not materialised.

18 June

Found some lovely monastery grounds today, and decided to stay there and write poetry. It is so quiet and secluded, far away from the noises of civilisation. Came across the place by accident as I was wandering across the fields.

There is an enormous field of wheat on my right, and a little dark wood behind me. Louvain is down there at the bottom of the hill and I can see the church spires. It feels so remote up here. It is lovely to get away by myself like this to relax and listen to the soothing sound of the wind rustling the corn, and watch the clouds sailing across the sky – no more bombers, just peace and sanctuary. One can never be lonely or unhappy when alone in the country. The sky and the birds and trees are always kind, no matter how cruel the rest of the world may be.

> In this world my mind has made
> to comfort me when I'm afraid
> to turn my loneliness and sadness
> all life's rush and hectic madness
> into naught but peace and joy.

19 June

This has been a lovely sunny day. Am attending lectures on tropical medicine, extremely interesting and obviously essential if we are to join SEAC.

The Registrar told me this morning that we should be in the UK by about 1 August but he does not know where we are going to re-mobilise. The married and non-tropical Sisters are being posted to BLA every day.

There has been an order from HQ to say that 50 per cent of the unit must be confined to barracks on alternate days. This does not bother me very much as nobody seems to notice that I wander off for a walk through the woods most afternoons. Got caught in a lovely thunderstorm today. It was so unbearably hot that the relief of getting soaked to the skin with nice cool rain was blissful. It was wonderful to see the parched earth steaming up to meet the rain, which came down in straight torrents. There was forked lightning like a magnificent display of fireworks, and then the thunder, which as a child I used to think was the voice of God in anger. I kept on walking and had a wonderful feeling of peace and release from tension. Was soaking wet by this time, but then suddenly the sun came out and it was all over. The quietness after the storm was so intense that I could easily distinguish the song of a blackbird some little distance away. He sounded so happy it reminded me of some lines of Tennyson.

I have sung many songs
But never a one so gay.
For he sings of what the world will be
When the years have died away.*

20 June

A lovely letter from M. He arrived back at his unit before Jeff due to the stopping of the Express at Malines.

Went for another solitary walk this afternoon and am now sitting near the little wood watching the clouds go by. They look so lonely, like lost souls condemned to spend eternity wandering in a land of nothingness.

Am happy today, less lonely now than I have been for years.

21 June

We have just had fifteen postings from here, but fortunately I am not amongst them. Connie has gone to Belsen and has promised to write and tell me what conditions are like there now. Connie has been a good friend and I shall miss her. Richard, too, has been fun to know, but we all grow accustomed to the lack of continuity in relationships. Army life is an interesting experience, if we are prepared to look at it objectively and take the bad with the good. People react to this way of life in different ways. A good soldier rarely makes a good civilian

* Alfred, Lord Tennyson, 'The Poet's Song'.

and by a good soldier I mean one who becomes an unquestioning cog in the wheel of military organisation. They tend to lose their individuality and begin to think that the big outside world is run on army lines.

Mess life is a strange innovation. It is much harder for M than it is for me. In the male Officers' Mess, it has long been considered the manly thing to drink oneself under the table every night of the week and heaven help the young subaltern who can't take his booze. It can be very hard for a young officer to feel much respect for a colonel whom he has had to watch dancing a jig in his underpants in the early hours of the morning. It was a release from tension during the active campaign, but what is it now?

I should be returning to England with the unit in July, always providing that my long posting elsewhere does not come to light. I was the first to pack in St Pierre and now appear to be one of the last to go.

Attended a rather amusing tropical lecture this morning in which the tutor described a little too realistically most of the more unpleasant creatures of the jungle. Hope M and I will not be too far apart out there. This Japanese war can't last very long anyway. It will probably be over by the time we reach SEAC.

25 June

This is a festival day here. There are flags and streamers across the streets, bands playing, boy scouts and the Salvation Army are marching up and down making a terrific noise. There are people dancing on the cobbled streets and others sitting on the doorsteps. I am told that it is a fiesta. Feel quite homesick as it reminds me of Dublin.

We are having a breaking-up party here in St Pierre tonight as there are so many girls leaving tomorrow – Connie and Driscoll amongst them – some are going back to the UK, others to Germany. There will only be a few of the old Normandy crowd left. This meeting and parting makes one feel like an actor on a stage.

26 June

Received several letters from M today. The APO [Army Post Office] seems to send letters out in batches. He and Jeff are still in Germany looking after a camp for Russian Displaced Persons. These DPs are really vicious and keep breaking out of camp to murder any Germans they can find and generally terrorise the neighbourhood. It is extremely difficult for a young officer to cope with these people, try to maintain law and order and keep cool enough to prevent [adverse] publicity from creating an international incident with our erstwhile Allies.

Poor darling, he spent over two years at Sandhurst training in various methods of assisting our Russian Allies in killing Germans, now he and Jeff and forty soldiers are given the job of protecting the Germans from the Russians. M goes on to say that this whole business is a very 'delicate diplomatic situation'. There is a camp curfew at night, but the Russians are allowed plenty of freedom during the daylight hours and are 'running wild in a thoroughly brutal way, going round to the local farms and demanding food and if they are refused, they murder the older people and knife the children and strip them of their clothing and valuables'. M sends out patrols round the streets at night, 'No German here will sleep or live alone in a house'. It is a difficult situation when the enemy one has been taught to hate is 'kind and courteous and one's allies are so barbarous and savage'. M writes that the Germans are admittedly rather over-anxious to please, and needless to say none of them ever supported the Nazi party (so <u>they</u> say) but they are at least reasonably civilised.

The language barrier is also a major problem for M. He has managed to find a 'buxom German blonde woman who speaks Russian and English, but unfortunately Maria, the German girl, will not merely translate, because she has some very strong political views and opinions of her own, and is constantly raising her voice and throwing her arms in the air.' M has enclosed a very amusing cartoon demonstrating the utterly hopeless absurdity of the situation.

27 June

My long-lost posting has come through at last. Tomorrow I am to go to the 108 in Brussels. This is a temporary posting, so I presume that I shall stay there for three or four weeks before returning to the UK en route for the Far East.

St Pierre is very quiet tonight, quieter than I have ever known it to be. Tomorrow we are all going our separate ways, and tonight everybody seems to be at the farewell party in the Officers' Mess. It will be the usual drinking affair and somehow I do not want to say good-bye to St Pierre that way. I shall go to visit Soeur Marie-Anselma and some of the other young nuns who have been such loyal colleagues and good friends to me over the past few months. They too will have to re-adjust their lives when we go away. Shall miss Louvain and particularly St Pierre.

Mary's new posting was to the psychiatric ward of the 108 BGH in Brussels. Her entries show an empathy with her patients' wartime psychological trauma that was at odds with much of the thinking of the time.

28 June, 108 BGH, Brussels

Arrived here this morning. It is a lovely hospital in Laeken outside the city. One can get in to town on a rattly No. 16 tram.

Have a room of my very own, such luxury after a year of sharing tents and dormitories. Soeur Marie-Anselma and all the St Pierre nuns and Belgian workers gave us a very affectionate send-off. Have promised to go back to visit them.

This place is so large that I feel quite lost. The building is magnificent with cool, wide corridors and bright, cheerful-looking wards. The Sisters' Mess is rather pleasant, very modern and comfortable, several bathrooms and masses of hot water. The view from my window is not spectacular but I've been told that the surrounding countryside is extremely pleasant. Shall enjoy finding new walks around here, but I do miss the homely friendliness of St Pierre.

30 June

Sister Ann Reeves is an enormous help to me on the ward. She is trained in psychiatric nursing and is a very understanding, sensible person. The mental suffering of these boys is painful to endure. The aftermath of war can be excruciating for people whose minds have been wounded. It upsets me to see so much ongoing suffering, and I feel strongly that it is all of us who are young now, who must shape the world of the future for ourselves. I am tired of the Churchills and the Pattons of this war who enjoy the power it gives them. It is a game to them; these boys are the victims, heroes today, forgotten tomorrow.

There is a lovely swimming pool here built by the Germans. This was their military hospital, too, during the occupation and there are still some German pin-ups on my bedroom wall.

1 July

This is a typical Sunday afternoon, very quiet and sleepy. Am writing this on duty and feeling rather bored as all the patients are asleep – or at least they were until a few minutes ago when a couple of very glamorous Belgian girls came into the ward. The conversation is all very one-sided I notice.

There is a funny young Polish boy here about fourteen years

old. We call him Paul and his only efforts at English are 'OK' and 'good-bye'. His vocabulary is certainly over-worked. I sometimes remember Chezzy and his cheerful usefulness as an interpreter in Normandy. The boy in the next bed to Paul is a young Italian called Vittorio. He too is a charmer with dark hair and deep brown eyes and has reached the 'OK' and 'Kaput' stage. Sgt James, a forty-year-old cockney, has just been into the office to ask if it might be possible to adopt Paul as he understands that the kid has lost all his family (Polish Jews). They died in Auschwitz. It restores one's faith in human nature to find so much kindness and understanding.

Went to see *Meet the Navy*, a lively Canadian show. Kathleen Aitken accompanied me. We both enjoyed it. Connie came along to my room afterwards and we talked and drank coffee until 3 a.m. Her temporary posting to Belsen was a most traumatic experience. She has changed, much quieter, less ebullient. Night duty there was horrific. There are still very high numbers of deaths, not from starvation now but the aftermath of starvation, which goes on for a very long time. The patients still steal food from the kitchen and from each other. They have been brutalised and many are totally deranged. The newspapers have not exaggerated the horror and suffering. Wally has been posted back to the UK en route for SEAC. She, too, had some very hard experiences in Belsen. Will the Germans ever live down the shame of these places?

4 July

The Sisters' Quarters are about ten minutes' walk from the wards. The garden with the avenue of trees looks beautiful at 7 a.m. The birds are singing, making the world of early morning a very bright and cheerful place, and then one leaves all of this and is immediately plunged into the problems of diets, medicines, breakfasts, and sick and hungry people.

3 p.m. Am writing this in the grounds near the ward. Have

spent an hour trying to persuade John, a young sapper, to stay out here in the sunshine. John fought his way bravely through the cauldron at Arnhem and is now suffering the after-effects of shell shock and the rejection of his physical fitness. He looks well but mentally he is a very sick boy and only twenty years old. He has convinced himself that he is paralysed from the waist downwards and crawls along the ground using his arms to propel himself forward and dragging his legs. He has had all the necessary neurological tests and is pronounced fit – there is no paralysis except in his mind. He has grown accustomed to me now and is just beginning to trust me a little. This type of nursing requires infinite tact and patience but it is very worthwhile. People are impatient of the mentally ill, particularly in the army, and think they are swinging the lead. The physically wounded can demonstrate their suffering, the mentally wounded are sad outcasts, whom nobody wants to know or care about. I suppose it is the unpredictability of mental illness that makes people suspicious and frightened of them.

Poor John is quite harmless, but some of the others have alarming swings of mood. I was talking quietly with Christopher yesterday (paranoic dementia praecox) in a perfectly rational way and suddenly he hit out at me and would have hurt me had not one of the other patients restrained him. Today I asked him why and he was perfectly charming and had forgotten the incident.

I spend most of my time here giving the boys pep talks, trying to calm hysterical outbreaks when chairs and even tables are thrown at one, the rest of the time taking blood samples from the purely medical patients in the ward. This war appears to have acted as a catalyst for psychotic illness in some of these boys. The strain has been too much, combined with enforced separation from their families.

7 July

Another glorious day. Writing this in the garden outside my ward while keeping one eye on the patients. It is very warm but with a mischievous wind that comes suddenly, snatches any papers in sight and scurries across the lawn with them. It reminds me of the fairy winds we have in Ireland sometimes. I remember watching and listening to these sudden gusts of wind, which make a strange whistling noise over the houses, sweep away any light articles in their path and then just as suddenly die away. Today I miss the cool, soft Irish rain and the green, green fields.

Went to see *French Without Tears* (Rex Harrison and Anna Neagle) with Connie and Kathleen Aitken. Brussels looked very gay and fascinating when we came out of the theatre, music and bright lights from every café and crowds of people walking along the boulevard looking for entertainment and escapism.

9 July

Several letters from M. He may be able to wangle a forty-eight-hour leave this weekend. A letter also from Michael. He, too, is coming to Brussels this weekend. It will be nice for him to meet M at last. Must apply to Matron for a forty-eight-hour pass.

Went to a violin and pianoforte recital this evening. They played superbly – 'Fantasie and Fugue' (Bach, I think) also 'The Spring Sonata' by Beethoven and Chopin's Nocturne in F Major. My musical education is very inadequate but I did enjoy this recital enormously.

10 July

We had a new contingent of Canadian patients admitted today, mainly medical cases. I was in my office admitting them when suddenly Vernon was standing there. We were both speechless with amazement. He looks the same although a little more strained. There is the same wide smile and reckless personality. He had a hard time in Nijmegen, a severe head injury followed by a temporary amnesia and he has come to us for neurological tests and a query disseminated sclerosis [multiple sclerosis]. He still possesses that same ease of manner, a young officer unselfconsciously comfortable and relaxed with everybody, regardless of rank and nationality. He is kind, helpful and cheerful in the ward. The other patients call him Canada. Ann Reeves is already in love with him! Tomorrow I shall tell him that I am engaged to Malcolm.

11 July

Told Vernon about my engagement, but he is determined to ignore it. It is an extremely difficult situation for me. He must allow me to treat him in exactly the same way as the other patients, but he is constantly bombarding me with masses of flowers and making cups of tea. I am knee deep in flowers and awash with tea. He is such an outrageous character that I don't seem to be able to get through to him. The past is over and he must stop imagining that he is in love with me. The other patients are beginning to notice, I shall have to ask for a transfer unless he stops this persistent courtship.

12 July

Told Vernon today that there can't be anything between us now. It is too late. He just smiles disarmingly and goes on pestering me.

Came off duty at 7 p.m. and Malcolm arrived a few minutes later. It is marvellous to see him again. I am so very happy. We went into Brussels and had dinner at the Plaza. Came back here on a No. 16 tram (I love trams) and went for a walk in the woods. It was such a beautiful night.

13 July

Started my leave. Met M at 9.30 a.m. Had some coffee and after lunch took a tram out to Waterloo. We had a picnic tea on the famous battlefield – a tin of fruit (which we had great difficulty in opening) and some sandwiches. M is looking forward to meeting my American brother on Sunday morning.

15 July

We waited in the hospital gardens all morning for Michael to arrive. M had to leave at 12.30 p.m. My big brother arrived twenty minutes later. They seem destined not to meet. The irony of it is that Michael would have been here much earlier had he not caught a No. 16 tram going in the opposite direction! Michael looks older than he did last time I saw him (fourteen months ago in Chipping Campden). We talked over lunch and he gradually relaxed. He has had a very hard time, particularly in the Ardennes, and is stationed in Berlin at present. The Russians are behaving as badly in Berlin as they are everywhere else. The German people are terrified of them, particularly the girls. There is an awful lot of trouble over the zoning areas too and everything seems to be rather chaotic there.*

I managed to persuade him to talk about the Ardennes. He spoke of the bitterly cold, icy snow conditions, shortage of provisions and fuel and the utter ruthlessness of General Patton. He lost several good friends there, young officers and senior

---

* Germany, and Berlin itself, had been divided into four zones of occupation controlled by the British, French, Americans and Soviets.

NCOs shot in the back, not by the Germans but by their own men. The orders from Patton were passed down the line and the junior officers who gave the direct order to attack rarely lived to give another order. It was all rather horrific. Two young lieutenants whom I knew in Chipping Campden died in this way. Michael thinks that Patton is a paranoic nutter interested only in playing the game of war regardless of the lives of his men.

Went to see Bing Crosby this evening in Brussels. He sang all the old favourites. We dined at the Allied Officers' Club and came back here afterwards. Michael is sleeping in one of the empty side wards. We sat in my bedroom, drank a bottle of wine and talked until 2.30 a.m. He told me a few months ago in a letter that he had been one of the first American soldiers to stumble across Buchenwald sometime in April. He still finds it distressing to talk about that awful place – the sheer horror of it all will remain with him all the days of his life. He described the 'breathing dead, conditions of indescribable filth, no sanitation, animal misery, the stench of sweat, dirt, menstrual blood and human excreta'. The women whom he first saw lay or squatted on the dirty floor 'moaning, coughing, spitting, silent or weeping'.

He and the other Yanks, hardened war veterans, vomited over and over again as they 'picked out the dead corpses from amongst the living and piled them in heaps on the lorries to be taken away for cremation'. The dead looked like 'shabby bundles of striped rags'.

He remembers the women fighting for the food and chocolate they were given, 'snarling like wolves at each other and then rushing off to hide the food'. The first few days 'were a nightmare'. Michael said 'We brought in piles of food and cleaned the place up but they kept dying on us, every day more and more dead'. It was not until the Medical Corps arrived that they were made to realise that they were killing the inmates of Buchenwald with kindness. Too much food, too quickly after starvation is a sure killer.

Michael is being demobbed at the end of this year, is having a holiday in Ireland and then returning to the States. I am very fond of this brother whom I have seen so rarely in my life.

He has given me a Leica camera – 'liberated' I think!

16 July

Michael returned to Berlin this morning. He has a long uncomfortable journey all the way up the 240 in a truck.

Have been feeling rather depressed all day. Vernon has been extremely tactful and understanding. The results of his neurological investigations are not yet through. Hope it is not anything serious.

20 July

The results of Vernon's tests have come and he is OK. He will be demobbed and returning to Canada soon. He spent ages taking snapshots of me this morning – most embarrassing. I hate being photographed and particularly by Vernon who makes no secret of his admiration.

This is a lovely windy afternoon. Have just been for a short walk and got caught in a glorious shower of rain. It has been oppressively hot and sultry all morning and it was wonderful to feel the rain pouring on to one's head and shoulders. The sun came out afterwards and made the raindrops sparkle like diamonds on the leaves of the trees. I love the fresh smell of the earth after rain and the birds too seem to sing more joyously. How dull life would be without the moods of nature, the seasons and the weather.

21 July

Vernon came along to my ward today to say good-bye and to wish me happiness in the future. He is returning to his unit en route for Canada. He tells me that he will get a job as a lumberjack and if I ever change my mind, he will be waiting. He is delightful and I am glad that we are parting on such good terms. He has promised to write and send me some snaps.

I feel that this ward of mine could well be designated psychiatric – so many of these skin conditions appear to be associated with anxiety states, reactive depression and shell shock. These poor boys receive very little sympathy from the powers that be. Skin diseases are considered rather embarrassing and unmilitary. The ward too is a dark, depressing place (the Germans used it as a mental block) and the other Sister here is a frightfully fussy old hen. She is about forty years old and worries incessantly about everything and nothing in particular. Don't think I am going to be very popular with her, as I refuse to run round in circles and am far too lazy to rush when I can do things at my ease. It is a tragic thing to have reached that stage of life without having developed any poise or calmness. Her mind is so cluttered up with petty regulations and military red tape that there is no room for all the beautiful and interesting things in life. I should hate to become a fussy, worrying type of woman.

The patients are extremely nice, all nationalities as usual. How international are our common ills!

We are having a sports day here on Sunday and one of my ex-friends has put my name down for a 100-yard race, a tug of war, and a slow bicycle race! Must try to borrow some shorts and a pair of sand shoes.

23 July

The sports were a great success. Came in last in the 100-yard race (such ignominy), but by sheer accident was first in the slow bicycle race (by coming in last!). It was great fun, but the day has been intolerably hot. They are still dancing in the open out there – a lovely warm moonlight night. I can hear the strains of

Victor Sylvester in the distance. It is on evenings such as this that I miss M most. He is still trying to protect the Germans from our Russian Allies!

24 July

There are innumerable rumours circulating about the movements of the 101. It is now supposed to be returning to the UK in the last week in August. I hate all these indefinite rumours and can't understand the necessity for such strict secrecy now that the war is over. There is still no news of my posting to SEAC. M is due for privilege leave soon. Hope we can arrange to be in England together. They are very busy with the General Elections over there now. Wonder if Churchill will survive, as people are sick of war and politicians associated with it.

25 July

Two lovely letters from M and some funny snaps taken on our forty-eight hours' leave. He has not received confirmation of his SEAC posting. If he were to remain in BLA I could apply for a compassionate posting in Germany, even though it is the eleventh hour. This day-to-day uncertainty about our movements is beginning to get me down.

26 July

Heard on the Home Service today that Churchill's Government is out. Attlee is in.*

Packing yet again. We are returning to the 101 Louvain tomorrow. The official bulletin states that the 101 is sailing to

---

* The General Election of July 1945 saw a Labour government come into power with a large majority, supported by a population who welcomed the Beveridge Report with its promise of a Welfare State, and the creation of the National Health Service.

England on 1 September. Wrote to M to say that he will find me in the Sisters' Mess at Sacré Coeur. It is impossible to make any plans about our leave yet, but if M is staying in BLA and I obtain a posting over there we should be able to have our privilege leave together, and if I am going to SEAC I shall certainly be in England until the end of October. Have also heard that we are going under canvas in England. October under canvas in biting winds and rain is something to look forward to. My brain becomes befuddled if I try to plan anything in advance these days. There is so much movement in the air. All conversations are riddled with the talk of postings, serials, transit leaves, etc.

27 July, 108 BGH, Brussels

The Mess Hall here is very impressive and rather intimidating. It is extremely formal, spotless white tablecloths and seating according to rank and seniority. The Matron and senior Sisters are all regulars and there is always an official with an eagle eye who notes with obvious disapproval if we are a few minutes late for a meal.

I made a wonderful impression this morning by arriving for breakfast twenty minutes late. The reaction was such that I thought it must be a court martial offence. The reason for my lateness was absurd. I was mesmerised by the notice board in the corridor outside. It was full of statutory regulations stating that Sisters <u>must not</u> do all sorts of extraordinary things. The regular army influence is very much in evidence.

Am working in an acute Medical Ward and was rather taken aback when I presented myself to the Sister in charge who looks about sixty, and has what the patients call a battle-axe expression. She looked at me over her spectacles (rather disapprovingly, I thought) and then smiled quite unexpectedly. We are now the best of friends and she really is a very amusing and original character – proves how impossible it is to judge people according to their appearance.

The patients are a fantastic mix-up of types and nationalities, cockneys, Canadians, Poles, Americans, Scots, Irish and several Russian displaced persons. The result is a hopeless hotch-potch of languages, even the cockneys are speaking pidgeon English, with a few foreign words thrown in. What a perfect solution for preventing future wars, a universal language and the opportunity for communication. More than 50 per cent of the patients are here for psychiatric treatment, post-war depressions, etc., many were shell shocked during the active campaign. There are several deeply disturbed young men suffering from psychotic illness such as dementia praecox. Their illness was probably precipitated by the strains and stresses of battle conditions and the problems of unsatisfactory relationships within their unit. The work is extremely interesting and the psychiatrist, Major Laing, is a most intelligent man and very involved in the work.

Am writing this at my bedroom window, the view is ugly enough to be almost unusual. There is a tall dirty-looking tower on the left and in front a mass of red brick buildings. The undulation of the ground gives them the appearance of being piled on top of each other and the only trees to be seen are three straggly looking birches (I think), which are holding each other up for support.

Mary's interesting work at the 108 BGH was short lived as she was sent back to her original hospital in Louvain, the 101 BGH. Here renewed military training and lectures on tropical diseases suggested that a posting to India or the Far East was likely.

28 July, 101 BGH, Louvain

Arrived back in Heverlee today – nice to see Louvain again. Shall have to put up my camp bed here, another thought that makes me groan. Am sharing a cell with Connie. The room is tiny and by the time the batman had put our valises, two trunks and hand luggage in here, there wasn't any room for us to get in. It was hilarious trying to put up our camp beds. My bed is directly under the window and I awoke at 3 a.m. soaking wet. I like thunder showers but not at that hour of the morning.

29 July

We had PT [physical training] for an hour after breakfast this morning. The instruction was given by a fat, jolly Welsh sergeant, who obviously does not take PT too seriously. We all wore slacks, which was another source of amusement. The variety of female shapes was amusing.

Looking at the recreational rota I notice that all our days are to be taken up with tent pitching, gas and squad drill. We have all had this before and it is very exasperating to have to waste so much time doing things that we are not interested in.

This has been a lovely windy day. Went for a walk round the familiar boulevards of the town. Was fascinated by the Beguinage. This is a group of attractive Flemish-type houses, a kind of long convent, where ladies under no vows live quiet, pious lives in a simple collegiate atmosphere. It seems to me the answer to loneliness amongst spinsters, widows and elderly ladies, who might otherwise live isolated lives in some lonely flat or bedsitter. The faces of the people here are very interesting. The physiognomy so reminiscent of the great Flemish painters.

30 July

Received three letters from M today. He has been trying unsuccessfully to find a fountain pen for me. This one is not too bad I suppose, but Connie moans about the scratching noise it makes. Ink is still in short supply. It is almost impossible to find.

More tropical lectures today. These diseases are rather interesting, certainly better than gas or squad drill.

M writes that he could never bear to hurt or lose me. I feel that inside of me I shall always love him. It is only outside influences that could ever separate us. He is a part of me and of my whole life.

31 July

This has been a dreadful morning – a dental appointment in St Pierre at 9 a.m., followed by three inoculations at the Sacré Coeur at 10 a.m. – physical training from 10.30 to 11 a.m. and squad drill and gas-mask fitting until 12.30 p.m. Am just pausing for breath before tent pitching at 2 p.m.

What a life! Am feeling very browned off and my arm is aching horribly. Must remember to be far more sympathetic next time I give a patient an injection.

Have just noticed what a lovely sunny day it is and the trees in the garden look so fresh and green. Went out to the 108 yesterday to collect my mail, only to find they had already posted it on. It will probably take a week to catch up with me, knowing the mysterious ways of the APO. The CO has stopped short leaves to Paris, etc. Do not know if this has any significance or not and refuse to make any further observations as to when we are or are not going.

1 August

M arrived here late last night. Had dinner at the Club and went for a walk – a beautiful night – very, very happy. Am going to apply for a BLA posting.*

---

* Since her training and inoculations suggested that she might be sent to India or the Far East, Mary applied for a posting with the BLA (soon to be renamed the British Army of the Rhine [BAOR]) in an attempt to stay as near as possible to Malcolm in Belgium or Germany.

2 August

Went out to the woods in Tervuren. M left at 1.45 p.m. I miss him very much. We must get used to saying good-bye but it is harder every time.

We are finally leaving Louvain on Sunday 5th. We shall travel by train from Brussels to the 115 BGH Ostend and shall remain in transit there until there is a ship to take us across to Dover. It will be super to smell the salt sea air again.

There is great excitement in the Mess this evening, everybody chattering excitedly and the dining hall looking unfriendly with bare boards and people clattering about with mess tins (memories of Normandy). It seems strange to eat out of mess tins again after so many months.

Received a letter from my Auntie. It has been raining solidly at home for four weeks. Poor old Ireland will be washed away.

There were four lovely letters from M this afternoon. Hope we can have some leave together in September. Am far less worried now about the difference in our age, religious and cultural background. I feel that we have both enough understanding and imagination to appreciate our individual point of view. Anyway it would be awfully dull if we agreed absolutely on everything. I do hope that we shall always have enough common sense to talk over any difference of opinion. We are going to make our life together beautiful and interesting and, with God's help, we need not fear whatever the future may bring. There will no doubt be joy and sadness and all the problems that make up one's daily life, but whatever happens we must not allow the petty unimportant things in the world to control our lives. We must live for the real things that we love. There will be so much fun bringing up our children and trying to understand them.

4 August

This place is in the most awful chaos at present, trunks and bed-rolls scattered all over the corridors and everybody dashing about getting packed. This happy carefree excitement and movement is one of the things that I love about army life – the fun of watching people and the pleasure of seeing new sights and strange countryside – of noticing how other people work and live and think.

6 August, Ostend (in transit)

We arrived here at 6 p.m. yesterday and the first thing I did was run down to the beach. The water was so cool and refreshing after the long, hot, sticky journey.

Am writing this sitting on a sandbank. There is a strong, fresh breeze trying very hard to blow the paper away. We came from Brussels by train. The countryside was rather flat and uninteresting.

We now have a rather amusing fat little Assistant Matron, who flaps continuously and gets everyone in an awful muddle by detailing half-a-dozen people to do one job. The noise and fuss at the Gare du Nord in Brussels and again in Ostend was terrific. There were contradictory orders flying about in all directions. I just sat tight and allowed them to get on with it. We are in transit here at 115 BGH but nobody has any idea of how long we are to remain here. We are sleeping right on top of the building (seventh floor). We have separate bedrooms but the odd thing is that none of the rooms have any doors. It is quite absurd, yet I can't find out the reason for this. There are four loud-speakers in the corridor and at least eighty noisy females on this floor.

This morning I woke up to hear the lovely sound of the sea, the roar of the breakers as they crashed on the shore. This sound always gives me a wonderful feeling of *joie de vivre*.

We had breakfast at 8.30 a.m. amidst a clatter of mess tins and enamel mugs. Went in to town afterwards. It was marvellous. There is an odd collection of gaily coloured boats and fishing smacks in the harbour, and there is a very cosmopolitan crowd of people in every type of wearing apparel, uniforms, sun-suits, cotton dresses, etc. There is very little bomb damage and the whole place has a happy holiday atmosphere. The price of everything is exorbitant, even for the black market.

8 August, Ostend (in transit)

We have been given warning orders and should be moving in a day or two. Another lazy day for me, time to think and dream and let the hours go by.

Went out to the village of De Haan this morning. It is a tiny, quaint little place, perched high above the pier, overlooking the sea, and gives one the impression that it was dropped there by accident.

After luncheon today we were presented with our service ribbons. It was terribly amusing and rather absurd to be one of thirty people queuing for a few pieces of ribbon. Connie sewed mine up most beautifully with a piece of cardboard at the back and covered it with cellophane. They look very impressive on our uniform but I haven't the vaguest idea yet of which is which. What a funny race of people we are and how we love our vanities.

9 August, Ostend (in transit)

Have just come from a walk on the beach in the pouring rain. It was wonderful to feel thoroughly soaked with rain and salt spray. Took my shoes off and walked across the wet mushy sand. The sea was very rough and the enormous breakers were sending up mountains of spray into the air. The bigness of the sea still fascinates me as it did when I was a small child on the coast of Galway.

We leave for England on Saturday 11th at 6 a.m. Why must they choose such an uncivilised hour? There are rumours that we are to go on embarkation leave as soon as we reach Netley. The noise here is deafening as usual, loud-speakers blaring forth discussing the appalling atom bomb and reminding us yet again that Russia has declared war on Japan.*

Went out to De Haan this evening. This little village reminds me of Salthill in Galway. It has a lovely peaceful atmosphere, particularly at night when the lights are shining all along the pier and one can hear music faintly in the distance. The brightness and gaiety of the lights on shore contrasted strangely with the rough sea and the flickering light of a little ship bobbing up and down on the waves and looking rather forlorn and sad.

11 August, Ostend (in transit)

Our movement order was cancelled last night because of the weather conditions. We may go in forty-eight hours if the weather is favourable. It has been very stormy all along the coast here and the rain has not ceased for two days. It is wonderful to realise that the Japanese War too may soon be over. Peace has almost lost its meaning for many of us. We have known so little of it. The realisation of what it means and of what we are going to make of it, will have to come slowly. If only we can remember the horror and futility of war then we may have the right foundation for peace.

---

* In February the US, British and Soviet leaders met at Yalta to agree on the occupation of Germany and on a date for the Soviets to join the war against Japan. In July the Allied leaders met in Potsdam and demanded the surrender of the Japanese. When this was not forthcoming they dropped atomic bombs on Hiroshima (6 August) and Nagasaki (9 August). Between these dates the Soviets invaded Japanese-held Manchuria.

15 August, 101 BGH, Royal Victoria Hospital, Netley

The last few days have been a miracle of organised chaos. We left Ostend at 7.30 a.m. on Monday without breakfast (as nobody had remembered to arrange it!). We waited on the quayside until 12.30 p.m. while a dispatch rider went to Louvain to collect our embarkation papers. He arrived back just in time for us to catch the boat. It was a troop carrier and there were about two thousand men on board, mainly troops for demobilisation. It was a most peculiar old ship, very ancient and dirty. The crossing was good, a beautiful day, but we were all ravenously hungry. We managed to locate some bully beef and biscuits eventually.* The white cliffs of Dover came into view about 5.30 p.m., a very impressive sight. Dover is an exceptionally attractive town. We waited there for a train to London, which arrived just after 10 p.m. One has to learn patience in the army. It was a most erratic journey, the train stopped at every little one-eyed station and in between also just for a rest. We reached London at 4 a.m. and there were some lorries waiting to take us to the YWCA for the few remaining hours of the night. London looked magnificent as we travelled through the West End. All the lights were blazing forth and Big Ben in full glory was striking the hour. The dear ladies at the YWCA were very kind and provided us with cups of tea and sticky buns.

We collapsed into bed at 5 a.m. and were up again at 8 a.m. We had breakfast and then came down here via Portsmouth. When we arrived at the station here we were all rather tired and browned off, and in the usual army fashion nobody knew we were arriving and there wasn't any transport to bring us out here to the hospital. We had to walk here carrying all our hand luggage.

The Royal Victoria is enormous; each corridor appears to be about a mile long. It used to be a peacetime mental asylum.

---

* Bully beef: tinned corned beef – a military staple in this war as in the First World War; biscuits (hard tack): military rations of rock-hard baked dough.

We are all sleeping in the Fracture Ward at present. It is rather amusing really as one needs a step ladder to climb on to the beds because they are so high. The beds have all the usual hoisting gear and fracture irons, etc., and each time one turns over in bed, there is a terrific clanking of irons. We were all in hysterics with laughter. The windows are barred too, of course, true prison fashion, and space is almost limited to inches between the beds. One needs to be an acrobat to get across the floor, jumping over trunks, valises, etc. I've been in lots of funny places but nothing like this before. It is so infuriating that one must laugh or cry. We laugh!

Have just realised that this is VJ Day. The war is over at last. It is I think a day for thanksgiving and remembrance rather than boozy celebration.

18 August, Royal British Nurses' Club, Queen's Gate, Kensington

Have just arrived here from Netley. My leave expires on the 28th. I must then report back to Netley for a posting. It looks as if I shall not be able to have my leave with M as planned.

London is terribly crowded and very gay with flags flying everywhere and military bands marching victoriously along the streets.

19 August

Went to Mass at Westminster Cathedral this morning. I was feeling rather worried by the difference in religious and cultural background between M and myself. Religion is such a vast and difficult subject to discuss. God gave us all a mind and free will, and something that may seem logical and reasonable to me may appear unreasonable and incomprehensible to another person.

Am happy that M agrees with the Catholic principles of marriage. There are few who do – other than practising Catholics.

It is not an easy way. I can't agree with divorce except in very special circumstances because people promise to marry for better or worse. Artificial birth control worries me considerably. I have been brought up to think of it as unnatural and sinful, yet I have seen the misery of too many babies too quickly in impoverished Catholic homes. The priest congratulates the father in Ireland, but it is the mother of an enormous family who suffers. She is drained mentally and physically by having a baby every year, and is fortunate to survive beyond the age of forty. The strain of ongoing pregnancies kills many a woman in Ireland today. It <u>must</u> be better to have fewer children and give them the time and mother's energy they need.

Received some letters from M at last. Hope he will not be sent to SEAC now that I have applied for BLA. I notice that Mr Attlee will not commit himself to any demobilisation manifesto.

Have been reading M's letters over and over again. One was dated 3 August. He had just attended an investiture where General Montgomery presented officers and men of the Division with Gallantry awards in the Opera House in Düsseldorf. Each regiment in the Division was represented by about fifty men and the Reconnaissance Corps contingent, which M happened to be in charge of, looked immaculate in cream blancoed [whitened] webbing including cross-straps. M of course, not bothering to read orders, turned up in battle dress and without a sign of blancoed cross-straps. Poor darling. He is not the army type. I gather that Monty wore so many medals that he looked like an advertisement for coloured paints. He made a good speech in his usual showman-like way, starting off by saying 'You may all cough now'. In that statement there lay a dire threat should any unfortunate soldier cough later. He told everybody in no uncertain terms what lay ahead for the Germans, what was going on in Potsdam as well as his personal impressions of Stalin, Churchill, Truman and the new Labour Government!

26 August

Heard on the radio today that the postal address BLA is to be changed to BAOR [British Army of the Rhine] – don't know how the 108 fits in to this. Brussels is a long way from the Rhine.

27 August, Richmond

Went to visit my future in-laws in Richmond. They were extremely pleasant to me, nevertheless it was a terrible ordeal. Auntie Bess loaned me an enormous nightgown and a toothbrush, as they insisted that I stayed overnight.

Mary spent from 29 August to 20 September 1945 waiting for her new posting, first at Netley and then at Wyke Hall, Dorset, arriving back at the 108 BGH on 22 September. A letter from Malcolm gave Mary an unvarnished description of the conditions of the Germans in the immediate aftermath of the war:

The Occupational Armies are living in extreme comfort, in the best surviving houses. The streets are silent, the shops empty, the only traffic the conquerors' cars and trucks. M tells me that the Germans scavenge for food in the pig bins. Their daily ration of food is two slices of bread, two potatoes and a spoonful of porridge.* There is a rampant black market. Antique furniture and even grand pianos are being sold in exchange for food and cigarettes and the furniture is then transported back to England, sometimes by the RAF. M tells me that the Germans seem to be a 'people without hope, and with an ongoing desperate fear of the Russians'.

---

* In June 1945 in the American zone, the official daily ration for most Germans was 860 calories.

21 September, 108 BGH, Brussels

Sailed from Dover at 6 a.m. and arrived here via Ostend this evening. Telephoned M. He is arriving here later this evening. Am very happy.

30 September

Have been put in charge of the isolation block here. It was discovered that I had fever training in the Brook at Woolwich. Am glad this did not happen last week as I would not have been able to spend so much time with M. I always want time to stand still when we are together.

2 October

Have just received a letter from home and they tell me that Michael is having a great time visiting all the relatives in different parts of the country. He is due back in Germany soon and may materialise here in Brussels any day.

I look very funny in the ward these days, dashing around in an enormous white gown that reaches almost to my ankles and wearing a hideous mask which is not at all glamorous.

Am paying in full measure for my week of leisure at Wyke Hall. There are almost a hundred patients and half of them have diphtheria and literally must not move a muscle. I myself contracted diphtheria while at the Brook and feel reasonably secure in that I have plenty of the relevant antibodies. This type of nursing is extremely hard work. The patients are given large doses of antitoxins as soon as the diagnosis is confirmed, but they have to remain on complete bed rest in order to protect the heart muscle from damage. Some of these boys are in a very serious condition when they arrive here and require emergency tracheotomy. Tracheotomy is a very distressing operation for the patient, and there is never time for an anaesthetic. The incision is made straight into the trachea and the tube inserted. The patient's colour and breathing improves miraculously, but he is usually very shocked and it also requires constant vigilance to make sure that the tube does not become blocked. There are three wards under my charge and it is very exhausting trying to keep an eye on everybody. I have some good orderlies and a few Belgian workers to help, but they are untrained.

4 October

Am just going on night duty. I will be on constantly for four weeks (twelve-hour shifts) and will then have four days off before starting back on day duty again. What a life, and with so much responsibility for a salary of £12 per month.

5 October, 12.30 a.m.

The last four hours have been both hectic and hilarious. We had an admission convoy with one hundred and forty patients. There were some cases for immediate total isolation and a few cases of suspected typhus and a query typhoid. Fortunately the rest of these men are not seriously ill. They have come in for observation and various tests. There are quite a few Russian DPs amongst this contingent – all of them without any knowledge of any language except their own. I rang round all the interpreters I knew, but no Russian speakers were available. These people are difficult at the best of times, but without an interpreter they were driving me crazy.

They are all asleep now, and the silence screams after all that noise.

I love this atmosphere of dramatic silence in a ward at night – the shaded lights, rhythmic breathing, and the weird ghostly shadows in dark corners as I take the torch and creep about stealthily to watch the ill ones, and to see that the drips are working properly and the airways clear in the tracheotomy tubes.

I try to write poetry and the night drags slowly on and then just before dawn the ward once more comes reluctantly to life.

5 October

There was an indescribable sunset as I awoke this evening. My room is at the top of the building and just beyond the row of pine trees in the distance the whole sky and the earth was ablaze with a reddish golden light. The variety and blending of the colours was superb. Sunsets and dawns become even more important to me on night duty, perhaps because the night and darkness seem so long.

My cosmopolitan patients are very exhausting. When I go round to see them in the evening they start gesticulating frantically, and speaking a strange language that sounds like a mixture of German and Swahili. One of the Russians was creating such an uproar this evening that I thought he was going to have an epileptic fit. It was so disturbing that I sent for the interpreter. They were jabbering away excitedly for about half an hour, and at the end of all that I managed to discover that he had a headache. We all had headaches by then!

6 October, 12.30 a.m.

My sweet little ATS orderly has been replaced by an Amazon ATS corporal. She is difficult to work with – a very large lady and too obviously a hard worker. She is so full of zeal and energy and purpose that it is exhausting just to watch her. I have managed to steer her away from the boys who are seriously ill and given her free rein with the Russians and Poles. She is so <u>noisy</u> I can hear clattering up and down the ward now with that awful air of purpose.

7 October

It is now 2 a.m. and all my bodies are asleep. How funny people look when they are sleeping and what a strange variety of expressions. There is one man who sleeps with his eyes wide open – quite terrifying. There are others who fight battles every night with monotonous regularity.

M's letters are overflowing everywhere, but I could not bear to destroy any of them as it will be such fun to read them again in about sixty years. I don't think we shall have changed very much by then, at least not inside. I shall be white-haired and wrinkled, but M will look handsome and distinguished in a white beard.

10 October, 4 a.m.

What a night this has been. This is the first opportunity I've had to sit down and even now I should be writing reports and filling in temperature and fluid charts. Another convoy of possible diphtherias about 9 p.m. and the MO and I have been rushed off our feet. Fortunately diphtheria has a distinctive smell and appearance, and our first job was to isolate the obvious cases of diphtheria from ordinary cases of tonsillitis. We have to rely on our experience in diagnosis, as it will take forty-eight hours to get the throat swabs analysed and by then a whole ward could be infected. The membrane can be seen quite clearly, covering the swollen vocal cords, thus reducing and finally blocking the airway. In this type of acute laryngeal diphtheria an emergency tracheotomy is usually essential.

There is a new male orderly now to help our energetic Amazon. He is quite the character. His name is Shufflebottom and he is tall and lanky with horn-rimmed spectacles and a permanent expression of solemn, bored indifference. He apparently considers it undignified to hurry under any circumstances, so the patients have ironically nicknamed him Flash. He rarely speaks, and when I ask him to do something he just nods profoundly.

There are twenty-five patients on penicillin three hourly and right on the dot of the hour he [Flash] presents himself at the door of my office with a torch. That is the cue for me to pick up my tray of syringes and away we go, through the dark wards, here a jab, there a jab! We both wear masks and long white gowns and one can imagine what a terrifying experience for the poor patient to be awakened in the middle of the night by such strange-looking silent apparitions. The study of expressions of both orderly and patient speaks louder than words.

This is a very interesting ward and I suddenly realise how very fond I am of this underpaid job of trying to soothe the fevered brow. The patients, on the other hand, must feel that I am some kind of sadist who enjoys sticking needles in their bottoms. Throat swabs are my other speciality. There are always so many and all of them must be very carefully tabulated.

Am feeling extremely tired at the moment and not in the least like Florence Nightingale.

13 October

The ward is absolutely hectic at present. We are short staffed and I am the only fever-trained Sister on night duty. The strength of staff here is chiefly maintained by Sisters in transit and the in-between periods such as at present are very difficult.

Flash and I have been moving Sgt James into a side ward and fixing up barrier nursing. His condition suddenly deteriorated about an hour ago. He has had a slight haemorrhage, has a dicrotic pulse and a high temperature, also a rose-coloured rash on his body. I've taken a sample of blood for culture and have sent for the Senior Medical Officer, as I fear it might be typhoid fever. The alarming thing is that he has been in the general ward with the other patients for several days.

17 October

We are having constant convoys of troops coming down from Germany. Judging by the number of confirmed cases of diphtheria and typhus we have here on this fever block at present, there could well be an epidemic starting in Germany.

I am rushed off my feet, Flash is walked off his feet, but anyway we just manage to keep abreast of the work load.

Sgt James is still under close observation as a suspected typhoid. The barrier nursing is very time consuming, but essential if we are to try and prevent the disease spreading to the other patients. He is a dear man in his forties, a patient, fatherly type of soldier. He has survived so many battles and was looking forward to demobilisation and returning home to his family. He feels totally helpless as we cannot allow him to do anything. He has to be turned every hour in order to prevent bed-sores, but it must be done very carefully as there is always the risk of haemorrhage. My hands are raw from scrubbing up in Dettol and I have a bath on the ward each morning before going off duty. I stink so much of disinfectant that everybody moves away from me in the Mess!

A letter from M this morning. He is coming here on the 18th on his way back from Krefeld. It will be lovely to see him, but am worried about all the infections that I am involved with. It would be awful to give M an infection. It is very difficult to have any social life while working on acute fevers.

18 October

Went to bed at 9 a.m. and was called at 11.30 to say that M had arrived. I was dizzy with a combination of joy at seeing him and unadulterated exhaustion.

19 October, 2 a.m.

Was late coming on duty tonight – nearly 9 p.m. when I arrived. The Day Sister had gone off duty and the MO and Flash were in an awful flap just because there were a few new admissions. This has been one of the busiest nights I've ever had here, but apart from a rather unreal sensation of working automatically, I did not feel tired. Sgt James is a little better, which is something to be cheerful about.

Flash has just brought me some toast and coffee. He is kind and thoughtful. The coffee is particularly welcome because now I <u>am</u> tired. There are three wards on this block and the penicillins take up an enormous amount of my time. Everything has to be done at the double and as one session of treatments ends, another begins. This isolation unit is not very well equipped. I think military hospitals pay more attention to providing facilities for wartime gunshot wounds, than to peacetime diphtheria or venereal disease.

20 October

Collapsed into bed at 8.30 a.m. to be called by Home Sister three hours later as M had arrived. It was lovely to see him but I felt like a zombie. We had lunch at the Plaza and went out to the country afterwards. It was so beautiful there and so peaceful that I fell asleep in his arms. M went back on the 7.30 p.m. train to Krefeld and I feel totally miserable. I try to be sensible but I can't help missing him and feeling depressed. It is going to be hard to get through tonight's duty.

22 October

Slept for twelve hours and am still tired. Sgt James is off the danger list. The wards are still extremely busy.

23 October

This is a lovely autumn night, and I've just been for a short walk in the grounds. There is a very large, pale moon moving majestically across the sky and there is that uncanny stillness so often associated with moonlight. I've just heard the low, muffled hoot of an owl and there is a dog barking in the far distance.

Flash has just interrupted this reverie to report that one of the Polish patients has drunk his thymol gargle and apparently gargled with his tea. Reassured Flash that it did not matter – the mouthwash is too weak to be a danger and the tea too foul to drink.

There was great excitement earlier tonight as four patients upstairs disappeared through the lavatory window. They were all under detention, four tough-looking Canadian commandos with suspected VD. They had one pathetic little guard with a rifle as large as himself. He apparently watched them all go to the latrines and could not understand why nobody came out! By the time he raised the alarm they had already scaled the wall and reached freedom. There will probably be a Court of Inquiry, and I shall probably have to give evidence. The army is a wonderful organisation. In order to compensate for their laxity in this affair they have sent four burly guards for another detention patient, a poor boy with diphtheria who is literally unable to raise his head from the pillow.

24 October, 3 a.m.

A cold, wild, windy night. I can see the moon and clouds moving rapidly across the sky, and outside my window the trees are making a mournful creaking sound as they are swayed back and forth by the relentless wind. I particularly love these wild, windy nights, although there is a poignant sadness in my memories of nights such as this, on the Atlantic coast of Galway.

Have a new orderly with me tonight and what a contrast to

Shufflebottom. The patients gasped with amazement as he whizzed by with their aspirin, gargles and hot drinks. My Amazon ATS orderly has been moved to another ward – but she and Clarke (the new one) would get on like a house on fire. His enthusiasm is rather endearing actually, or at least it is until about 2 a.m., but after that I hate having to find answers to intelligent questions about anatomy and physiology etc.

Poor patients, what a lot they have to put up with: me tearing about madly in one direction giving injections and sticking tablets and thermometers in their mouths before they are half awake, while the orderly dashes about with gargles and uninviting-looking bowls of tepid water for washing. All of this activity starts on the dot of 5 a.m. It is very funny really, but oddly enough I seem to be the only one who is amused.

25 October

Letter from M. He has been made Intelligence Officer of his unit. Brussels is no longer his leave centre, so he has invited me to visit him in Germany. The 77 BGH is somewhere in that area and Joyce Bale is still with the 77. They are under canvas, but Joyce may be able to arrange for me to stay for a few nights. M would like me to apply for a posting to 77 but I dare not make any requests for a little while. If my name appears at the War Office once again, they will post me to SEAC!

We are still very busy on the ward but it is great fun. Flash and Nobby Clarke keep me perpetually amused. There was a party in the Officers' Mess tonight and Nobby disappeared from the ward, returning later with a plate of sandwiches and other goodies. He very wisely conjectured that they would all be at that happy stage of intoxication when nothing appears strange – so he just walked in and helped himself.

26 October, 2 a.m.

This place is terribly eerie at night. I almost jumped to the ceiling just now. It was all quiet and peaceful and then suddenly the door burst open and a gust of wind blew in, driving a few dead leaves before it. If this was Ireland I would say that the place was haunted. Shufflebottom alone is enough to make one a nervous wreck. One never hears him come or go. He just appears out of nowhere with his long white gown and long white solemn face. The man's expression seems to be permanent. I've only once heard him laugh and that was a terrifying throaty chuckle, without any change of expression on his face. Perhaps night duty is making me morbid.

27 October

Went for a long walk yesterday morning. I miss M on these walks. He is such good, happy company. Have never seen him angry about anything. I get angry occasionally but I do not think that I possess the notorious Irish temper. Actually I dislike people who dramatise themselves by getting into a rage and chucking things around. Nursing has taught me the futility of being annoyed by petty details.

29 October, 7.30 a.m.

Last night was desperately busy. We had several new patients in, all from units in Germany – suspected typhoid. Flash and I did not sit down throughout the night. Very tired this morning.

1 November

It is now 2 a.m. but judging by the row in the ward it might as well be the middle of the day. I have just admitted an incredibly black Abyssinian, and have not yet fully recovered from the shock of seeing the black face and wide white grin in the semi-darkness of my office doorway. He too is a suspected typhoid, but he seems very cheerful to me. I had to put the lights on in the ward in order to get him to bed. There was a chorus of amazed comments, even the flat diphtherias sat up and had to be reprimanded. It is not so much the colour of Ahmad's skin that surprised the patients. He is at least 6 foot 5 inches tall and will probably come in for an awful lot of teasing. He has a wonderful deep Paul Robeson voice.

Have been sleeping all day as usual. It seems such a waste of time and I get quite peeved when people tell me what a lovely day it has been.

One of my patients has had a mild heart attack tonight but seems OK at the moment. His treatment entailed wheeling an oxygen cylinder through the ward – so once again everybody is wide awake. One precise little man has just asked me very politely just when he is supposed to sleep around here. He has a point as I shall be waking him and a large majority of the others for their penicillin jabs in twenty minutes!

5 November

Finished night duty. Hurrah! M arrived at 4 p.m. Am blissfully happy.

8 November

M went back to Germany at 2.30 p.m. Feeling utterly miserable and lonely. It is pouring with rain. He should be back at RHQ [Regimental Headquarters] by now, probably having dinner. The whole world seems so dark and cold and cheerless without him. The rain is pattering on the window panes and I wish we were having tea together in front of a glowing coal fire.

14 November

This is a cold, dark night with a sharp, biting wind. Christmas will soon be here – our first peacetime Christmas in what seems like a very long war.

15 November

Had a letter from M. He has been posted to Salisbury Plain to do a gas course. Astonishing – but at least he will be home for Christmas. I shall miss him. Poor M, he sounded rather unhappy and worried about the shortness of life, and the fact that there is so much that he wants to achieve. I must write and point out that he is not exactly on the edge of decrepitude, that he is going to have a long and happy life with me and plenty of time to do everything he wants to do.

17 November

Two letters from M. He is extremely incensed by the compulsory church parades at Salisbury Plain. He is quite right. No man should dictate another's actions where religion is concerned. It is just stupid hypocritical presumption to make church parades compulsory and must eventually be detrimental to the Church itself.

We had our Fancy Dress Ball last night. I went as a crinolined Victorian lady wearing the most magnificent feathered hat. The preparations took weeks and the amount of bribery and corruption that went on in order to obtain the hoops and feathers was quite exhausting. It was great fun, but very uncomfortable to wear – embarrassing moments too. How did Victorian ladies manage to spend a penny? My prize – second – was a pair of khaki stockings. What an anti-climax!

19 November

Have just been to a Mess meeting re the arrangements for Christmas activities. It was incredible. There were suggestions and counter-suggestions and innumerable silly discussions until now, two hours later, we are no nearer any fixed ideas than we were before. It was all so futile. Any original ideas were quashed by the remark that 'we have never done that before'. We shall end up by having the customary formal dinner, followed by a dance, to which the medical officers will be invited. Am tired of formal functions where Matron presides, and carefully scrutinises the behaviour of each individual.

One of the things that I do enjoy at Christmas is decorating the wards – wading through piles of gaily coloured paper and tinsel, and having enormous bowls of shiny green holly with red berries scattered around the place. It is much more fun on a Children's Ward of course, but the men do seem to appreciate it.

Two letters from M today. He is now living in the lap of luxury at the Army School of Chemical Warfare near Salisbury. This is a sharp contrast to his first night in England in a transit camp under canvas. There was a heavy frost and they were all frozen almost solid by morning.

M tells me that the gas lectures are as big a farce as he had anticipated and to quote from his letter – 'It is hopeless to expect a class of officers, which includes majors who have three or four years' overseas active service, and with numerous campaign medals, to listen with much interest to a sergeant instructor who has never been out of England.' He goes on to say that 'when these sergeants get up and recite in all seriousness two methods of rolling a gas cape, and other elementary things (which they have been teaching at the same school since 1939), it is painfully obvious that all they say is based on inadequate text book theory without any knowledge of active service conditions.' He concludes by saying 'I am beginning to talk like an old soldier – do forgive me and God forbid that I should ever be one.'

20 November

Have just come off duty and feel absolutely dead beat. What a day it has been. The orderlies mixed up the special diets, the diphtherias did everything they should not do, the geyser in the kitchen blew up, somebody let a bath overflow, I dropped a bowl of thermometers, and in the midst of all this the CO decided to do a ward inspection. He started off by looking in a cupboard and being almost knocked backwards by an avalanche of books and jigsaw puzzles.

Looked at myself in the mirror and decided that I look awful. Am looking forward to leave and the pleasure of wearing civilian clothes again. My battle dress covered in the honoured stains of Normandy combat looks less than glamorous thrown there on my bed. It never did fit me properly.

Must get some sleep as I must be up at the usual unearthly hour of 6.30 a.m., ready for an uncivilised breakfast at 7 a.m.

21 November

A parcel and two letters from M. The parcel contained some ghastly undies, mainly cami-knickers and slips. The material is parachute silk – extremely nice but the garments were obviously produced with a buxom Fräulein in mind. It is almost impossible to obtain underclothes at present other than khaki knickers with elastic in the legs!

M talks about homes and house designs in his letters. We must find the perfect place by the sea or an old cottage in the country – the one place in the world that will always be home to us. Home to me must mean something permanent. There is something precious about familiar things. They always hold so many memories. It would be lovely to build happy memories for recall when we are both very, very old.

23 November

Heard today that the 108 is disbanding next March. I shall probably be posted somewhere in Germany. Another letter from M. He is still in Winterbourne Gunner near Salisbury. He will most probably go to the Slade* after demobilisation. Shall certainly encourage him to do so. His work is important to me.

28 November

Have just had a beautiful bunch of roses sent to me from the patients of A block. I feel moved – almost to tears – particularly as I am always ticking them off.

29 November

Gee and I went to see Deanna Durbin in *Lady on a Train* last night. We had a rather amusing return journey to Laeken. There were very few passengers and the driver, a genial old boy, consented to allow Gee and me to drive the tram for a little way. Have always loved trams and it was enormous fun to drive it. They are now starting to speed up our demobilisation. I should be out of the army by September 1947.

5 December

I have been specialling a very sick man for the past three days. He has been so ill that I could not take any off duty. It was quite a problem to just snatch a quick meal break. Sgt Walters came in on Saturday last, with a diagnosis of acute tonsillitis. The 'tonsillitis' became rapidly worse by the late afternoon. It was obviously a very severe diphtheria. He had to be isolated at once, while we pumped antitoxins into him. His condi-

---

* The Slade School of Fine Art, now part of University College London.

tion deteriorated rapidly, and by early evening an emergency tracheotomy was performed in the ward. The membrane is still growing like a nasty weed over his tonsils and vocal cords. Poor man, it looks as if he will have to put up with a tracheotomy tube *in situ* for a long time.

7 December

The sky looks very lovely at the moment – masses of beautiful cumulus clouds. Wish I had time just to stand and stare, but my clock tells me that my one-hour break is over and I must go back on duty.

Sgt Walters is slightly improved, but he has to keep very still in bed – absolutely no exertion. There appears to be an epidemic of diphtheria at present. There are desperately ill men coming in at all hours of the day and night. The work is extremely hard and very tiring. Gee, who has been helping me here, went off duty at lunch time with a sore throat. I do hope it is not anything worse.

9 December

This has been another hectic day on the ward. Sgt Walters died this morning. We did absolutely everything possible, but the nasty dirty grey membrane kept on growing despite all our efforts. It was heartbreaking to watch his deterioration, the rapid onset of toxaemia and the eventual heart failure. The early diagnosis and treatment of diphtheria is vital if their lives are to be saved. I hate the smell of this disease. It is so foul and sickly.

12 December

My off-duty is practically non-existent at present as the ward is so busy. It is always about 10.30 p.m. when I come off the ward at night – a fifteen-hour day. It is sheer necessity in order to get through the huge volume of work.

This afternoon I dashed out for an hour in order to find some Christmas decorations for the ward, and had a wonderful time being trampled on in the Bon Marché. I could have spent hours there, particularly in the toy department. It is the type of fairyland of wonderful toys that I used to dream about when I was a child, lovely shiny things, woolly dogs with faces full of expression and all kinds of things that rattle and squeak and perform tricks. What fun it would be to find some poor scruffy little children who had never seen such toys, bring them here and buy them anything they wanted just for the pleasure of watching their faces.

Brussels was packed with people of all nationalities, dashing here and there, dodging cars and gazing in shop windows. The street vendors were shouting their wares and above it all the furious clanging of the tram cars.

15 December

The ward has been extremely busy for the past few days and we are under-staffed as usual. We have been admitting German prisoners from a camp here in Brussels. I am appalled by the condition of these prisoners in peacetime Europe. Starvation, filth and acute fevers are always hard to see and we all feel a sense of righteous indignation about the cruelty and sadism of the Germans in Belsen and Buchenwald, but what are we to feel or say when prisoners come in from our own POW camps suffering from the most advanced stages of starvation and smelling so badly that we have to wear double face masks? A young corporal who accompanied today's batch of prisoners tells me that they have been having 'an average of fifteen deaths per day for some time'. How long is this hate and cruelty and bestiality going to last? This little episode will be covered up very nicely, nothing of it will reach the newspapers or the people at home. This has really shaken me. It is not very nice to see human beings reduced to the level of beasts. We must believe that this war was fought and won in order to preserve decency and humanity and sanity in the world. The condition of these poor German boys is too pitiable for words – despite all our efforts, they are dying of starvation and dysentery. They are too far gone for help. They are just skin and bone – not enough elasticity in their veins to get a needle in for drip feeding. I feel ashamed and angry and depressed. We have all been working a twelve-hour day trying to save them. Why has this happened six months after the end of the war – and who is responsible? It looks as if we too have our war criminals.

Listened to Doris Arnold's *These You Have Loved* this evening in an effort to soothe my shattered nerves.

16 December

It is now 11.30 p.m. and I have just come off duty. My last task was to lay out the bodies of five young German prisoners. They were just skin and bone.

17 December

Dashed into Brussels this morning to buy some more decorations and a Christmas tree. I managed to find a tree after a great deal of physical and mental exercise. Was most unpopular on the tram returning to Laeken, in fact I created quite a disturbance by knocking off people's hats and scratching their faces (with the tree!).

Another letter from M. He writes that 'wars bring out the courage and self-sacrifice in people's character.' That may be true in some instances, but after nursing these German prisoners I now think that it brings out the worst traits in some people. Courage is very difficult to define, and the truly courageous ones rarely receive any medals. The awful thing is that the after-effects of war go on for years after the war is ended.

19 December

Some of the up patients have started to decorate the wards, but they keep coming along to me for advice and encouragement every few minutes. I have spent a great deal of time trying to persuade our German patients to become involved in the ward activities. Some are too weak to do anything, but a few of them are painting egg shells for me to decorate the tree. These POWs need a great deal of loving care – they are so frightened. The other patients are very kind to them. They are becoming enthusiastic about the Christmas festivities now and even the diphtherias who have been on a light fish diet for weeks are asking to see the menu for Christmas dinner. It is lovely to see the bed patients lying there happily cutting up strips of coloured paper. The ward is in a state of happy chaos – most un-military. The CO would have a fit – but I am determined that this ward will be a happy place this Christmas. I feel such a sense of guilt when I look at these poor German boys.

21 December

Have just finished decorating the Christmas tree despite the criticisms and unhelpful suggestions of the onlookers. Am trying to tell myself that it looks fine. There is a peculiar little fairy perched precariously on top and the branches are filled with an astonishing collection of little birds and bells and coloured egg shells.

This decorating business is becoming quite nerve-racking. There is a civil war going on between the Tonsillitis Ward and the Diphtheria Ward and all because one ward pinched a few lamp shades from another. Some men are like little children.

Our German patients are improving slightly. They are given

small hourly milk feeds. I warned the orderlies and the other patients that food other than the prescribed quantity could kill them.

Received masses of Christmas cards today. One from Richard Kelvin, an enormous one from Vernon and a letter and card from Connie. Connie is in Burma and becoming more and more suntanned each day. There is practically no work for the 101 there. Connie has five patients to look after, all of whom get up. How crazy to send them all out there when there is such a staff shortage here and in the UK. A letter from Driscoll. She is back in England now after a spell as a Prisoner of War in Sumatra.* Several people died in captivity there, including some nuns. She writes little of her experience. It is probably still too painful.

What an enormous change one year can bring. The girls whom I spent last Christmas with in Louvain are scattered all over the world. Time, when one looks back, always seems to have gone by so quickly. It is good to have plenty of interesting work to do, but I sometimes think that our lives are far too cluttered up with petty problems and worries. These things can rise to such a height that people can't see above and beyond them. Am working with a Sister at present who almost drives me crazy by worrying and nattering all day, both on and off duty. She is quite a sweet person, but she is continually looking for trouble and so naturally she finds it. Gee is on night duty. I miss all the fun and laughter we had together, regardless of how hard we had to work.

* Nurses and civilian women and children were held separately from men in Japanese POW camps in Sumatra, where deaths were caused by starvation and illness in addition to deliberate killing. The Japanese withheld medicine and food and potentially life-saving Red Cross parcels and letters, and dealt out life-threatening punishments for perceived offences.

25 December

Went to midnight Mass at the Sacré Coeur in Louvain last night. It was beautiful. The familiar little chapel, marvellous singing and the sweet faces of the nuns. It was good to see Soeur Marie-Anselma again. Her English and my Flemish have not improved, but we manage to communicate very happily. She is as plump and jolly as ever.

Have been on duty all day since 7 a.m. The patients have had a very good time. They had enormous quantities of food for dinner, lots of beer and two glasses of champagne each. I gave our German patients small amounts of everything so that they might not feel left out. We've had no more starvation deaths for several days and are hoping that the remaining POWs will survive. We are gradually gaining their confidence, but I still do not understand why this happened.

The ward has been extremely jolly all day – two gramophones screeching forth some awful jazz, champagne corks popping and some people throwing streamers around. The decorations too look rather grand. There is always a great deal of friendly rivalry between wards at Christmas in order to establish which one has the most original decorations. The main thing is that we tried to make the patients forget that they are away from home and not spending Christmas in the way they would like to spend it.

Have been invited to several parties tonight but am going to bed early as I feel very tired.

26 December

Another Christmas has gone. Our first peacetime Christmas in six years. I should have gone to bed early last night but decided to go round to A block to see Gee and help her to put round the small personal gifts for the patients. We tried to do it very quietly but giggled so much that by the time we had finished most of the men were awake. We then cooked ourselves spam and eggs and eventually I went to bed at 3 a.m.

29 December

Received a letter from Ireland. My Aunt is ill. She calls it a 'bad cold', but because I know her so well it must be much worse to keep her confined to bed. I have applied for compassionate leave in order to go home. Am very worried about her.

It will soon be a new year. I love the exciting feeling of anti-cipation that a new year brings, wondering what is round the corner, all the noble resolutions one makes and breaks, and the brand new diary with its snow-white pages. How wise God is not to give us the power to foretell the future. Life would lose all its excitement and promise and adventure if we knew exactly what lay ahead.

30 December

The papers for my leave have not yet come through. It will probably be a few days before I am allowed to go to Ireland. This waiting is terrible. My Auntie is a lovely person, the most unselfish human being I have ever known. She is so warm and loving and until I met my dearest M, she was the only one who really mattered to me.

31 December

The last day of the year always seems a little sad to me. One remembers all the incidents of the past year, all the joy and happiness and sadness, which will now belong to the precious memories of 1945. I am especially reluctant to say good-bye to 1945, the year I met and fell in love with my darling M.

Our German patients are making steady but slow progress. Sgt Adams, a man recovering from acute diphtheria, asked me today if he might borrow my Gerald Breen book on fevers. He returned it this evening before I came off duty. He wondered why all the medical terminology was so obtuse. It was a good question and difficult to answer. It may be that technical terms and elaborate high-faluting words and phrases tend to impress the lay mind. The medical profession is not above such subterfuge in an endeavour to maintain the charisma of 'I know more about your body than you do'.

My papers have come through at last. I should be leaving here for Ireland on 2 or 3 January.

1 January 1946

Spent a very frustrating morning doing the ward inventory – checking equipment etc. One of the things that I dislike about military hospitals is that Sisters are held individually responsible for all equipment and we must pay for any deficiencies out of our meagre salary, which is £12 per month. It is fortunate that I enjoy the work otherwise the responsibility of a fever block (two large wards and several isolation units) might be too much at times, particularly while we are so under-staffed. I have some good friends in the QM's [Quartermaster] office and they came to my rescue by producing sheets and blue blankets to make up our ward stock deficiencies. I hear that there are high prices still being paid for our hospital blue blankets in Brussels.

The patients gave me a very amusing Christmas present, a large wooden doggie that moves along the floor on a piece of string and wags its tail furiously up and down. It is so fascinating that I could play with it for hours.

2 January

This evening I should be going on leave but I find myself a patient instead. Woke up this morning with a face that was not at all symmetrical and a throat that refused to swallow break-fast in a way that a normal throat should. The result is that I find myself in this tiny room, sitting in bed foolishly in the middle of a sunny afternoon. They have taken a throat swab (never again shall I take a swab without considering the unfortunate patient's feelings) and are now giving me three-hourly injections of penicillin. Shall be OK in a day or two, and were I not so worried about my Auntie, I should probably enjoy it. Everybody is so kind and helpful here. It is quite an experience to see hospital life from the patient's angle.

A letter from M. He is back with his unit in Germany. He was unable to disembark from the train in Brussels as the place was crawling with military police. One of his most unpleasant duties since his return to Germany was to assist at the trial of a young German civilian, accused of murder. He was convicted and subsequently beheaded. It sounds macabre and horrible.

3 January

Seem to spend most of the day sleeping and just wake up for meals. The food is marvellous. It would be, of course, just when I'm on a diet of jelly and aspirin gargles. For lunch today they brought along a delicious-looking chop with roast potatoes and peas and, feeling really martyred, I had to send it away and in exchange received a minute piece of pathetic-looking fish, which any self-respecting cat would ignore.

When I woke up this afternoon there was an enormous bunch of tulips on my bed from 'all the garglers and pin cushions on A block'. It reminded me of happier days when I was the one dishing out the penicillin and gargles. They are such a lovely crowd of patients on A block. I am very fond of them.

Am hoping every day to receive a letter from Ireland to say that my Auntie has recovered. If, in fact, she is better, then I shall try to arrange my leave duties to coincide with M's in February.

5 January

A lovely letter from M, which cheered me up enormously. He has been doing quite a lot of watercolour painting and house designing. Am pleased that he is such a versatile, creative person. It is good to have a real purpose in life, something totally absorbing. Many people waste years of their life groping about in a fog of doubt and uncertainty, not knowing what they want to do or what they want to achieve in life. Sometimes I feel that I am one of those people. There are times when I love nursing, other times when I hate it and feel that it deprives me of the time and opportunity to find the intellectual excitement which might lie within the study of history or philosophy and all the other interesting subjects in the world. I do not seem to be at all creative. Have tried to write but the ideas in my head will not convey themselves to my pen. Am feeling very inadequate this evening – can't even do a rotten crossword. Have spent hours of painful agony today trying to do *The Times* crossword – just one stupid little word of seven letters eludes me. It will probably wake me up at 2 a.m. if I ever manage to sleep.

6 January

They allowed me to get up for an hour today and the first thing I did was to peer out of the window at the outside world, just to make sure that it was still there.

Have just been reading a letter from Peter Waller (in India) in which he was describing the heat there very graphically. What a contrast to the scene outside my window. The cold, foggy, lifeless atmosphere and the trees looking so bare and empty and forlorn, not a speck of colour or a ray of sunshine anywhere. Was feeling rather depressed and miserable, when suddenly Gee blew in with a glorious bunch of yellow mimosa. I can't describe what a difference these flowers make to my room and to my life at the moment. Their gay colour and clear earthy smell bring a breath of spring, and a glorious promise of life and colour and long, lazy summer days.

9 January

Was allowed out on pass yesterday. The day was bright and sunny but bitterly cold. Felt like a newly liberated prisoner, good to be out in the fresh air again and to feel the hard crunchy ground beneath my feet.

10 January

Have just been told that I must take my leave allocation on the 17th. My Auntie is still very ill so I must go to Ireland, but I would love to spend at least some of this leave with M.

A letter from Kathleen Aitken from Canada enclosing a lovely pair of fine nylon stockings. She is a dear. Haven't seen anything so pretty since my last pair of pure silk stockings in 1939.

12 January

Went out to dinner at the Rue d'Arlow Club with Chezzy. He turned up out of the blue. It was fortunate that he was passing through Brussels but he had some difficulty in locating me. It was fun to see him again. We talked about Normandy and all our mutual friends. He is being demobbed in six weeks' time and is going back home to Poland. Chezzy is such a kind, caring person, so helpful to everybody, vulnerable too in a way that makes me want to protect him against hurt. He is so self-deprecating, and lacking confidence in himself and his future. He is fearful too of what the Russians and their ideology might do to destroy the culture of his native land. It is impossible to convince him that they are our allies not our enemies.

We both enjoyed watching the other people in the Club. The majority of them were senior regular officers and their glamorous Belgian girlfriends. The rest were voluntary services in varieties of exotic uniforms that we had never seen before (where were they during the war?). The place reeked of artificiality, the officers (obviously with wives at home) were trying rather pathetically and not very gracefully to regain their lost youth. Brussels is obviously a pleasant place for the desk wallahs.

Told Chezzy about my engagement to M. We drank coffee for hours and talked and talked and then it was time to say good-bye. He asked to be invited to our wedding. On my way back to Laeken in the taxi I remembered his dear, ugly face, generous smile and warm humour.

17 January

Am in the midst of packing and chaos. I seem to be the only one going on leave tonight.

22 January, Galway (in transit)

Am in the train to Galway at the moment, passing through the Bog of Allen. There is a fine rain falling, just enough to add an air of mystery to the miles and miles of wild, open, boggy marsh land, a paradise for wild birds, so lonely and uninhabited by man. In a little while we shall come to the very green fields of the midlands, which look so calm and peaceful, and then as we go further west the mountains will begin to emerge on the horizon, and we shall see the tiny white-washed cottages dotted here and there. I love the variety of the Irish countryside, the vivid emerald green fields, and that wonderful feeling of relaxation and remoteness, which is a part of the easy-going way of life here. Nothing changes and any signs of progress are treated with suspicion.

I've had to spend the weekend in Dublin at the Grosvenor.

There is an acute coal shortage over here and there were not any trains going anywhere.

The journey from Euston to Holyhead was quite comfortable. Met an Irishman (a British Army officer on leave) and he told me that the boat situation across the Irish Sea was pretty good now, so I was rather dismayed on my arrival in Holyhead to see the very old and all-too-familiar *Hibernia* moaning and groaning on the quayside. The seagulls looked so much at home sitting on her bow that I began to wonder if they were nesting there! The crossing was the worst I have ever known, a howling gale and enormous waves washing over the deck. Everybody was ordered below and it was hell. I was violently sick and my only hope at the time was that we might hit a mine and be blown to smithereens! How Rupert Brooke could even bear to write a poem about sea-sickness is beyond my understanding.

The lights of Dublin came into view after what seemed like centuries. The inexpressible joy of removing myself from that awful stinking boat! I went through to the train and then suddenly my bags were snatched up and I was practically pushed into a carriage by a funny little porter with spectacles perched precariously on the end of his nose. When I was inside he promptly locked the door. I was a little alarmed until I noticed that he was doing this to everybody. The chaos can be imagined, a crowded platform filled with people who had spent a hellish night coming across, all of them yelling for seats and this little man darting about with his enormous bunch of keys, locking and unlocking doors. This train was on its way to Dublin from Kingstown – not exactly an elaborate journey – but this is Ireland – one never bothers to reason why!

Dublin was packed with American and Canadian servicemen in uniform. It still annoys me to see all these people wandering around O'Connell Street while Irishmen serving in the British forces must wear civilian clothes.

The food at the Grosvenor was superb – lots of lovely bacon, eggs, butter, etc. and one can buy oranges and chocolate ad lib.

24 January, Galway

There was a telegram and heaps of letters from M awaiting me when I arrived home. My Auntie is much better, thank God, and she met me at Woodlawn Station with the ass and trap. It was lovely to drive along the almost empty lanes in the old trap – so completely tranquil and relaxing.

Am writing this in front of an enormous turf fire. There is an Atlantic gale blowing outside, and the trees are almost bent double against the force of the wind. There is a brown pot of tea brewing on the hearth and there is a smell of damp dog as Collie lies across my feet. It is all so dear and familiar to me, including the face of my Auntie, which is lined with the cares and the laughter of all her years. She must have been a beautiful woman in her youth, but I love her as she is and however she is. This is a rather special leave for me. My life is changing. I must make my own life soon with my dear M but all this will be a part of me for as long as I live.

25 January

It is still raining here although the storm has abated. Cycled to Killasolan to visit my father. He is far from happy at the idea of my proposed marriage to a British Army officer. His Ireland versus England bitterness still goes on. He seems to think that all Englishmen are like the 'Black and Tans'.* It seems so unfair, for M is such a gentle, artistic person. He is just not interested in politics. My father will never change now. He will want to fight the British until the day of his death, and all because of his dream of a United Ireland.

---

* Members of the Royal Irish Constabulary (many ex-British Army) especially detailed to fight the Irish Republican Army during the Irish War of Independence. Known for their brutality, especially against civilians, they were called 'Black and Tans' because of the colours of their mismatched uniforms.

26 January

There was another tremendous storm last night. Was awakened about 2 a.m. by the neighing and stampeding of the horses. They were trying to kick down the stable doors in their terror. A piece of galvanise had blown off the chicken house, and the hens were screeching their heads off, and a tree had fallen across the cowshed and everything was in chaos. I could see Tom and Cormac out there – struggling to calm the frightened animals and cutting the horses loose before they broke down the doors. My Auntie and I made the fire and put on the kettle for tea. The place looks as if it has been bombed this morning.

Mary managed to squeeze in a few days with Malcolm at the end of her leave before returning to Brussels. She now applied to be posted to Germany so that she could be closer to Malcolm.

6 February, 108 BGH, Brussels

It seems strange to be back in this familiar little room again, and at 6.30 a.m. it was too uncomfortably familiar to be awakened by the loud clanging of the bell, no tea in bed and no more lunch-time breakfasts.

We had a rough Channel crossing. Stayed on deck most of the time and was literally soaked to the skin with rain and spray. What a dilapidated wreck I was on arrival in Calais. Am convinced that the lowest ebb of mortal misery is to be seasick, cold, wet and tired all at the same time and in my case one could add extreme loneliness and despair at being parted from M. Was feeling too sorry for myself to realise that all the other passengers were in the same predicament. I can't find words glowing enough to describe the Officers' Mess in Calais – the sheer joy of abundant hot water, coal fires, a good meal and best of all, <u>terra firma</u>.

Arrived here at midday yesterday, but did not really wake up until this morning. Have been plunged into a completely new ward – a busy surgical block. What a hectic day this has been, specialists visiting patients and asking innumerable questions about them, telephones ringing constantly, trolleys clattering by taking people to and from the operating theatre, drugs to be checked, complex dressings to be supervised, accident cases coming in. I've had to hold on to the top of my head just to make sure that it is still there.

This is probably a very nice ward with very nice patients, if only I could find time to look at them. Am finding it very hard to adapt to this hectic way of life. At present, most of me is still on leave and there is only a small part on duty here in the midst of all this chaos.

They are very short of Sisters here. Matron will have a fit when I apply for a posting to Germany.

7 February

Another extremely busy day on the ward and to add to my worries I have laryngitis. My voice has gone completely. It is terribly funny as all who talk to me whisper in sympathy. The telephone is my greatest ordeal as people want to know why on earth I am whispering. This ward is usually very noisy, but tonight by the time I had finished the usual inspection round with the MO, both he and the patients were talking in ridiculously loud whispers. The voice also has a disconcerting habit of coming back to normal at odd intervals much to everybody's astonishment.

9 February

Two letters from M, one written in Dover, the other in Calais. He is on his way back to Germany. He is a dear to write from these transit places. They always depress me too much. On the

English side there is the unhappy anticipation of the crossing and on the other side my half-conscious mind is concentrated on food and the appreciations of a world that stays in one position.

10 February

Feeling a little depressed today. There is so much paper-work to be done, a great deal of it quite unnecessary. It was much better in Normandy where all our time was spent caring for the patients and forms in triplicate could be ignored. We are now functioning as a peacetime military hospital with all the bull that goes with it – Colonel's inspections, beds and patients lying to attention – so much absurd minutia. It is a battle to obtain a cradle to protect a man's stump or injured leg from the bed-clothes. I fight on regardless for the sake of the patients' comfort, and usually manage to win. I love dashing about the ward, looking after the men, and listening to their problems and cheerful grumbles. They love to talk about themselves and their families. This is, in my opinion, an important part of my job, yet in training days we were discouraged from wasting time by talking to patients. People in hospital are extremely vulnerable. They become their real selves and are stripped of the veneer and show that they put on for the outside world. All nurses should have a spell as a patient in order to understand the other side.

13 February

M has been posted to Wuppertal. Have submitted my application for a posting to 77 BGH. It has to go through normal channels before reaching the War Office, so we can only wait and see.

The CO did an inspection of the ward this morning. There was the usual flap: people tearing around tidying and re-tidying and the poor patients looking uncomfortable and miserable.

My voice has almost returned to normal, so I was astonished when the CO told me after his round that he had arranged for me to spend a week at the Officers' Convalescent Home in Waterloo. Feel an awful fraud but am going out there on Friday morning.

15 February

My birthday, twenty-five today. Feeling very old. My sojourn at the Convalescent Home has been postponed until next week as there are not any vacancies at present. Gee and I went shopping in Brussels this afternoon but did not make any exciting purchases. There are very few troops here at present, and consequently the black-market prices are dropping rapidly. Noticed that watches are half the price they were at Christmas.

17 February

Went to a concert at the Palais des Beaux Arts this afternoon. The theatre was packed tightly, but I had a good seat with an excellent view of the orchestra. The streets of Brussels were filled with noisy crowds when we came out of the theatre. It seems to be election fever, but judging by the hoardings everywhere the Communist Party appears to be the only one interested in getting into power. It is frightening to see how rapidly Communism is gaining a foothold in Europe. We seem to have won a war against one type of tyranny only to be faced with another that is equally formidable.

18 February

The ward is still very busy. Am trying to find time to talk and listen to the men as much as possible. It is sad to hear of so many broken marriages. The strain of being apart for so long during the war. It is easy to understand this problem really. The ordinary pre-war moral and social standards were swept away during active service days. There was suffering and loneliness and unhappiness then, but also a strange euphoria of excitement – the uniform seemed to give us a special status. We were in the Services and tended to look down a little on mere civilians. It is very difficult to keep a sense of proportion and a firm sense of values when the world is rushing by – here today, gone tomorrow – nothing seemed to matter then except the shortness of life and the proximity of death.

21 February, Officers' Convalescent Home, Waterloo, Brussels

Arrived here just before lunch. Had a drink in the Mess. Everybody extremely friendly. An excellent lunch – food much better than at the 108.

Mary's convalescence allowed her to socialise and enjoy life in Brussels for a brief time before she returned to the 108 at the end of March.

23 March

Saw the MO this morning. Am definitely to be discharged on Tuesday or Wednesday. The Convalescent Home is closing down in a few weeks.

This is another sunny day. I can just see a farmer ploughing with his team of horses, a few fields away. There are a few seagulls hovering around and they swoop down gracefully now and again to catch the fat wriggling worms. I love the smell of newly ploughed earth.

We had a farewell dinner here last night. There were several brass hats present but nevertheless it was most enjoyable, very friendly and informal.

25 March

Gee came here to visit me yesterday morning. Eric drove us all back to Brussels for lunch and afterwards he took me to Louvain to say farewell to St Pierre and Soeur Marie-Anselma. The Officers' Club is closed down, but it was a strange nostalgic feeling to wander again along the familiar cobbled streets. Wonder if M and I will ever be together in Louvain again.

Am returning to the 108 tomorrow. It is going to be difficult to adapt to a normal routine after all this delightful leisure. Am writing this outside the lounge facing the lake and can just see the narrow stretch of water between the trees. If I close my eyes I can imagine the sea down there, stretching away to the horizon, smell the salt tang of the air and hear the rumbling of the breakers dashing against the rocks.

26 March

Discharged from the Convalescent Home.

31 March, 108 BGH, Brussels

Am writing this on duty while waiting for a patient to come round from an anaesthetic. Hank is an American detective who was chasing a suspected murderer through the streets of Brussels last night, and became involved in a frightful jeep accident. He has fractured both legs and some ribs.

The ward is very busy as usual, but it is the problem of communication that makes life rather trying at times. My ward orderlies at the moment are Belgian women and a few German men. They do not understand each other and I do not understand them. The women are Flemish speaking and always in a flap. The German orderlies are surly and unco-operative, but reasonably efficient at times.

8 April

Tonight I start night duty again. It is going to be difficult to sleep through this lovely sunshine but at least I shall have the semblance of more free time. Two nights off each fortnight is very inadequate really, as one becomes so unbearably tired.

11 April

Commenced night duty on Tuesday and have been working and sleeping alternately since then. There are only four Night Sisters to cover the whole hospital. I am running the surgical block, including officers, at present. The wards are widely separated, which means that most of the night is spent walking from one ward to another and checking drips, giving drugs and antibiotics and supervising post-operative patients. I love it and all the patients in at the moment are absolute darlings. This is a lovely moonlight night. The peacefulness of the whole scene is almost incredible when contrasted with the noise and bustle of the day.

There is some kind of vague charm about tip-toeing round a quiet ward of sleeping people, people who are blissfully unconscious of their day-time worries and anxieties, and then going out across the quadrangle into the quiet night, where the moon with her cold, unreal beauty transforms the whole scene and makes one hold one's breath for fear of destroying the magic of it all. I like night duty because there are always moments when one can stand and stare or think and dream.

Tonight I am thinking of M and the uncertainty of our future together. We have no money and no home. We both realise the difficulties and responsibilities that lie ahead of us. We want our marriage to be everything in the world to us and we have to consider our unborn children. We must be able to give them the things in life that they have a right to have. I suppose we could be married and wait to have a family until we could afford them, but that is not very simple. I have a religious and natural repugnance for artificial birth control. It seems wrong and it destroys the beauty and spontaneity that there should be in the physical relationship between two people who love each other.

Tonight I feel grateful for all the lovely people whom I have met in my life, friends whom I never want to lose.

12 April

There were four letters from M in my pigeonhole this morning. The APO seems to be making a habit of collecting several of his letters and then dispatching them all at once. Poor M. He is being posted to command the 94th Club in Düsseldorf. It is an enormous place and he is so obviously the wrong person for the job. It will be so artificial and noisy, no time for painting and poetry, and so far away from the peace of the countryside, which he loves.

Have been told that this has been a lovely sunny day. On night duty one has the alternative of missing either sleep or sunshine, so it is usually the latter.

14 April

It is now exactly midnight and all my patients are asleep. The orderly is making the inevitable cup of tea in the kitchen, and so far everything is quiet and peaceful.

We are commencing the evacuation of the patients from here on the 23rd and should be closed down by the end of this month. Our postings should start coming through then.

Gee woke me up at three o'clock this afternoon and literally dragged me out to tea. Was so tired that I was sitting down in Smiths eating waffles before I really woke up. Brussels was hot, stuffy, and over-crowded. It was one of those days that make me long for a pair of sandals and a cool linen frock. Collars and ties and berets are too much. How lovely it will be to dress in civilian clothes again, the joy and comfort of feeling like an individual, having the choice of colour and style. Khaki is particularly depressing in weather such as this.

16 April

There is a Polish patient here who has been very depressed recently and suddenly threatened suicide. Have been talking to him for nearly two hours (with the aid of a sleepy interpreter). We both know that he has no intention of doing anything drastic, but I could be wrong and dare not take the risk. This man seems to be suffering from an endogenous type of depression: he knows it is unreasonable to feel this way, yet there is no way in which he can help himself. He is to be demobbed soon and will be returning to his family in Poland. I always try to resist the temptation to tell a man in this situation to snap out of it or cheer up. This type of reaction merely adds to their feeling of guilt, and increases the depth of depression.

An emergency call came through from E Ward on the other side of the quadrangle and, as it was pouring with rain, I grabbed a ground sheet to put over my shoulders. The emergency was a fifty-year-old sergeant with severe chest pains – a possible coronary. I gave him some morphia and stayed until the MO arrived, still in his pyjamas and looking pleasantly dishevelled. Sgt James was sitting up and feeling much better by then.

The American detective has made an excellent recovery and is to be discharged tomorrow on crutches.

19 April

Sgt James is quite well tonight. He is a regular soldier and told me earlier that he was one of the hated 'Black and Tans' in Ireland in 1916. Told him that my father was one of the Sinn

Féin who was on the run. They seem to have had an exciting time all round.

20 April

Private Smith, my chatty cockney orderly, is a wizard with food. He disappears down to the kitchen every night and re-emerges with a practically cordon bleu meal. Tonight I had two fried eggs, chips, tomatoes and mushrooms. I did not dare query their origin as I know only too well that the official meal is bully beef, beetroot and dehydrated potato.

21 April

Easter Sunday. What lovely childhood memories it conjures up – arising early to watch the sun dance as it comes up on the horizon (an old Irish custom). Wish I had something new to wear. We are now permitted to wear civilian clothes occasionally.

This will be our last night duty session at the 108. In a couple of weeks we shall be posted around Germany.

22 April

A lovely surprise this evening, M telephoned, but I wish we had not been cut off so abruptly. There were dozens of things to say but I foolishly could not think of them in the excitement of hearing his voice.

25 April, 4 a.m.

Was very peeved to find myself in charge of the whole hospital tonight. What a night it has been, admissions and theatre cases on the surgical side and people having attacks of cardiac asthma and epilepsy on the medical wards. Trying to cope with the Belgian volunteer nurses on the Women's Ward was bad enough, but the German orderlies were even more dense than usual. Things should be better tomorrow night, as there are several sea evacuations to the UK tomorrow and another Sister coming on duty.

This is a brilliant starlight night, the air dry and crisp. Jemmie, our lovely Persian pussy, likes to accompany me on my rounds. She watches with interest while I give the penicillins etc. but tonight she was extremely naughty. She jumped on to the bed of one of our more excitable Polish patients, who yelled that he was being attacked or the equivalent in his language, and within a matter of seconds the ward was a hubbub of noise and chatter – all this at 4.20 a.m.

Time seems to go on endlessly on night duty, one loses track of dates and even the days of the week. It is a sort of active hibernation – unless that is a contradiction in terms.

1 May

Our postings came through today. I am to go to 25 BGH in Münster. It is disappointing that I shall not be nearer to M but Matron told me today that 77 is closing down and 6 BGH is being reduced to two hundred beds.

The majority of the others are going to Berlin, Hamburg or Hanover and a few to a FDS [Field Dressing Station] in Calais. We are all being widely separated. Gee left for Berlin last night. I shall miss her.

I shall probably be leaving here after night duty ends on the 7th. 25 BGH is about 50 kilometres from M, but at least it is better than Berlin or India.

Tonight as I looked out of my window at the cherry blossom and lilac in full bloom and the church spires of Brussels in the distance, I felt just a little sad at leaving here, my friends and all the happy memories of the past year.

2 May

A ladybird has just walked across this paper – that means good luck. A lovely letter from M. He is to have a temporary acting promotion to Captain and is being posted to Hamburg as Public Relations Officer for Hamburg district. He will be working closely with the British Forces Network there, writing up stories of a local boy makes good angle and feeding material to the BFN and various newspapers in the UK. It sounds quite creative and interesting, far more suitable for him than managing the 94th Club.

6 May

This is my last night on duty here. It seems almost too wonderful to realise that I shall be able to sleep tomorrow night.

Am suffering from brain fog at the moment. Have just completed an article for the *Nursing Mirror* on 'Why so many nursing recruits leave the profession before completing their training'. It is doubtful if my strong views on the subject will be published, but I enjoyed getting it off my chest. I blame the attitude of so many hospital Matrons towards young nurses. These Matrons are in my opinion too often dogmatic, autocratic and totally lacking in sympathetic understanding.

The 108 is gradually assuming a sad, neglected atmosphere. The almost empty wards look cold and unfriendly after the crowds of noisy, jovial patients who have passed through. It would be much better to close quickly, this slow demise is painful.

8 May

The movement order came through this afternoon. Am leaving here on Friday 10th and should reach 25 BGH by Saturday afternoon.

Today is the anniversary of VE Day. I was sitting in the little Mess at St Pierre then listening to the church bells and watching the flags through the window. How this year has flown by.

A letter from M. He is most anxious to speed up our wedding day. Wish we were together to discuss our marriage. This is such a big decision. My only reason for wishing to postpone our marriage is that we might have a baby before we could afford to save enough money for a home. There is a form of birth control based on the ovulation period which is allowed by the Catholic Church, but we would have to discuss these things carefully.

The sky is so blue this evening. I wonder if M is watching it too. My one ambition is to make him happy, to understand him and share everything in our lives together.

Six

'It is good to be out of khaki'
Germany

A home in Hamburg

12 May 1946, 25 BGH, Münster

We left the 108 at midnight on the 10th, went to Schaerbeek and waited there until 2 a.m. when the train came in from Calais and already over-crowded with leave personnel. The journey was far from comfortable and it was impossible to sleep or read, but the sun began to rise at 4.30 a.m. and it was fascinating to watch the countryside in the roseate glow of early morning. We flashed across the Belgian frontier and into the flat Dutch terrain dotted here and there with old windmills.

We reached Krefeld at 9.20 a.m. and had an excellent breakfast of bacon and eggs. I was reprimanded by the RTO [Rail Transport Officer] there for giving away my stale sandwiches and some issue chocolate to the German children who were asking for bread and looked thin and hungry. I do not see why I should not give these children food that would otherwise be thrown away. These children shocked me and it was another shock to see the appalling destruction of the towns and cities on our way to Münster. The problem of finding accommodation for the homeless must be tremendous.

Arrived in Münster at 2 p.m. The others went on to Berlin and Hamburg. The whole place here is uncanny, just masses of ruined buildings and hungry dogs, cats and children. The sun was shining brilliantly and everything was so quiet and dead. I wandered about the ruined streets while waiting for transport to the hospital. It was utterly depressing. I was relieved to come away from there and out into the country. The hospital is about half an hour's journey from the railway station and the surrounding countryside, although rather flat, looks wooded and attractive.

Our Mess here is rather shattering by contrast with the luxury, comfort and spaciousness of the 108. Am sharing a room with three other Sisters and by the time I had put my luggage into my allocated area of space, it was impossible to turn around. We haven't any cupboards and spend a great deal of time frantically diving in and out of trunks in search of various garments. We also have to lock everything away as there is a notorious burglar around. He apparently goes into the bedrooms while people are sleeping and steals cigarettes or anything of value, as there are not any locks on the doors. We barricade our doors at night with trunks piled on top of each other. The bed next to mine is occupied by a Theatre Sister who is on call during the night and each time they come to call her, there is a terrific upheaval of banging and scraping chairs and the removal of the door barricades. Throughout this zarabanda there are people falling over things and keeping up a most irritating conversation in loud whispers. It is certainly eventful.

The Sisters here are in constant dread of their boyfriends being posted elsewhere as there aren't any cinemas or theatres or even a shop. We are not allowed out without a male escort. What an embarrassing situation, to be at the mercy of a mere male to take one out for a walk – rather like a dog.

The farmhouses here and the cows grazing in the fields remind me of home. There is a pond beneath my window here, with two ducks floating about aimlessly. 'Two ducks on a pond, a green field beyond'. The Matron here is very pleasant. She has put me in charge of the Resuscitation Ward – all accidents and seriously or dangerously ill cases. There are only six patients at present but they are very ill and require very intensive nursing care.

15 May

Have started German classes and am just as enthusiastic as I was about French last April. The tutor is an ex-Wehrmacht officer with a rather attractive aesthetic appearance. He speaks English with a slow, concise accent, a rather formal, correct man in his forties. Herr von Stroehem is also very fond of bowing and clicking his heels on every possible occasion. The execution of all these polite formalities takes so much time that we do not seem to be making much progress with my German. The most startling thing about this man is that occasionally, without moving a muscle of those aquiline features, he comes out with the most astonishing American slang. He spent two years as a POW with the Yanks, and genuinely believes that the correct expression for a person in higher authority is a 'big cheese'. What a guttural language it is – worse than Gaelic. Hate having to make queer noises in my throat while trying to pronounce their Rs.

18 May

M arrived at 5 p.m. on a motorcycle. He looked tired and scruffy – lovely to see him. I found him a bed in the ward and put some screens around. This is all very unofficial. Hope I am not found out.

Went for a ride on the back of M's motorbike. It was great fun but terribly bumpy. The roads are full of pot holes. We were laughing at the bumps when suddenly there was a terrific thunderstorm. The rain came down in a deluge and we were soaked by the time we reached the hospital. I managed to find some dry clothes (an old suit of blues for M, which looked hilarious) and we sat in front of the window listening to the patter of the raindrops. There was a strange hush in the darkness outside and then quite suddenly a bird began to sing. It must have been a nightingale. It is impossible to describe the exquisitely beautiful sound. It was for me one of the few most perfect moments, which are as intangible as life itself. Our perfect moment was rudely shattered a few minutes later as the three other girls came off duty. Poor M had to go downstairs to his ward bed. There is no accommodation here for visitors, yet we are severely penalised if a boyfriend is found anywhere near a Sister's bedroom, regardless of how over-crowded with other Sisters that room may be.

27 May

This hospital used to be a Wehrmacht HQ and yesterday I found a map of the South of England in a cupboard in the ward. It is, I think, not quite the same as the one I came across in Poix. That particular map was never returned to me so I was delighted to find this one.

On opening it out and examining it carefully I find that it is a remarkably accurate chart of Southern England. Every city, town and hamlet is clearly marked, although some place names are misspelt. It shows the major British defensive positions, sea depths and approaches to the coast. The coast of Kent was marked in red as were several other coastal areas. The chart bears the stamp of the Oberkommando der Kriegsmarine, Admiral Doenitz. Felt very grateful that the war was over.

3 June

My leave allocation has come through, commencing on Saturday next. Hope M will be able to obtain leave at the same time. We shall miss all the excitement of the Victory Parade. It will probably be a most interesting and spectacular scene, but I feel that in view of the sad state of chaos and food shortages in Germany and England, the whole thing might be rather ostentatious and distasteful. How can the British taxpayer celebrate with his inadequate ration book?

On leave together at last, Mary and Malcolm set off for a camping and cycling holiday in the Cotswolds.

9 June, Richmond

Arrived Victoria at 5 p.m. M, his father and brother were there to meet me – very tired – lovely to be on leave with M.

11 June

Bought our camping kit and helped to fix up the bicycles – very exciting. Went for a walk with M across Sheen Common, one of his boyhood haunts.

13 June

Commenced on our cycle tour. Went through Maidenhead along the Great Western Road. Pitched our tent in an isolated spot outside Reading. Sheep and cows in the field and a little babbling brook close by.

This tent is our first home and we have christened her Mrs Walters so that we can truthfully say to the family at home that we have stayed with Mrs Walters. Very happy.

14 June

Woke up in our lovely little tent to hear the cry of a cuckoo and a cock crowing in the distance. We splashed each other in the brook, and had a hilarious time trying to cook breakfast on the tommy cooker.

The sun was shining as we cycled through to Charlton, but it started to rain quite soon. It poured and poured, and we sang as we peddled along to keep our spirits up. We could not find a field to pitch our tent, but the friendly landlord of a small country pub took pity on us and said that we could camp on his chicken run. He obviously had not consulted his hens, for they made a frightful rumpus as I helped M to erect the tent. We laughed until the tears got mixed up with the rain pouring down our faces. It was happiness to lie close together listening to the patter of the rain on the canvas roof, and the angry squawking hens outside. Was so happy that M yelling 'Don't touch the inside of the tent or the rain will come through' was just a part of the great adventure of our green tented paradise.

15 June

Cycled through Chipping Norton and Moreton-in-Marsh – lovely West Country names. Raining as usual. We camped in a super spot on top of one of the Cotswold Hills. It was blissfully peaceful – apart from the intrusion of an inquisitive cow at 2 a.m. She pushed her head through the tent flap to have a look at us and then went away.

17 June

A warm sunny day. Posed for M while he did a sketch of me. Cycled along to Worcester. It was such bliss to ride along the almost empty roads with M beside me – the sun on my face – a gentle breeze blowing through my hair and inside me such a feeling of perfect happiness. In future years if we ever feel that we are becoming too dull and sedentary we shall take 'Mrs Walters' with us and go right out in the country, far away from petty conventions and irritations, and in the quietness of our little tent we shall again see life in its true perspective and re-capture the magic loveliness of being alive and together in a beautiful world. I want M to stay as happy as he is today – unconventional, not too self-confident or too worldly wise.

18 June

Caught the 12.15 p.m. train from Worcester to Paddington and cycled from there to Richmond. The end of our perfect holiday. We shall always remember the lovely days when we cycled across England discovering the Cotswold Hills, the Vale of Evesham and the hamlets clustered along the Thames – the clean breath of fresh country air, and the magic of nights spent in the cosy warmth of our little green home.

21 June

M came with me to Victoria Station. Caught the midday train to Dover. His train leaves Liverpool Street at 2 p.m.

On her return, Mary was once again immersed in twelve-hour days.

22 June, 25 BGH, Münster

Have just arrived here feeling tired, dirty and missing M very much.

23 June

It is strangely peaceful here tonight and the steady patter of the raindrops on this window makes me long for the warm, intimate cosiness of our little tent. I loved to lie beside M in the greenish semi-darkness and listen to the rain and the birds and the rustle of the leaves on the trees. It was another world.

We are very short of Sisters here. Have been on duty twelve hours today – nobody to take over the ward.

25 June

Back on Resuscitation. We are extremely busy and under-staffed. This is a small intensive care unit, twelve beds in all. They are mainly accident cases, dispatch riders with the Royal Signal Corps. The roads are lethal around here, full of pot holes and other hidden hazards. These young soldiers do drive their motorcycles very fast and the results can be extremely tragic. Nine of my patients are on blood transfusions, all are bed-cases on traction for broken legs etc., and almost completely immobile. Most of them have also suffered severe head injuries.

28 June, Möhne Zee

M arrived at 2 p.m. with a borrowed jeep. We arrived here at tea time and are staying at the Officers' Club. Went canoeing after dinner. It was great fun and such a beautiful sunset.

29 June

Hired a sailing dinghy after breakfast and went out on the lake. The boat was over canvassed and rather frisky and as the wind got up we found it more difficult to handle her. We sailed on her ear, leaning as far out as possible, but we almost capsized several times. Had a nasty bang on my head from the boom as we went about. It was all very exhilarating.

It is lovely here – very difficult to associate it with the 'dam-busting' operation.*

2 July

Have a bedroom of my own at last. It looked very empty and dreary yesterday when I first saw it – just four bare walls, and a little iron bedstead – rather like a cell, but at least a cell of my own. I went to the Quartermaster and persuaded him to give me a wardrobe, a table and a chair. It looks much better now and I can unpack my trunk at last. The window faces west and I shall be able to watch the sunset each evening after duty.

---

* The Möhne Zee dam was the site of the dam-busting operation led by Wing Commander Guy Gibson in May 1943.

6 July

There was a great flap here this morning. I almost burnt the place down. Was sterilising small dressing bowls by lighting them with methylated spirit over the Bunsen burner, when suddenly a large dish containing instruments in spirit went up in flames. It was terrifying – the orderly rang the fire alarm and there were people shouting 'Fire', the patients I think. I quickly closed the nearest window and threw sand and a blanket over the flaming dish, and just as half the hospital arrived to view the excitement it went out quite peacefully. The fire picket crew arrived half an hour later complete with hoses and all the paraphernalia.

The patients were superb, most of them remaining calm. Thank God they are OK. There will probably be an official enquiry and I shall be reprimanded for negligence.

9 July

M's posting as PRO [Public Relations Officer] to the Hamburg District has come through. Have applied for a seventy-two-hour leave there on 9 August.

13 July

Went shopping in Enschede again yesterday. For some inexplicable reason we are the only unit allowed a pass across the frontier. One of the men obtained the currency for me as usual. It is amusing to see the way they do this – they have that furtive black-market look written all over their faces. Some of them trade directly in cigarettes, using them as currency. I did not buy very much, just some lace mats and lots of fruit. I listened to some extraordinary tales of big-time black marketing. An RAMC Major alleged that he had bought a luxury sailing yacht in Kiel, purchased with cigarettes and whisky, and an RAF Officer said that he took home a baby grand piano in his aeroplane. The spoils of war I suppose, but it is astonishing how quickly greed makes criminals of us all. There are people going on leave every day who are exchanging more marks into sterling than they could have earned legally in a year. The authorities seem to have discovered what is going on at last, and we are to have a special currency, BAFS [British Armed Forces banknotes], in the future. That should put an end to the fiddling with marks.

The black market is still thriving of course, and it was amusing to see how like a Sunday School outing the bus seemed on the way back, people chattering away, eating fruit and looking excitedly at each other's purchases.

Food is very plentiful in Enschede – some people had a whole chicken each for their dinner.

There was an amusing incident on the frontier on our return journey. The Dutch guards came on the bus quite unexpectedly to check our identity cards and to my horror I realised that I did not have any identification with me. There were a few panic-stricken moments while I had visions of being detained under suspicion and thrown into a Dutch jail, but just at the crucial moment somebody, realising my predicament, casually dropped a Red Cross card at my feet. I guessed at once that the guards could not read English and with a hopeful smile presented a card identifying myself as John Henry Campbell. The guard looked at it with what he presumably thought was a wise and intelligent expression, nodded and passed me on. I was very grateful for the quick-wittedness of J. H. Campbell.

21 July

M has just received his third pip. It may be 'temporary acting and provisional' but at least it is not unpaid and we need the extra money.

I miss him very much and wish it were possible for me to

be posted to Hamburg. 94 BGH is on the outskirts of the city but there is little hope of getting there. Some of the girls here applied for postings elsewhere six months ago, and they are still here. 25 is notoriously the dead end of BAOR and it seems to be a case of 'abandon hope all ye who enter here'.

We have two very ill men on the ward at present. Sgt Hodgson has multiple injuries and sadly is unlikely to recover. They are both on the danger list. Private Johnson has a fractured skull and has been unconscious now for nearly three weeks. They are both on drip feeds. Was furious with the orderly today as he talked about Private Johnson's 'poor chance' while standing at his bedside. Why do so many people assume that an unconscious patient is unable to hear what we are saying? How awful to be unable to speak and hear somebody say that you're dying. The horror of that situation is intolerable.

Have been on duty all day, and as I sit here holding Sgt Hodgson's hand I feel tired, sad and lonely, and remember some of the lines from Walter de la Mare, 'Look thy last on all things lovely'. This man has a wife and two small babies. Why is life so wretched?

23 July

What a day this has been. Have just staggered off duty at 10 p.m. having started at 7 a.m. Sgt Hodgson died at 7.30 a.m. and my first duty was to lay him out. He looked so young. I have written to his wife.

Private Johnson has some eye pupil reaction at last, which is a good sign. We can only hope that he is not brain damaged.

I had to have my compulsory jabs at 10 a.m. (TAB and typhus). They made me feel quite ghastly and then Matron came flapping around to say that the General and some Brigadiers are doing an inspection tomorrow – and the place 'must be spotless'. The military mind seems to have an obsession with tidiness. It may be a type of insecurity, I suppose.

I've had a new orderly on with me today, a gentle, timid private in the Pioneer Corps. The poor boy was so petrified by the blood transfusions and nasty accident cases that he is asking to return to his unit tomorrow.

There were four very bad accident cases brought in this afternoon. There was so much blood everywhere that the place looked like a slaughter house. The main problem is trying to reassure these boys. They are usually screaming with terror.

25 July

There is a most exciting thunderstorm at the moment, loud crashes of thunder, brilliant streaks of lightning, and rain pouring straight out of the skies. It is so cool and refreshing, such a blessed relief from the sultry heat of last night.

Am a patient on Officers' Ward at the moment. It is not very serious, just a rather painful infection of the antrum, which I may have picked up on Resuscitation Ward. Colonel Hearn insisted on me resting here for a few days, much to Matron's annoyance. Have just had my head X-rayed – quite interesting really as I watched the plate being developed afterwards, and was able to see the shadow that indicated an infection of the sinus.

Two letters from M. He seems to be having an interesting time as PRO for Hamburg. It must be great fun poking one's nose around (in the name of the Press), finding out how various places are run and meeting interesting people. I would love it as it would be an excuse for endless curiosity.

27 July

Have applied to spend my seventy-two-hour leave at the Atlantic Hotel in Hamburg. M writes to say that he has been looking round the docks in Hamburg. I love the sea ports, the variety of old tugs and boats of every description, the romance and excitement of ships that travel all over the world. As a child

I watched the great Atlantic liners going out of Galway Bay en route for the distant land of America. Despite the anguish of weeping relatives on the quayside, I watched the big ships disappear over the horizon and made up my own exciting fairy tales about the people living in those far-off lands.

1 August

Back on duty on Resuscitation. The patients were delighted to see me. The ward is not quite so busy today, and most of the boys are improving.

Came off duty at 5 p.m. and as some of the other girls were in the Mess we decided to liven up the evening by having a dress rehearsal in my bedroom. This is all in preparation for the big night of our dance. It was great fun, putting in darts, lengthening and shortening hems, pirouetting in front of the mirror, etc. The noise and chattering was deafening. We are all wearing evening dress tomorrow night. I have managed to borrow a simple, stunning Grecian frock and it will be so exciting to wear evening dress for the first time in so many years.

2 August

Wish M could be here for our dance tonight. Have been helping to decorate the Mess this afternoon. It looks marvellous, lots of flowers and tropical palms etc. The food, too, is super, masses of cooked chickens and hams, and great bowls of colourful fruit making delightful table centres.

4 August

Our dance was a great success. The band was excellent and played all my favourite waltzes and tangos, including 'Jealousy'.

The profusion of flowers and pretty dresses blended beautifully with the men's dress uniform, and the addition of a warm moonlight night lent an atmosphere of gaiety and animation. The music and dancing drifted out of the French doors and across the lawn to the lake. I thoroughly enjoyed myself. The men were amusing and attractive and best of all they complimented me on my dress (the simplest there). I do love a little flirtatious blarney and flattery now and again – find it quite stimulating in fact.

Received a letter from Gee from Berlin this morning. She had nights off last week and managed to obtain some transport and a driver to take her sightseeing. Anyway, for some inexplicable reason she found herself in the Russian zone. The car was stopped and she was yanked out and marched at bayonet point to the Area Commandant's office. Nobody there could speak English or German and she was detained in a cell for six hours without food or drink until an interpreter arrived. The interpreter managed to disentangle the muddle, but the Russians needed a great deal of persuasion to accept the fact that Gee and her driver were not spies. Needless to say, Gee enjoyed the incident. She is always happiest in awkward situations.

15 August

Another letter from M with the proposal that we should be married in England, probably in October. Wedding dresses are impossible to obtain so I had the bright idea of writing to Gainsborough Studios [London film studios] and pleading with them to allow me to hire one of their Elizabethan gowns.

17 August

A letter from M enclosing printed instructions under the heading of 'Marriage'! I never realised that getting married entailed such a lot of fuss. We shall be in a state of mental and physical exhaustion by the time it is over. How annoying it seems that we are destined to live our lives according to so many rules and regulations. Must we spend all our lives conforming from the cradle to the grave? I shall never make a good conventional citizen. It must be the rebel blood of my ancestors that makes me so antagonistic to an ordered, routine way of life. I shall probably be a most inefficient housewife, will refuse to do washing on Mondays, and will be ridiculously annoyed with M if he always hangs his coat on the same peg.

18 August

Have a ticket for the Military Tattoo in Dortmund on Thursday next. Am looking forward to seeing it. The unit is providing transport.

Applied for marriage leave today as from 7 October. I would like to spend a few days at home with my Auntie before we are married, as it may be a long time before I have the opportunity of seeing her afterwards.

21 August

We are extremely busy on the ward at present. There is the usual shortage of Sisters, no relief for off duty, so it is once again a twelve-hour day. It is difficult really as I have so much planning to do and so many letters to write.

Am feeling a little frightened of all the fuss and rituals, but then I remember it is M I am marrying and everything is alright again. Will he be able to put up with having me around for the rest of his life? It is a long sentence.

Received a charming letter from Gainsborough Studios. They will allow me to hire the white Elizabethan gown worn by Flora Robson in her recent film. There is also a beautiful full-length veil, which sounds marvellous.

2 September, Night Duty on the Officers' Ward

Feel rather depressed tonight. The twelve-hour night duty is so long. I feel desperately empty and lonely. It is foolish to be like this but I love M so much that I can't bear to be away from him. I should hate to become the type of wife who completely monopolises her husband. I always want him to have complete freedom in all his interests. His happiness and well-being is very important to me. Will I be able to make him happy? My mind is a whirl of contradictions tonight as I sit here in the dimly lit ward. Wish he were here to talk to me. I want to be so many things that I am not.

Thank God we are to be married soon. It is so difficult and unnatural for us to be separated physically when we love each other so much. M is such a perfect lover, so unselfish and full of laughter and with a wonderful delicacy and understanding. He understands me so well, my quick changes of mood, sometimes even the fleeting thoughts that go through my mind. He is the one person in the world with whom I am in complete harmony.

It is now 5 a.m. My patients are still sleeping and I can see the first streaks of dawn on the horizon. Suddenly I am unaccountably happy. The dawn is so wonderfully symbolic of everything that is new, fresh and hopeful in life. The morning of our wedding day will make me feel this way.

8 September

Still on night duty. The ward is very busy and there is only one orderly. Private Smith, RAMC orderly, is a lovely quick-witted cockney, but just lately he has been coming on duty yawning his head off. Discovered the reason for his permanent state of exhaustion tonight. He and some friends have managed to wangle some transport and instead of sleeping during the day as all good night orderlies should, he and his friends have been swanning, that is travelling round the factories all day armed with cigarettes and booze and buying under the counter. Private Smith tells me that they have stacks of loot hidden away, everything from dress material to cameras and watches. The black market over here is becoming big business. Told him that my business was to see that he was in a fit state to look after the patients.

21 September

My marriage leave commences tomorrow. M and I spent most of the day making exciting and wonderful plans.

Mary travelled to London ahead of Malcolm to begin preparations for her wedding and honeymoon.

23 September, London

It was good to see and smell England again – never realised before what individual smells countries have got.

London loomed into view about 8 p.m. It looked so ghostly in the semi-darkness. This city gives me a strange mixture of feelings, loneliness and fear, and yet pride and wonder at the stupendous bigness of it all. Am staying in a Club near Victoria.

24 September

Dug out my mufti. It is good to be out of khaki. Lunched with [Malcolm's sister] Dorothy and M's father and afterwards went out to the Studios in Shepherd's Bush. My Elizabethan wedding dress will not be available until 8 October (cutting things fine as we are to be married four days later), but I found an attractive bridesmaid dress for Dorothy.

25 September

Spent most of this morning chasing around the West End of
London on the back of a motorcycle. He was a most terrifying
driver. We missed buses, taxis and pedestrians by inches, and
turned corners on one wheel. Never have I been more scared
in my life. He told me that he used to be a wall-of-death per-
former before the war, as if I had not guessed!

The reason for all this gallivanting is that I need to have
special papers made out at the ATS HQ in order to travel to
Ireland. I went to the usual place in Gower Street but they had
moved, so I found the RTO [Railway Transport Officer] and
he gave me another address. Anyway the address was incor-
rect but when I arrived there some REME [Royal Engineers]
chaps were fixing something or other. My desperation must
have been apparent by then, for they made the astonishing
remark that they knew where ATS HQ was but did not know
the address. One of them offered to take me there, hence the
hair-raising motorcycle ride. He did find the HQ and I had
my papers made out – then dashed out to Richmond on the
District Line to see the local Registrar in Sheen Road. What
a depressing-looking place. I sat on a hard chair for nearly an
hour, looking at a wall covered with notices informing people
of the dire consequences of neglecting to register a birth, death
or marriage. There were half-a-dozen unhappy-looking people
sitting there also, and I quite expected them to burst into tears
at any moment. I never realised how difficult it is to get married – can see why living in sin could appear to be an attractive option. When I eventually saw the Registrar he informed
me dolefully that 11.15 a.m. was the only suitable hour for <u>him</u>
on that particular date. We shall have to catch a later train to
Cornwall (our honeymoon venue) than we had planned.

26 September, Galway

The Irish Sea lived up to its usual reputation. It makes me feel sick just to think about it. The huge waves were washing right over the deck. Arrived feeling forlorn and looking bedraggled. It was 7.30 a.m. but dear Tommy was waiting patiently at the barrier in Westland Row.

After lunch I caught the train for Galway. My Auntie was waiting at Woodlawn with the ass and trap. It was lovely to see her dear old familiar face, so lined with care and laughter and years of hard work. She is such a grand, unselfish person, just happy to be near the people she loves. We had a superb Irish tea when we got home, brown new-laid eggs, fresh wholemeal bread with home-made butter and a dark, rich fruit cake.

7 October

Left Dunleary on the night ferry. Felt very lonely saying good-bye to my Auntie and Tommy. Future homecomings will never be quite the same again.

Marriage is a big change in one's way of life. My upbringing has been that of the average Irish Catholic girl, a strong emphasis on religion and purity of mind and body, yet with a strange freedom from pettiness and interest in trivia. As a child I roamed the fields, coming and going as I pleased. Meal times were completely flexible. We ate when we were hungry, and such things as housework had a very low priority in our lives. The door was always open, and hospitality provided to all, be they tinker, tramp, neighbour or friend. People were important, not possessions. There was little money but a great deal of laughter and simple kindness.

M, on the other hand, comes from a middle-class English family, with the more laissez-faire attitude of the Church of England, yet surrounded by his strictures of nice manners and good behaviour at all times. His home has always been ordered and well cared for, whereas my home has often been a refuge for tinkers and passing tramps. My Auntie believes in acting out her strong Christian principles. Are we perhaps an ill-assorted couple? Will we be able to overcome the problems of our different cultures?

8 October, Richmond

Arrived in Euston at 7 a.m. Met M in King's Cross at 5.30 p.m. Wonderful to see him. Very, very happy.

12 October, Bude, Cornwall

My wedding day. Was almost blown up in the bath by the antiquated gas geyser! Had a leisurely breakfast. The gown is beautiful and the lace veil full length. The car arrived and we reached the church just after 11.15. I forgot to lower the veil over my face as M's father and I walked down the aisle.

M was in uniform and looked terrific, his blond hair shining in the sunshine that came through the stained-glass window. He looked round at me as Uncle Leonard started to play the organ. I shall always remember him as he was at that moment.

The reception was at M's home and everything went extremely well, apart from Auntie Bessie's refusal to allow us to open my bottle of champagne. Arrived here in Bude this evening. It is a lovely spot and we are both deliriously happy.

14 October

Went for a walk along this lovely rocky coast. Slipped on seaweed in my efforts to climb Chapel Rock. M had to carry me over the rocks and hire a car to the nearest Casualty Department. Had an X-ray, nothing broken just a bad sprain.

Discovered on return to our room that M has lost his wallet (probably on the beach) containing £20 and all our sweet coupons.

Mary and Malcolm's wedding day, with Mary
in her dress from the Gainsborough studios.

We are broke now and without a toffee to cheer us up. It could have been worse. I might have had my leg in plaster.

21 October

Went to Tintagel. Saw King Arthur's Castle. Wonderful view from the top of the tall cliff. Had tea and home-made scones in Boscastle. Walked along the famous smoking rock.

There was a letter for me at the hotel forwarded by M's father. It was from Peter, newly returned from Burma – and asking if I might consider marrying him!

22 October

Went to Clovelly, this is a most delightfully quaint place – steep, narrow, cobbled streets leading right down to the little harbour. Walked on to Hartland Quay afterwards, lovely high cliffs. We walked for miles, as M always wants to know what is round the next bend and there were a lot of bends.

This is such a lovely holiday and a wonderful honeymoon. I must be the luckiest girl in the whole world.

26 October, Richmond

Left Bude at 8 a.m. – the end of our very happy honeymoon. Arrived Waterloo at 2.30 p.m. Staying with M's family.

After their honeymoon, Mary and Malcolm travelled back to Germany separately. On her return Mary found out that she would be posted to the 94 BGH in Hamburg, which meant that she and Malcolm would finally be in the same place at the same time. Yet as Malcolm was under twenty-five, the marriageable age for an officer, they were ineligible for married quarters, and faced an ongoing struggle to be able to live together.

1 November, 94 BGH, Hamburg

M met me at the railway station with transport and his driver, Jock. Jock is a stocky cheerful Scot who calls M 'The Gaffer' and is very well in with all the local black-market rackets.

94 BGH is on the outskirts of the city in a semi-rural setting, quite pleasant and apparently spacious grounds. I have a rather bleak single room.

Do hope that M and I can find somewhere to live together. The British Army is refusing to acknowledge that we are married, despite a marriage certificate as proof. The result is that we are NOT allowed married quarters or a marriage allowance. This is because of the age ruling for officers and if M remains in the army our marriage will not be recognised for another four years! M has written to his MP about this. This means that he has broken another regulation – no soldier is permitted to write to his MP. The War Office is totally inflexible and in the meantime we must live apart.

How ironical that M would have been considered old enough to die for his country at eighteen, yet not old enough to marry for another seven years.

2 November

Am in charge of K1, a very international Officers' Ward. We are fairly busy. I have a German-trained nurse as my assistant. She comes from Bavaria and is a very pleasant person and an excellent nurse. She speaks very little English and my German is minimal, but we manage and I think we are going to be friends. Her name is Helda.

Met M this evening and we walked around the lawn. Hamburg is comparatively undamaged in the vicinity of the Alster. There are several large international company buildings that are totally intact. The outskirts of the city, on the other hand, have been severely bombed. The people look pale and depressed. There is a severe food shortage.

3 November

On duty at 1 p.m. The officer patients are very pleasant with the exception of three Russians who are an awful nuisance. They are distrustful and suspicious of everything and everybody. Two of these men are on penicillin three-hourly and each time I have to instruct the interpreter to tell them yet again what the antibiotic is for and why it is necessary for them to have so many injections. It is very exhausting and time wasting. Their table manners too are excruciating. The up patients eat in the Officers' dining room adjoining the ward and, to everybody's amazement, the Russians eat all the cheese on the table. They just grab everything in sight. There are constant incidents, which are a great strain for me. There are two French officers and an American who are particularly intolerant of the Russians' boorish behaviour. The Russians are of high rank and I feel that I am not just a Ward Sister but a mediator in a very delicate diplomatic situation.

We had a new patient in today and to my delight it was Jack Wyper, an old friend from Normandy days. He has a minor infection, nothing serious, but I shall be glad of his support in coping with these voluble officers.

Jack, ranking as a Major, worked as a General Surgeon with the 101 but is in fact an obstetrician, a calling that is not in great demand in a wartime army. He is looking forward to meeting M. We spent ages talking about our Normandy experiences and wondering about friends and where they are now.

13 November

M is still battling away with the War Office in an effort to get them to recognise our marriage. It is ironical that young soldiers (other ranks) are now marrying German girls and are having nice homes provided for them outside the city. Some of these girls are really marrying a British passport and the food and perks that go along with being an army wife.

15 November

Jack Wyper is now recovered and is on the surgical staff here.

15 December

Helda is still terrified of our Russian patients, and I try to protect her from them as much as possible. There is still a great deal of hardship here for the German people. The weather is very cold and there is no fuel for heating. Food is still severely rationed.

17 December

M and I went to the Ravensbrück Trials today. He was there in his official role as HQ Observer Officer.[*]

My first impression was that we were in a theatre. The Judge Advocate sat on the dais (or stage) in full regalia flanked on both sides by senior army officers, probably from the military legal division. The defendants had their own German Counsel. The proceedings were conducted in English, with interpreters to keep the defendants informed.

The army of international journalists scribbled away as first a butch-looking woman went into the dock. She was the type of person we expected to see there, but the next girl, the 'blue

[*] The first of seven trials in Hamburg of the camp staff at Ravensbrück, a concentration camp for women (the trials ran 5 December 1946–3 February 1947). As well as being subjected to starvation and ill-treatment, prisoners at Ravensbrück worked as slave labour for German corporations and underwent quasi-medical experiments. Several of the women Mary would have seen on trial were nurses who had participated in the medical experiments and brutality at the camp.

angel', was quite different, with long dark hair and a very glamorous appearance. The trials go on.

1 January 1947

Saw the New Year in at the Four Seasons Hotel. We had a wonderful evening as there were lots of our friends there. Wonder what 1947 will hold in store for M and me – still no hope of married quarters or even a room that we could share.

6 January

The weather is bitterly cold here, heavy snow and black ice. We had dinner at the Atlantic and afterwards walked across the frozen Alster in the moonlight. It was so beautiful and so cold. There are ten-foot walls of snow and the army three-ton lorries are crossing the ice-covered Alster as if it was a public highway.

Came back here to the hospital on the train this evening. I was very conscious of the cold, hungry misery of the German people. I feel particularly sorry for the children and feel that the international military government could and should do far more to help.

10 January

M has his office in the Four Seasons (HQ Hamburg District). They are a small, jolly unit. Sergeant Covey, an excellent photographer, Sergeant Clarke, who helps to find material for writing up, Lotte, M's German secretary, and Jock, his driver.

The band was playing 'Die Fledermaus' as we walked into the Atlantic Hotel for dinner. Odette Churchill* was sitting at

---

* Born in France, Odette Churchill (née Brailly, formerly Sansom, later Hallowes) moved to Britain in 1933. In 1940 she joined the Special Operations Executive (SOE) and was sent to France in 1942 to work with the French resistance. She and a colleague, Peter Churchill, were betrayed by a double-agent. Although they were not married at the time (they married in 1947), she used the name to persuade her

a table near the window with several young subalterns in tow. M had interviewed her yesterday morning. She almost looks too fragile to be a war heroine.

16 January

I am pregnant or at least I think I am. Will tell M this evening.

Our short leave starts tomorrow evening. We are going to Berlin. Feel happy and yet rather frightened. We have so little money and no home. If only the War Office would recognise our marriage, we could look forward to having our baby without anxiety. A pregnant woman needs many things, but particularly good food, fresh milk and fruit. Most of our food comes out of tins and, as fresh fruit and milk are unobtainable, I shall have to manage without them.

18 January, Berlin

Dear M, I told him that I was pregnant on our way here last night. He was genuinely pleased, and cheerfully optimistic as usual.

Arrived here at breakfast time. The city is an awful mess, so much bomb damage. M took photographs. It is far worse than London. We went out to visit the Stadium – the erstwhile stage for Hitler's strutting and posturing in the Olympics of 1938. What a lot has happened since then. It is a magnificent place, over four-hundred acres of deserted snow-covered ground.

It is bitterly cold here too – heavy snowfalls everywhere and the people look so cold and dejected. It is very embarrassing to see proud people begging for cigarettes.

German captors that they were related to Winston Churchill and saved them both from execution. Tortured by the Gestapo and sent to Ravensbrück camp, she was subsequently an important witness at the Ravensbrück and the Nuremberg Trials.

19 January

Wandered around this ruined city most of the day. It is now jointly administered by the four ruling powers. We had to show our identity cards each time we travelled from one zone to another. The heart of Berlin lies in what is now the Russian sector, but so much is destroyed. This was the centre of the metropolis – Berlin on the Spree – and it was here between the Brandenburg Gate (still standing), the Friedrichstrasse and Alexanderplatz that the life of the city pulsated. The elegant buildings, consulates, embassies, universities, banks are razed to the ground. The only life and sound here this evening is the clatter of a rifle as the Russian soldiers change their guard. These Russians are very surly and took their time before permitting us to go through.

Feeling rather ill and depressed this afternoon. It is still snowing.

20 January

Went on another tour this morning but this time by car. We drove down the Unter den Linden. The University is still standing, but a mere shell of a building. Went to Lustgarten via the Dome Cathedral (designed by Raschdorff). Was saddened to see the amount of damage done to this beautiful edifice. Most of the buildings here were destroyed by Russian shells. We walked through the Reichstag and went below to look at the bunkers. This building, once the scene of important decisions in German politics, is now a very impressive skeleton.

21 January, Hamburg

Returned here at 6 a.m. The journey by train was bitterly cold and very uncomfortable. Feeling very sick and feverish.

22 January

Came on duty this morning feeling far more ill than any of the patients. We had a new man in this afternoon. He was found by the Military Police unconscious in the snow. They thought he was drunk and brought him in here. He was wearing a khaki uniform with ENSA on the shoulder lapels. He did not smell of alcohol, so the MO asked me to take a blood sample and have it tested. The resulting blood sugar was so low that we realised at once that he must be a diabetic and in an insulin coma. We gave him intravenous sugar and he regained consciousness dramatically. His name is George and he is the Controller of ENSA in Hamburg. I put him on a stabilising diet, and asked why he did not carry some lumps of sugar in his pocket in case of an emergency such as today, when he was unable to obtain a meal. He promised to do so in future, but he will remain here for at least a week in order to get his diet and insulin properly stabilised. He is a very pleasant, amiable man in his mid-forties. It was fortunate that he was found so promptly by the MPs. He could so easily have died from hypothermia.

24 January

George is much better today and, as he speaks a little Russian, he is a great help with our recalcitrant Allies.

Told him about the problems that M and I are having in finding any type of married quarters. He told me that we can have a double room at the Reichshof, a building used occasionally by visiting ENSA artistes. Grateful, delighted and happy about this.

28 January

I had to apply to Matron for permission to sleep out, which was granted – reluctantly.

George helped M and I to move our belongings into the Reichshof this afternoon. He is quite well now and delighted to be able to help us.

The room is on the first floor with a window overlooking the ice-bound Alster. It is a rather forbidding room, with plain white walls, a bed, a chair and a polished table. There are no cooking facilities or heating appliances, but at least we shall be together. It is so marvellous to have a room of our own.

30 January

Have to get up at 6 a.m. in order to be on duty one hour later. Felt very cold and sick this morning. M came to the station with me. Poor darling, he does not have to be at his office until 9 a.m. but it was still dark and he did not want me to walk to the train alone.

Arrived on the ward to hear that the Russians were complaining about the breakfast and demanding to see me at once. I summoned the interpreter and went into my usual routine of apologies, and they simmered down.

Felt rather angry afterwards, angry, sick and hungry, but there was no time for breakfast or self-pity. We had several new admissions in the night and there was a busy day ahead.

9 February

Matron told me this morning that I am to go on night duty tomorrow night on Pavilion A, one of the busiest surgical units in the hospital. This <u>would</u> happen just as M and I had found a room of our own. He is working during the day and I need to sleep, so I must now move back to the Sisters' sleeping quarters.

6 March

Off night duty at last, thank God. It has been so long and miserable. A busy surgical ward is not the easiest post when one is feeling constantly nauseated and having to dash off to vomit periodically.

10 March

We are back in our room at the Reichshof. M has been telling me about the Ravensbrück Trials. Odette Churchill gave evidence. There were such horrific tales of woman's brutality to woman.

We are going on leave tomorrow to Ireland. Am looking forward to fresh milk and fruit. I dream of bowls of fruit and gallons of lovely creamy milk.

On leave between 12 and 28 March, Mary and Malcolm visited his family in London and she brought him to meet her family in Ireland for the first time. On their return to Hamburg in April, they renewed their efforts to have their marriage recognised and be eligible for married quarters.

16 April, Hamburg

M and I are still unable to persuade the War Office that we are married and entitled to married quarters and allowances, and we are living in our one room here at the Reichshof.

The morning sickness has ceased, but I am very conscious of my body's need for fresh fruit and vegetables. The diet here is always out of a tin and I worry about my baby. Am just beginning to show a little and Matron has moved me from Officers' Ward to FR2, which is for army wives and children. I was happy to see the back of the Russian patients, but the others were extremely nice and always good fun.

There are only two English wives here, all the others are German. There is a small Babies' Ward attached, with eight children at present. The work is extremely hard. Sick babies require a great deal of time and attention.

20 April

The morning sickness has returned. It may be purely psychological. My first task here each morning (without breakfast) is to bath, feed and do the dressings for the sick babies. We have two very ill children. One has encephalitis. His head is enormous. The fluid has to be withdrawn by syringe periodically. The other is a very severe spina-bifida. These babies are so fragile and deformed that it is frightening and distressing to handle them. The parents never visit these children.

Genetic abnormalities are always frightening, but particularly so when one is pregnant. What if M and I should have a physically or mentally abnormal baby? Would our marriage stand the strain? Would we survive? The other babies here are underweight – one I feed every half-hour from the pipette of a fountain pen. There is also a two-year-old girl with meningitis. She screams almost continually, like an animal caught in a trap. I have a German nurse to help me now, a charming girl called Elsa.

24 April

We have four German wives here at present, all suffering from pregnancy sickness. Ironical really, as I feel just as sick as they do – their blood pressure etc. is OK. They are big, strapping blonde girls, but they lie in bed all day moaning and vomiting. Their young English soldier husbands come in each evening, bringing fresh milk and fruit and vegetables flown in from Denmark. Am going to suggest to the MO tomorrow that these young women would be perfectly capable of looking after themselves at home. They are not ill and most of them have relations here in Hamburg. The army has provided Married Quarters for other ranks in a rather nice area just outside the city.

26 April

Jack Wyper was full of commiseration over my homeless state. He reminded me that he would be looking after me during the baby's birth if we were still in Hamburg. I told him that M and I would like to have a home here at least until after the birth of our baby. I shall have to submit my resignation to the War Office soon. They require three months' notice.

12 May

Handed in my formal resignation to Matron today. She will dispatch it to the War Office.

She always makes me feel rather indecent and distasteful, not to mention inconvenient. A QA Sister beginning to show her pregnancy is not Matron's idea of good form.

22 May

We had a new girl in yesterday. Her name is Jean and she is married to a sergeant in the Sappers. She has salpingitis, the result of a back-street abortion in England. She is a very sick girl, semi-comatose since admission. We give her two-hourly injections of penicillin. She is on an intravenous drip and we try to persuade her to drink as much fluid as possible. She is acutely toxic. Hope she pulls through.

Our other sick patient is a blonde German woman, called Anna, who came in two days ago looking at least seven months pregnant. An X-ray revealed not the baby she was hoping for, but a huge ovarian cyst. She was whipped down to the theatre straight away and Jack Wyper performed the operation. It was a macabre cyst, weighing nearly five pounds and containing tufts of hair and some bone material. She is on a blood transfusion at present and still suffering from post-operative shock.

28 May

The ward is a little easier now. Jean is up and walking around the ward. This abortion and the resultant toxaemia has been an emotional and physical shock for her. It is still considered very improper to discuss birth control. There is a great need for sensible advice on this subject.

Anna will be discharged next week providing that she makes steady progress.

7 June

Saw Jack Wyper this morning. He tells me that I am looking exhausted and must have some rest, so here I am on Officers' Ward doing absolutely nothing but listen to the patients quarrelling with each other in the Common Room nearby. I can hear the controlled accent of a British officer with an underlying note of desperation and despair, a French voice almost in high contralto, and a Russian bellow. The Russians must be devouring all the cheese as usual.

16 June

Back on duty again. The ill patients are very good, but I find these neurotic self-pitying young German girls very tiresome.

11 July

Matron sent for me today. I am to cease duty at once and will be shipped back to the UK. Desperately unhappy. I do not want to leave M and we need to be together when our baby is born. I have nowhere to go in England, no bed booked for the confinement. What a dilemma. The army red tape is such that in their eyes we are not married.

It would have been so marvellous to have this baby here in this hospital amongst my friends and with Jack Wyper as my obstetrician. Having a first baby is always a frightening experience, but without a home, my husband and my friends and without reasonable hospital facilities, it will be terrifying.

14 July

A memo from Matron this morning to say that I will be 'dispatched to the UK by hospital ship as soon as possible'. Feel very depressed. M and I need to share the experience of being together when our baby is born.

15 July

Went to see Jack Wyper. He is appalled by the way we are being treated by the army. He has offered to help me obtain local release.

17 July

Jack came along to see me in the Sisters' Mess this morning. He has written to Matron and the War Office to say that I am not in a fit condition to return to the UK and recommended that I should be granted local release. He tells me that I must spend a few days in bed as I am suffering from nervous exhaustion.

What a good and kind friend he is. There are few people who are willing to go to so much trouble to help another person. Feeling much happier. M will be delighted.

18 July

Here I am back in bed on Officers' Ward. Am feeling quite fit, but rather nervous of Matron's reaction to having her plans for packing me off to England foiled. Jack was with her as she did her rounds, and his professional composure was quite superb. He really is a darling man.

26 July

Left the hospital at 11.30 a.m. M and his driver Jock came to collect me. There was further marvellous news. We are to have a family suite at Streit's Hotel. This was arranged by the kindly help of M's CO. We deposited some of my things at Streit's, had lunch at the Atlantic and then went on to Schaerbeutz by car. A lovely ride and we are so happy. My only problem at the moment is maternity clothes. I have one smock which I must wash and wear, and have had to cut a large piece out of my khaki skirt in front in order to accommodate the bump. It is impossible to obtain maternity clothes anywhere. Clothes are still on coupons in England and, as I am not a civilian living in the UK, I am not entitled to coupons anyway.

27 July, Schaerbeutz

Today I am a civilian. It is so wonderful to be away from nursing and hospitals.

29 July, Streit's Hotel

My trunk arrived from the hospital. Had a lovely day unpacking and getting organised. The bump is still very active, continually kicking, a strange and exciting sensation.

Some hard-earned relaxation:
Malcolm, Mary and 'the bump'

6 September

There is a hubbub of excitement in M's office today. There is a tremendous flap on about two or three cargo ships full of European Jews who were on their way to Palestine via Cyprus and the Mediterranean. Britain, I believe, is policing the Palestine area, and on the order of Ernest Bevin the ships have been intercepted and diverted back here to Hamburg.* They are to be disembarked here and transferred to camps, until it is decided where and how to settle these displaced persons. There are enormous numbers of DPs here in Germany, including young children. They are mainly Jews of all nationalities. I feel extremely sorry for these people. They are chivvied about from pillar to post, and nobody knows what to do with them. They have lost their homes and their country and many have lost their families. There is a shortage of food here too, and these poor people are an embarrassment to the occupying powers.

7 September

Went along to M's office to take him out to lunch at the Atlantic. They were all rushing around in a flap. M, Sgt Covey and Lotte the secretary were answering the telephone to callers from all over the world, making enquiries about the Jewish ships. They were mainly Press, many of them American.

Went along with M to the BFN as he wished to talk to some people there. British Forces Network here is an excellent wireless station, with a wide variety of programmes. It is run by the Forces for the Forces. There are local and foreign news items, and plenty of classical and contemporary music, personal profiles, etc.

* The British were responsible for the repatriation of Jewish displaced persons. They felt their only option, however unpopular, would be to return Jews to the British-controlled zone in Germany, while many Jews, on the other hand, hoped to found a Jewish state in Palestine. In Operation Oasis, the ships bound for Palestine, still under British administration, were intercepted and the passengers were removed.

The Jewish ships will provide plenty of excitement, as it is obvious that the passengers will not be anxious to disembark. There are bound to be problems.

8 September

M has had an extremely busy day. HQ decided that appeals should be made to the Jews to disembark quietly, first by the Military Government (the Civil Authority) and if that met with no response and they decided to dig their heels in, the situation would then be handed over to the army. A special compound was erected at the foot of the quayside gangway. This would house the World Press who could then describe what they saw without the opportunity to interview. It was also decided that, because of the danger of Jews acting up, no Press photographers would be allowed. M tells me that this decision caused a great uproar at the pre-operation Press meeting today. The noisy meeting went on and on until a compromise was reached. One army cameraman would be allowed to take photographs, but he must be kept completely out of sight. The *Daily Mail* correspondent undertook to fly the films back to London for processing. All the prints would be put on display in the *Daily Mail* offices for selection and use by any other newspaper that wanted them. M proposed his Sgt Covey for the job as he is an excellent photographer. The ships should be here tomorrow. This whole operation is designated 'Oasis'.

9 September

Spent the day with M at the quayside. We were all there at 6 a.m. – the journalists chatting and grumbling to each other. The Military Government chaps were there too, looking slightly embarrassed and out of place in their white collars and Town Hall suits.

M had a crane gantry moved to just the right position above

the gangway and Sgt Covey (more than a little nervous) was hoisted up with his camera. He crouched down inside the gantry and waited for the action to start.

The first ship arrived in the harbour about 8.30 a.m. and a Military Government official went aboard to ask the Jews to disembark quietly and promised them food and accommodation. They refused to move, so now it was over to the army. The Military Government official told us that it was obvious to him that many of the Jews would have accepted the inevitability of their situation, but there were several fanatics in the hold who were preventing the others from leaving.

In view of this situation the army personnel were formed into snatch squads. They went aboard, peered through the mesh of the holds, identified a ringleader and then the Squad would burst in, grab the leader, and bundle him unceremoniously ashore. This procedure was repeated several times, after which it was no longer necessary, and the other Jews filed ashore, quite unaware of Sgt Covey's camera clicking away above their heads.

Occasionally a woman or a child would stop half-way down the gangplank and resist well in view of the world's Press. A gentle coaxing was all that was necessary at this stage. Poor people – they looked so tired and depressed. I was standing next to the BBC's Godfrey Talbot as he scribbled away. I wonder if anybody really cares – or is this another circus that makes the headlines?

I looked over the shoulder of one American lady reporter as she filled her notebook with the most astonishing account of events which were <u>not happening</u>, Jews being 'bludgeoned by British soldiers' etc. She was obviously colouring and distorting the facts to fit pre-conceived ideas. This was obviously an editorial political situation and truth played a very small part.

10 September

Went along to M's office at HQ about 10 a.m. He and Sgt Covey were pacing up and down and Lotte was making her usual ersatz coffee. The newspapers had not arrived. Sgt Covey looked hollow-eyed and haggard, not at all his usual cheery self. He kept saying 'Supposing I've made a mess of it all, forgotten to wind on the film or adjust the focus'. We were all biting our nails by now, when suddenly Jock burst into the office unceremoniously and dumped a pile of newspapers on the desk.

It was tremendously exciting. The papers carried innumerable photographs and we set a precedent in *The Times* by having a photograph on the front page. The American and European papers also covered the story. The story lines were astonishingly dissimilar of course, some reporters could not have been there, but we were not worried as we opened a bottle of Scotch at 11 a.m. to celebrate the power of Sgt Covey's camera and also to wish good luck to displaced persons everywhere.*

18 September

M and I went to see the film *Freda* in Blankensee. Labour pains commenced at a rather interesting point in the film, so we returned to Streit's and ordered an ambulance.

Arrived here at 10 p.m. Admitted by Mac, who warned me jokingly about 'making a fuss'. Feel both excited and frightened.

They made M go away. Husbands are not permitted to stay. It would be so marvellous if he could just sit here and hold my hand.

There is a very kind middle-aged German cleaner lady who rubs my back occasionally and makes soothing noises in German. This is very comforting, but alas she has just been shushed out of the room.

---

* A specific report of the event Mary describes can be found in the *Guardian*, 9 September 1947.

19 September, 2 p.m.

Had a forceps delivery and general anaesthetic. Woke up to see Jack Wyper smiling at me and to my great and incredible joy he said 'Congratulations. You have a handsome son.'

Malcolm, Mary and their 'handsome son'

Mary and Malcolm named their first child Michael. After his birth they remained in Hamburg waiting for Malcolm's demobilisation, but their housing problems continued so they decided Mary should take Michael back to England. When Malcolm returned they set up home in Twyford, Berkshire. The next few years were tough financially as Malcolm became a student at the Chelsea School of Art (now the Chelsea College of Art and Design), but they were also exciting and fulfilling as they added three more children to the family in rapid succession, Maureen, Jennifer and Kathryn. From the late 1950s to the 1970s they lived in Brighton, with Malcolm making a living from commercial art and writing advertising copy. Mary returned to nursing after having children and would regale her family with stories of the characters she met in her work. Unafraid to challenge ideas and eager to be a force for change, Mary spoke up when she saw the need. In the 1960s, she was a keen instigator in the campaign to carry resuscitation equipment on board emergency service vehicles: a legacy that undoubtedly saved many lives. She and Malcolm later moved to the Wye Valley. Mary died in 1997; Malcolm died in 2008. They are survived by their four children and eight grandchildren.

POSTSCRIPT

Kathy Lowe (Mary's daughter)

It was early in the 1960s and I was about seven years old. It was a hot day and I was digging in the sand. I looked up and there was my mum, she was sitting there on the beach, resplendent in her best bra and pants. I ran up to her, pink with embarrassment. 'You can't wear your bra and pants, Mum, not on the beach!' (I was starting to understand the ways of the world.) She smiled, then laughed and said 'What nonsense. It's just the same as wearing a bikini.' I always knew that my mother was a rebel.

Her rebellious streak, her 'bloody-minded' determination and her great sense of humour must have helped her to get through the horrors of nursing in Normandy, in that tent, just after the D-Day landings. I remember, I must have been about twelve, going into her bedroom and searching through her dressing-table drawers for her pile of old diaries. Her handwriting was a flamboyant scribble and in places difficult to read, but I was fascinated by the descriptions of war, and the people caught up in it. I'd also search through the pages to find the part where Mum met my Dad, trying to imagine them when they were young.

As a child in rural Ireland, her life had been basic and austere, yet full of love and warmth. Just a matter of weeks after her birth her own mother died so she was raised by an aunt. This aunt lived on a small farm, and there was a lot of hard work to be done. My mum loved to tell stories of bringing in orphaned lambs to be fed and cosseted by the fire. Her sheepdog, Sammy Laddy, would keep one eye open in case a young lamb tottered too close to the fire, then he'd gently nose them away. She rode to school each day in a pony and trap, and she'd come home to play with her pet pig, Muck. Her father visited only occasionally as he was busy raising five other children while running his own small farm. He had also been deeply involved in the politics of the time, namely working for a free Ireland. So when my mother decided to come to England to qualify as a nurse and to help the English in a time of fast-approaching war, it was in the teeth of family opposition. To her family, the English were the enemy.

It must have taken great courage for my mother to come to a country where she knew no one and at a time when war was looming. Maybe she came through a sense of adventure, or to be free of the oppressive Catholic culture, or maybe because she loved to help people, people of all cultures, races and backgrounds. She had great empathy for others and was determined to do something useful. And she did.

Anna Wood (Mary's granddaughter, Kathy's daughter)

By the time I knew my Grandma she was in her sixties with white hair. She lived with Malcolm in an old one-bedroom stone cottage deep in the woods on the hillside of the Wye Valley. It was a tranquil and enchanting place; the cottage was like something from a history lesson. It wasn't connected to mains water or gas, it had electricity but no central heating, just a log and coal fire. There was no driveway or even a road outside the house. You had to park in a layby on the single-track lane that wound steeply through the woods then down a path to the cottage. Inside, the walls were covered with enormous sculptured wall plaques: art that my Grandpa had created over the years. A small winding staircase led to the only bedroom, and outside was a summerhouse at the end of the garden and a large wooden art studio. The garden itself had a waterfall, a pond with a bridge over it, numerous clay sculptures and views across the valley. When we were small, my brother and I stayed in the little house at the end of the garden and I remember being excited and terrified as we listened to the owls hooting only feet from my head at night.

My earliest memory of Mary is when I was about three years old: every time we went up any stairs or steps together she would sing 'Up the airy mountain, down the rushy glen, we daren't go a-hunting, for fear of little men'. I always felt she was singing about leprechauns. I remember her always laughing and chatting. She loved long walks through the fields and woods. She would beat the stinging nettles aside with a walking stick that she appeared to use for that singular purpose. If she cooked for us, the food was usually still frozen in the middle or burnt black. Sometimes she would put nasturtium flowers in our food; I remember watching her eat some straight from our garden and thinking her quite mad.

Grandma was a prolific reader: if she had any spare time she would settle herself in bed with a book and a bowl of apples. She used to recommend books to me – *Anna Karenina*, Somerset Maugham, *The Rubaiyat of Omar Khayyam* and poems by Coleridge.

I had always been fascinated by personal accounts and fiction from the First and Second World Wars. Then, when I was twenty years old, I was lent Grandma's diaries. I was amazed to read about her life in the war. I knew she had been a nurse but she never told me about her experiences. I stayed up all night reading them from start to finish.

Not only were the diaries exciting to read, but they also helped me to get to know her as a person rather than just a grandmother. That she could live through the horrors of the Second World War and afterwards still find beauty in the world is testament to her strength of character. She has taught me that no matter how dark life gets, it is possible to feel joy, to laugh and to live life again. I have no idea how she coped with being a nurse at that time. It was incredibly difficult and exhausting for long periods. We should be indebted to her generation not just for the lives that were sacrificed but also for the long hours, the physical, mental and emotional effort they put into protecting their country and loved ones.

The last time I saw Grandma she was seventy-six years old and was in the last few months of her life. She was in a bed made up for her in a summer room just off the main cottage. It overlooked the hills and River Wye below. She had a glass of wine and talked animatedly about her home in Ireland, something she'd never done before. I asked her if she could speak Gaelic and she said she had excelled at Gaelic as a child and had been rewarded with a trip to Inishmore, staying with a family who only spoke Gaelic. She wasn't convinced that this was a great reward, but she was always ready for an adventure and in the end she had a lovely time and never forgot it. Then, in her native language she sang for us. That final time is how I will always remember her: smiling, laughing and singing in Gaelic.

FURTHER READING

GENERAL

Beevor, Antony, *The Second World War* (London: Weidenfeld & Nicolson, 2012)

Judt, Tony, *Postwar: A History of Europe since 1945* (London: Penguin, 2006)

Nicholson, Virginia, *Millions Like Us: Women's Lives in War and Peace 1939–1949* (London: Penguin, 2011)

Shephard, Ben, *After Daybreak: The Liberation of Bergen-Belsen, 1945* (New York: Schocken Books, 2005)

THE MEDICAL WAR

Andrews, Lucilla, *No Time for Romance* (London: Harrap & Co. Ltd, 1977)

Harrison, Mark, *Medicine and Victory: British Military Medicine in the Second World War* (Oxford: Oxford University Press, 2004)

MacGregor, Mildred, *World War II: Frontline Nurse* (Ann Arbor, Michigan: The University of Michigan Press, 2008)

Mawson, Stuart, *Arnhem Doctor* (London: Orbis Publishing, 1981)

Mayhew, E. R., *The Reconstruction of Warriors: Archibald McIndoe, the Royal Air Force and the Guinea Pig Club* (Barnsley: Pen & Sword/ Frontline Books, 2004)

McBryde, Brenda, *Quiet Heroines: Nurses of the Second World War* (Essex: Cakebreads Publication, 1989)

McBryde, Brenda, *A Nurse's War* (New York: Universe Books, 1979)

Mortimer, Barbara, *Sisters: Memories from the Courageous Nurses of World War Two* (London: Hutchinson, 2012)

Phibbs, Brendan, *The Other Side of Time: A Combat Surgeon in World War II* (Boston: Little, Brown & Co., 1987)

Starns, Penny, *Nurses at War: Women on the Frontline 1939–45*
(Gloucestershire: Sutton Publishing, 2000)

Tyrer, Nicola, *Sisters in Arms: British Army Nurses Tell Their Story*
(London: Weidenfeld & Nicolson, 2008)

Website of the QAIMNS/QARANC (Queen Alexandra's Royal
Army Nursing Corps): www.qaranc.co.uk/qaimns.php
www.qaranc.co.uk/d-day-normandy-landings.php

The Blitz

Collier, Richard, *The City that Wouldn't Die: London May 10–11 1941*
(London: Collins, 1959)

Gardiner, Juliet, *The Blitz: The British Under Attack* (London:
HarperCollins, 2011)

Mortimer, Gavin, *The Longest Night: Voices from the London Blitz,
10–11 May 1941* (London: Weidenfeld & Nicolson, 2005)

Online sources for the nights of 10 and 11 May 1941:
www.westendatwar.org.uk/page_id__24_path__op28p.aspx
(includes photographs of the damage to the Alexandra Hotel)
www.westendatwar.org.uk/page_id__205_path__op28p.aspx

The RAF

Higham, Robin, *Unflinching Zeal: The Air Battles over France and
Britain, May–October 1940* (Annapolis: Naval Institute Press, 2012)

Holland, James, *The Battle of Britain: Five Months that Changed
History, May–October 1940* (London: Bantam Press, 2010)

Online sources:
Biggin Hill: www.wartimememories.co.uk/airfields/bigginhill.html

'Paddy' Brendan Finucane: A wonderful tribute to Finucane can be
heard in this RTE documentary:
www.rte.ie/radio1/doconone/finucane.html
More information, including photographs, is available at
www.acesofww2.com/UK/aces/finucane

Wing Commander Douglas Bader: Photographs of Bader and
further information can be found at
www.dailymail.co.uk/news/article-2292943/Douglas-Bader-
Incredible-footage-WW2-fighter-ace-fought-Nazis-false-legs-
goes-display.html

D-Day

Ryan, Cornelius, *The Longest Day* (London and New York: Simon & Schuster, 1959)

The Battle of Arnhem

Harclerode, Peter, *Arnhem: A Tragedy of Errors* (London: Caxton, 1994)

Nichol, John and Rennell, Tony, *Arnhem: The Battle for Survival* (London: Penguin, 2011)

Online sources:

www.bbc.co.uk/history/worldwars/wwtwo/battle_arnhem_01.shtml

www.pegasusarchive.org/arnhem/frames.htm

This site includes a photograph and biography of Sgt Louis Hagen. In 1945 Hagen published an anonymous account of his Arnhem experience, *Arnhem Lift: A Fighting Glider Pilot Remembers*. This was reissued with additional material under his name as *Arnhem Lift: A German Jew in the Glider Pilot Regiment* (Gloucestershire: The History Press/Pen & Sword Books, 1993)

Ireland and the War

Doherty, Richard, *Irish Men and Women in the Second World War* (Dublin: Four Courts Press, 1999)

Doherty, Richard, *Irish Volunteers in the Second World War* (Dublin: Four Courts Press, 2002)

Grob-Fitzgibbon, Benjamin, *The Irish Experience during the Second World War: An Oral History* (Dublin: Irish Academic Press, 2004)

Muldowney, Mary, *The Second World War and Irish Women: An Oral History* (Dublin: Irish Academic Press, 2007)

Wills, Clair, *That Neutral Island: A Cultural History of Ireland during the Second World War* (London: Faber and Faber, 2007)

The Ravensbrück Trials

Tickell, Jerrard, *Odette: The Story of a British Agent* (London: Kaye & Ward, 1949)

Online sources:

www.jewishvirtuallibrary.org/jsource/Holocaust/WarCrime49.html

Film of the trial is available on the British Pathé site:
www.britishpathe.com/video/ravensbruck-trial-ends

OPERATION OASIS

A specific report of the event Mary describes can be found in the
Guardian, 9 September 1947
century.guardian.co.uk/1940-1949/Story/0,,105124,00.html
Further online sources:
www1.uni-hamburg.de/rz3a035/exodus1947a.html
newspaperarchive.com/lowell-sun/1947-09-08/page-18

EDITOR'S ACKNOWLEDGEMENTS

My thanks must go first to the Imperial War Museum, London, and the unfailingly helpful staff in the Department of Documents where the typescript of the diary is held. Thanks are also due to my institution, St Jerome's University, Ontario, for the financial support that originally enabled my archival research. On the editorial path I have been supported by many individuals, not least by my agent, Andrew Lownie, whose encouragement, professionalism and patience brought me through the stages of the proposal and led to a wonderful editor at Weidenfeld & Nicolson, Bea Hemming, who has put so much work into shaping this diary for publication.

I owe much thanks to others who played a role at various stages of the process: Andrea McKenzie for prodding me to find a publisher; Jane Potter for never saying a word when I reneged on my promise not to take on any more work until our book was finished; Megan Drysdale for much fast and accurate typing; Carolyn McCormick for her careful work on the map; members of my family for listening to my endless diary talk and also for other contributions, Rachel for typing, Pierre and Marc for historical discussion and information, and my nephew Cian for his ongoing enthusiasm.

Above all, my greatest thanks go to the Morris family for entrusting me with editing the diary. I have been enormously fortunate in having the opportunity to take on this project, and could not have done it without their generous permission. Especially I must thank Mary's granddaughter Anna Wood, whose email query about an article I had written on the diary dropped into my in-box when I had all but given up tracing family members; and Anna's mother, Kathy Lowe, Mary's youngest daughter, who welcomed me warmly into her home, took out the family photographs, and having clearly inherited the ability to tell a good story, regaled me with accounts of her mother.

blog and newsletter

For literary discussion, author insight,
book news, exclusive content,
recipes and giveaways, visit the
Weidenfeld & Nicolson blog and
sign up for the newsletter at:

www.wnblog.co.uk

For breaking news, reviews and exclusive competitions
Follow us 🐦 @wnbooks
Find us **f** facebook.com/WNfiction